MW01224614

INTELLIGENCE: NEW RESEARCH

INTELLIGENCE: NEW RESEARCH

LIN V. WESLEY
EDITOR

Nova Science Publishers, Inc.
New York

NOTICE TO THE READER

The Publisher has taken reasonable care in the preparation of this book, but makes no expressed or implied warranty of any kind and assumes no responsibility for any errors or omissions. No liability is assumed for incidental or consequential damages in connection with or arising out of information contained in this book. The Publisher shall not be liable for any special, consequential, or exemplary damages resulting, in whole or in part, from the readers' use of, or reliance upon, this material.

This publication is designed to provide accurate and authoritative information with regard to the subject matter covered herein. It is sold with the clear understanding that the Publisher is not engaged in rendering legal or any other professional services. If legal or any other expert assistance is required, the services of a competent person should be sought. FROM A DECLARATION OF PARTICIPANTS JOINTLY ADOPTED BY A COMMITTEE OF THE AMERICAN BAR ASSOCIATION AND A COMMITTEE OF PUBLISHERS.

LIBRARY OF CONGRESS CATALOGING-IN-PUBLICATION DATA
Intelligence : new research / Lin V. Wesley, editor.
    p. cm.
Includes bibliographical references and index.
ISBN 1-59454-637-1
1. Intellect. I. Wesley, Lin V.
BF431.I547   2006
153.9--dc22   2005037328

Published by Nova Science Publishers, Inc. ✦New York

CONTENTS

PREFACE

The research projects presented in this book are the most recent studies of intelligence. They will improve our understanding of the human's ability to learn, understand or deal with new or trying situations and how people apply knowledge to manipulate one's environment or to think abstractly as measured by objective criteria (as tests). Understanding intelligence is important because it improves our understanding of how the brain works and could potentially be a gateway to improving education on all levels from individual teaching methods to widely used curriculums.

Spearman (1904) introduced the concept of general intelligence (g) to describe the universal positive correlation among tests of different abilities. He later defined g as a "mental energy" that could be applied to any and every kind of task (Spearman, 1927). What g is and which role it plays in cognitive processing is still under debate (Jensen, 1998). From a psychometric point of view g is the result of two main factors called gc (crystallized intelligence) and gf (fluid intelligence) that reflect the amount of knowledge and the ability to educe relations, respectively. Recently a large number of studies focused their attention on the biological basis of g and its relationship with other cognitive functions. The leading idea is that g could be strongly linked to the executive control system (Deary, 2000). This idea is supported by some behavioural, lesions and bioimaging studies. The activation of the lateral prefrontal cortex during fluid reasoning tasks (Duncan, Seitz, Kolodny, Bor, Herzog, Ahmed, Newell, and Emslie, 2000) and the involvement of a domain-independent working memory system in problem solving, localized in the prefrontal areas (Prabhakaram, Smith, Desmond, Glover, and Gabrieli, 1997), give a great contribution to the supposed link between g and some frontal lobe functions. The data obtained on frontal patients seem to go in the same direction: the dysexecutive syndrome caused by lesions in the lateral prefrontal cortex is often associated with a decline in fluid reasoning (Duncan, Burgess, and Emslie, 1995). On normal subjects, some authors find a significant correlation between executive abilities and performances in gf tests (Duncan, Emslie, Williams, Johnson, and Freer, 1996). All these data will be largely reviewed in chapter one and integrated in a unique framework.

While the original studies in Mendelian genetics focused on unit characters, traits that could be classified as present or absent, it later became necessary to deal with quantitative attributes, such as size or intelligence, assessed by a series of measurements. Polygenic inheritance has long been accepted as the principal model applicable in that field. It now appears that sometimes a different approach may be appropriate, based on hybrid vigor as a chief force in individual variability. The present analysis in chapter two is an attempt to illustrate that intellectual differences may at times be related to individual mutant genes that exist at levels much higher than would be expected on the basis of mutation pressure counteracted by natural selection. The emphasis is thus on genetic abnormalities known to remain quite frequent. The first itemized segment describes psychotic disorders, analyzing the evidence for heredity and evaluating the probable genetic mechanism. Relationship to creative forms of thinking are then discussed in detail. The second part assesses the genetic basis of myopia and its connection to learning ability. Finally the influence of these factors on personality traits is summarized. This leads to a view of the need for natural selection to ensure retention of intellectual gains achieved in the past.

The neurophysiological research of ability has mainly focused on the verbal and performance components of intelligence, and has, only recently, paid some attention to emotional intelligence. The explanation of individual differences in ability was an efficiency theory. Neuroscientists have, despite the acceptance of the 'Big 5' model of personality including extraversion (E), neuroticism (N), openness to experience (O), agreeableness (A) and conscientiousness (C), been mainly interested in extraversion. It was suggested that extraverts have relatively low levels of cortical arousal, by contrast, introverts are assumed to display comparatively high levels of cortical activity.

The present study in chapter three investigated neuropsychological differences in verbal/performance intelligence (IQ – measured with WISC-R), and emotional intelligence (EIQ – measured with MSCEIT), as well as the 'Big 5' personality traits (measured with BFQ). For that purpose the EEG of 70 individuals (38 females and 32 males) was analyzed in two conditions: resting with eyes closed, and while solving a figural task. The EEG was analyzed in the time and frequency domain. Correlations between EEG parameters and behavioral measures were obtained. The findings can be summarized as follows:

The major finding of the study is that males and females differed in resting brain activity related to their level of general intelligence. Brain activity in females increased with the level of intelligence, whereas an opposite pattern of brain activity was observed in males. In males an even more pronounced correlation between EIQ and EEG power measures was observed. High emotional intelligent males in all three alpha bands showed more synchronous oscillations equally distributed over both hemispheres and three brain areas.

The M.I.N.D project expects to explore the best combinations of sensory stimuli that create emotional connectivity, create techniques to evoke more effective emotional links and measure these stimuli and techniques for validity and develop guidelines for future emotionally encoded training scenarios. Just as the VRML97 standard advanced virtual environment development by creating a guideline to unify the work done in dozens of individually developed virtual reality team training systems, neuroergonomics standards can help us develop systems that are compatible with natural human behavior for creating safe and comfortable training environments. In addition, methodologies and tools for measuring human behavior, understanding and accumulation of measured behavior, and assisting human behavior, will be developed. This study in chapter four investigated the relationship between virtual training, physiological coherence, heart-brain synchronization, and cognitive performance in 36 healthy individuals. Subjects performed explosive ordnance disposal (EOD) task with an enhanced VE intended to instill a positive emotional state and increase physiological coherence inside a virtual incident exercise scenario of EOD Training. One VE was using the explicit biocybernetic interface that challenged the self-efficacy and team decision making of the operators in an EOD scenario by linking their heart rates (ECG), electrodermal activity (EDA) and electromyogram measurements of facial muscle tensions (EMG) with a Force Feedback Joystick of controlled "ease" of movements while engaged in a joint task. The second VE was the same EOD situation environment as the above, but without the introduction of the advanced biocybernetic interface. In both the scenarios the operators had the freedom to communicate verbally while engaged in the common task. Two performance measures were computed: (a) RMS error, and (b) number of groundings. Analyses of RMS error scores indicate that performance improved over the three repeated runs with each VE, as evidence of specific-channel learning. Similarly, performance improved on the first run from Day 1 to Day 2, as evidence of near-transfer learning. However, the advanced biocybernetic interface provided to the first experimental group, provided an additional important statistical performance improvement relative to the "simple" VE group and the control groups. The mapping between the type of user - operator state and the type of medium response also had an influence on the level of presence. This project suggests that social-psychophysiological measures and team biocybernetics merit further investigation in sociotechnical systems that demand high proficiency and self-efficacy

Emotional intelligence (EI) has been one of the most controversial topics in both practitioner and academic communities since its first introduction by Salovey, Mayer and their collaborators in the early 1990s (Salovey and Mayer, 1990; Mayer, Dipaolo, and Salovey, 1990). Fervent discussions and severe debates have been raised on the meaning and domain of this concept and its validity and utility to the academic field. Proponents of the EI construct claim that it affects important individual life outcomes and has utility in various areas, such as education and organizational behavior. Empirical evidence has accumulated in support of these claims (Mayer, Salovey and Caruso, 2004; Law, Wong and Song, 2004b). However, there are also researchers who dispute the scientific credibility of the concept of EI and conclude it as an "elusive construct" (Davies, Stankov and Roberts, 1998; Matthews, Roberts, and Zeidner, 2004).

After about fifteen years of research, it is a good time to review what has been done in the field and whether EI deserves future attention. As an emerging topic, there are very few comprehensive reviews of the construct, which offer a big picture of the current state and future directions of EI research. This is what the authors want to achieve with chapter five. Specifically, they start with a review of the development of the EI concept and the main works in the field. Following this, they discuss the debates on three major aspects of EI: the nature and domain of the EI construct, its construct validity, and its measurement problems. They then suggest what we see as the most important directions for future development of the field. In particular, they call for research that focuses on the construct validity and measurement of EI, and efforts on the outcomes and antecedents of EI toward developing an EI theory that could guide the field to move forward. This review is concluded with their overall evaluations of the field and suggestions for future development.

Chapter six reviews the basic neuro-anatomic foundations and psychological concepts of intelligence, aptitude, talent and giftedness and their relevance to music. There are several academic traditions with different approaches which are based upon various scientific paradigms. Starting with a brief survey of the historical contribution of differential psychology and the European tradition of investigating musicality, different concepts of intelligence from the g-factor paradigm (Charles Spearman) up to the theory of multiple intelligences (Howard Gardner) are reviewed. The neural correlates of intelligence introduce into the discussion to what extent (if ever) music abilities and general cognitive competences interact. For this, the debate on the Mozart effect is critically viewed. From a meta-analysis it can be stated that although a moderate positive correlation between studying the music and academic achievement is observed, there is no empirical evidence to suggest a causal relation between music and verbal or math advancement. In the last section a hierarchical structure of the different aspects of intelligence and how they relate to and possibly interfere with music is outlined. An integrated model of general intelligence and music achievement is finally elaborated

In chapter seven, to obtain clinical clues for differential diagnosis of high-functioning (i.e., IQ of 70 or over) pervasive developmental disorders (HPDD) from attention-deficit/hyperactivity disorder (ADHD), the authors compared 79 HPDD children (15 autistic disorder [HFA] [M = 9.3 years, 13 males]; 45 PDD not otherwise specified [HPDDNOS] [M = 8.1 years, 37 males]; 19 Asperger's disorder [AS] [M = 10.3 years, 17 males]) and 37 ADHD children (M = 8.6 years, 30 males) on the Japanese version of Wechsler Intelligence Scale for Children Third Edition (WISC-III) and the Childhood Autism Rating Scale—Tokyo Version (CARS-TV). Compared with the ADHD children, the HPDDNOS children scored significantly (p < .05) lower on Verbal IQ (90.5 vs. 103.5) and Verbal Comprehension (90.3 vs. 103.8). The HFA children scored significantly higher on Freedom from Distractibility than the HPDDNOS children (111.9 vs. 97.4). After controlling for Full Scale IQ, the HPDDNOS children scored significantly lower on Comprehension and significantly higher on Block Design than the ADHD children. The HFA children scored significantly lower on Vocabulary than the ADHD children. Although all of the three HPDD subgroups showed the similar profile of low score of Comprehension and high score of Block Design, the AS children showed relatively high verbal ability and troughs on Coding. The latter profile was also shared by the ADHD children but not by the other two HPDD subgroups. Although both HPDD and ADHD groups partially shared some clinical symptoms, the HPDD subgroups were more abnormal in social interaction but less abnormal in hyperactivity and near receptor responsiveness. These findings might reflect underlying brain dysfunction in the three HPDD subgroups and ADHD and may help professionals to distinguish clinically between them.

In: Intelligence : New Research
Editor: Lin V. Wesley, pp. 1-22

ISBN 1-59454-637-1
© 2006 Nova Science Publishers, Inc.

Chapter 1

FLUID INTELLIGENCE AND EXECUTIVE FUNCTIONS: NEW PERSPECTIVES

Aristide Saggino[1], Bernardo Perfetti[2], Grazia Spitoni[3] and Gaspare Galati[4]

[1] Laboratory of Psychometrics, Department of Biomedical Sciences, University "G. d'Annunzio", Chieti-Pescara, Italy
[2] Department of Clinical Sciences and Bioimaging, University "G. d'Annunzio", Chieti-Pescara, Italy
[3] Department of Psychology, University of Rome "La Sapienza", Roma, Italy; Laboratory of Neuropsychology, Santa Lucia Foundation, Roma, Italy
[4] Laboratory of Neuropsychology, Department of Clinical Sciences and Bioimaging, University G. d'Annunzio, Chieti, Italy; Imaging Laboratory, Santa Lucia Foundation, Roma, Italy

ABSTRACT

Spearman (1904) introduced the concept of general intelligence (g) to describe the universal positive correlation among tests of different abilities. He later defined g as a "mental energy" that could be applied to any and every kind of task (Spearman, 1927). What g is and which role it plays in cognitive processing is still under debate (Jensen, 1998). From a psychometric point of view g is the result of two main factors called gc (crystallized intelligence) and gf (fluid intelligence) that reflect the amount of knowledge and the ability to educe relations, respectively. Recently a large number of studies focused their attention on the biological basis of g and its relationship with other cognitive functions. The leading idea is that g could be strongly linked to the executive control system (Deary, 2000). This idea is supported by some behavioural, lesions and bioimaging studies. The activation of the lateral prefrontal cortex during fluid reasoning tasks (Duncan, Seitz, Kolodny, Bor, Herzog, Ahmed, Newell, and Emslie, 2000) and the involvement of a domain-independent working memory system in problem solving, localized in the prefrontal areas (Prabhakaram, Smith, Desmond, Glover, and Gabrieli, 1997), give a great contribution to the supposed link between g and some frontal lobe functions. The data obtained on frontal patients seem to go in the same direction: the dysexecutive syndrome caused by lesions in the lateral prefrontal cortex is often associated with a decline in fluid reasoning (Duncan, Burgess, and Emslie, 1995). On normal subjects, some authors find a significant correlation between executive abilities and performances in gf tests (Duncan, Emslie, Williams, Johnson, and Freer, 1996). All these data will be largely reviewed and integrated in a unique framework.

INTRODUCTION

What intelligence is and how the human brain produces an intelligent behavior is a matter largely debated in psychological literature. Although many theories have been proposed to describe and understand what is certainly one of the most important sources of individual differences, complete agreement is still lacking. Probably the most important source of variability lies on terminologies: What do we mean when we refer to intelligence? As the conspicuous number of studies has shown, we can approach this question from several points of view. We can refer to intelligence in its psychometric structure or consider it as an expression of human creativity; otherwise, we can talk of intelligence as a cognitive function. It doesn't mean that we are talking of different things. It just means that intelligence is a complex construct that cannot be studied only from a single point of view.

In this chapter we shall focus our attention on the interesting debate about intelligence and its relationship with other cognitive functions. Our main goal is to understand the link existing among intelligence and executive functions (EF). To reach this goal we shall consider behavioral, lesion, and bioimaging studies that can provide a path to a future theory on this topic. In particular, we are interested in the growing idea that intelligence is a reflection of frontal lobe functioning and executive control.

The first part of the chapter will be dedicated to the genesis of the concept of intelligence and its psychometric aspects. A brief description of factor analysis will be necessary to understand the meaning of the "g factor" and the differences between fluid and crystallized intelligence. A closer look at the most important intelligence tests will help us to understand why some of these tests are more correlated with executive control, and others are less.

We will then briefly review the literature on executive control and the psychometric aspects of executive functions. The specific human executive abilities and the important role of attentional control will be considered together with their anatomical and functional localization in the prefrontal cortex and the broad disorganization of behavior following frontal lobe lesions. This will provide some important concepts, as adaptation to task-demands, cognitive shifting, goal setting, etc., which are fundamental in understanding recent issues on intelligence.

Following, we will discuss the relation between intelligence and executive function considering the contribution of some psychometric and neuropsycological studies. We will analyze the open debate on this topic and the contradictory data due to different methodological approaches.

Fundamental is the contribution deriving from neuroscience. Bioimaging and neurophysiology of single cells underlined the role of executive control and prefrontal functioning as the possible linking bridge between intelligence and executive function .

INTELLIGENCE AND G: A DEFINITION

Intelligence has been defined in different ways, for example, as what is measured with psychological tests of intelligence (a tautological definition used by Boring, 1923, cit. in Kline, 1991). Wechsler (1975) defined intelligence as the capacity to understand the world and meet its demands. It is also defined as the ability of abstract reasoning.

All the above-mentioned definitions are just "verbal definitions", therefore, they have no scientific value. Only psychometric definitions of the term "intelligence" should be considered scientific. Spearman, who discovered both intelligence and factor analysis, in his seminal paper '"General intelligence": objectively determined and measured' (Spearman, 1904) defined "intelligence" as the tendency of all human abilities to be positively correlated (law of Universal Unity of the Intellective Function). This definition means that there is a general tendency: if a person is good at one thing he is also generally good at others things. According to Spearman (1904), this correlation among different abilities is accounted by general intelligence (or "g"). Psychologists, and especially psychometricians, prefer the term "g" (or "g factor") to "intelligence", because the first one is considered to be more scientific and less popular psychology. G is considered a general ability common to all tasks. For example, mechanical ability depends on g plus a specific mechanical component; mathematical ability depends on g plus a specific mathematical component. The g factor is common to all problem solving abilities. Factor analysis was the method invented by Spearman to uncover g. For this reason, factor analysis and the general ability factor are deeply related. You cannot completely understand g if you are not acquainted with at least the general aspects of factor analysis.

According to Kline (1991), we can accept the Boring definition ("intelligence is what is measured by psychological tests of intelligence"), only because these tests are constructed to measure g. In a more objective way, g is defined from its factor loadings. Kline (1993) defines intelligence "...the basic reasoning ability of an individual which she or he can employ in problem solving of many kinds" (p. 172). This definition is the chosen definition for the present paper.

Different critiques to g have been presented in the literature by different authors. Just to give a general picture of these critiques we will discuss the following:

1. the cognitive critique to the g concept (see, for example, Sternberg, 1977). According to this critique, g is a descriptive concept, because factor analysis is a descriptive method. Therefore, this concept has no explicative value. In other words, it does not permit us to understand the basic psychological processes underpinning human abilities. This critique is of no value because we first need to have a picture of a construct before we can understand the processes on which it is based.

2. the behavioral critique (see, for example, Skinner, 1953). According to behaviorists' black box hypothesis, intelligence is a redundant concept and it has no utility in psychology. This critique is definitely disconfirmed by the fact that intelligence is a construct able to predict behavior in real life situations (e.g., in the education; see Kline, 1991 and Jensen, 1998). Furthermore, today behaviorism is not so rigid in his theoretical formulations.

FACTOR ANALYSIS: A SHORT EXPLANATION

Factor analysis is a statistical method of data reduction. In factor analysis scores' variations on a series of variables (V) are expressed in a smaller number of dimensions (F), called factors, so that F < V. Factor analysis shows the correlations of each variable with the corresponding factors. We can define a "factor" as a construct operationally specified by its factor loadings. From a mathematical viewpoint, factors can also be defined as linear combinations of variables. The discovery of factor analysis and general intelligence are strictly connected. In fact, factor analysis represents the statistical method used by Spearman to discover the g factor. The starting point of factor analysis is represented by the correlation matrix among all the variables (that is, abilities if we are studying intelligence). There are two main types of factor analysis: exploratory factor analysis and confirmatory factor analysis. *Exploratory factor analysis* is used when you need to explore a new field, for example when you have to construct a psychological test starting from a pool of items. In this case you need to select the best items to use in the final form of the test excluding the items which simply does not work. *Confirmatory factor analysis* is used when you need to test which hypothesis is able to better explain your data. Obviously, you need at least two hypotheses to confront.

Exploratory factor analysis is constituted by the following steps:

1) choosing the initial factoring method (e.g., principal components analysis);
2) selection of the number of factors to rotate (e.g., using the scree test);
3) selection of an appropriate method of rotation (orthogonal rotation against oblique rotation);
4) interpretation of factors.

We can use different types of initial factoring methods: principal components, principal factors (or principal axis analysis) and maximum likelihood analysis. *Principal components analysis* uses all variances, including an error variance (that is the casual error which characterize all the psychological measurements); on the contrary, principal factors analysis excludes the error variance by estimating communalities. *Maximum likelihood factor analysis* is the only method which is based on a test for the significance of the number of factors to extract. In general, with matrices of more than 25 variables there is no difference between the different methods.

In regards to the selection of the number of factors to rotate, there is no generally accepted method, even if it is a crucial point in factor analysis. According to Cattell (1978), rotation of too many factors causes factors to split, whenever rotation of too few factors tend to produce second order factors. The scree test and the parallel analysis seem to be the best methods at the moment. Statisticians tend to prefer the maximum likelihood method (ML), because it is the only method based on statistically significant factors. As all the probability based methods, the ML depends on the number of subjects in the sample. This is the reason for which the scree test or the parallel analysis should be preferred. Using different methods to evaluate their convergence is usually a good way to approach this problem.

If the factors are uncorrelated, an orthogonal rotation is to be preferred, and whenever they are correlated an oblique rotation is better. Anyway, we suppose that all the variables in the abilities' domain are correlated. For this reason, an oblique rotation is to be preferred, even if it is usually more difficult to interpret.

Interpretation of factors is the last step in factor analysis. It depends on the factor loadings, that is, the correlations between the variables and the factors (at least in principal components analysis). Anyway, any interpretation based on the factor loadings needs to be confirmed by external objective criteria. An easy explanation of factor analysis can be found in Kline (1994).

An example of the factor analysis of abilities is represented in Table 1. This table represents an unrotated one - factor principal axis solution for the Wechsler Adult Intelligence Scale (WAIS-R; Wechsler, 1981) and the Corsi's block tapping task (Corsi, 1972) for a sample aged 65-74 (N= 200; Saggino, Balsamo, Grieco, Cerbone, and Raviele, 2004). This solution explains 52.32% of the total variance. As shown in Table 1, all the variables present loadings higher than .50. Both the WAIS-R subtests and the Corsi's test load on the only factor. Therefore, this factor represents the g factor. The fact that all the variables have high loadings on this factor means that they are all a good measure of general intelligence.

Table 1. Unrotated first principal factor loadings for a sample aged 64-75*

Information	.823
Digit Span	.601
Vocabulary	.835
Arithmetic	.663
Comprehension	.733
Similarities	.771
Picture Completino	.753
Picture Arrangement	.672
Block Design	.696
Object Assembly	.689
Digit Symbol	.860
Corsi's test	.507

N= 200

*Table taken from Saggino, Balsamo, Grieco, Cerbone and Raviele (2004).

FACTOR ANALYSIS OF HUMAN ABILITIES

Extensive work was done on factor analysis of human abilities, particularly by Cattell and Horn. Recently Carroll (1993, 2003) attempted to realize a complete map of all human abilities. Cattell (1971) considers human abilities subdivided in strata. He found many primary factors in the abilities domain (as, for example, flexibility of closure, verbal ability, inductive reasoning and spelling). Five factors were found at the second order level: fluid intelligence, crystallized intelligence, visualization, retrieval capacity or general fluency and cognitive speed. The first two factors are considered by Cattell as the most important. *Fluid intelligence* (g_f) mainly depends on the neurological aspects of the brain (e.g., the neuronal efficiency) and represents the individual reasoning ability. It is the basic reasoning ability and it is close to Spearman's general ability factor. G_f mainly loads tests as the Culture – Fair Test

(Cattell and Cattell, 1959), and primary factors as intellectual speed, memory span and induction. Fluid intelligence is also genetically determined.

Crystallized intelligence (g_c) is dependent on the culture of the person, that is on his/her environment. G_c mainly loads on primary factors as numerical, verbal and mechanical abilities. Being different from fluid intelligence, crystallized intelligence is influenced by the culture and can be different from one culture to another. According to Cattell's (1971) investment theory, fluid ability is a general relation-perceiving ability which is linked to the associational neuronal development of the cortex. Crystallized ability represents the result of investing g_f in learning experiences. Crystallized ability and fluid ability are highly correlated in two- to three-year-old children. They become less and less correlated as they grow and become more involved in the cultural environment (e.g., school and family).

According to Cattell and Horn theory (e.g., Cattell, 1971; Horn, 1998) the existence of g at the third strata is questionable.

Carroll (1993, 2003) assumes the existence of three principal strata (or levels) in human cognitive abilities: a first (lower-order) level containing about 50-60 linearly independent narrow abilities, a second stratum containing about 8/10 linearly independent broader abilities and a third stratum comprising only the general ability factor (g).

According to Carroll (1993), three theories exist in the domain of cognitive abilities:

1. the view of Spearman (1927) which includes the existence of a general factor and a group of non general broad factors. Carroll calls this theory "the standard multifactorial view of cognitive abilities".
2. The view of Gustafson (e.g., 2001) and others which includes the existence of a general factor but considers it substantially identical to the second-order g_f but independent from the second-order g_c. This view is called by Carroll the "limited structural analysis view".
3. The view of Cattell (1971) and Horn (1998) that there is no general factor except two levels, the second broader one, mainly characterized by g_c and g_f. Carroll calls this latest view the "second stratum multiplicity view".

Even if current evidence tends to strongly support the standard multifactorial view, a final decision cannot be reached (Carroll, 2003).

INTELLIGENCE TESTS

There are many intelligence tests, including both group and individual intelligence tests. We just want to present the most important tests, that is, the Wechsler scales, the progressive matrices and the Cattell's Culture Fair Tests.

The *Wechsler scales* are a group of intelligence tests constructed by David Wechsler, the oldest being the Wechsler Bellevue Scale of 1938. Actually, there are three forms of the Wechsler scales: a pre-school form (WPSSI), a primary school form (WISC) and an adult form (WAIS). They permit the measurement of intelligence beginning with the age of 4 through the age of 89. They are all individually administered. Just to give an idea of the Wechsler scales we are describing the form for adults, that is, the Wechsler Adult Intelligence

Scale Third Edition (WAIS III; Wechsler, 1997). The WAIS III is constituted by fourteen subtests, two scales (performance and verbal) and four index scores (Verbal Comprehension, Working Memory, Perceptual Organization, and Processing Speed). Therefore, it is possible to obtain not only three total scores (total IQ, verbal IQ, and performance IQ) but also four index scores and fourteen subtests scores. Only eleven out of the fourteen subtests are used to calculate the four index scores. Comprehension, Picture Arrangement, and Object Assembly are not included. As with the three IQs, the four indexes also have a mean of 100 and a standard deviation of 15.

The verbal scale is formed by the following seven subtests: Vocabulary, Similarities, Information, Comprehension, Arithmetic, Digit Span, and Letter-Number Sequencing. The performance scale is constituted by seven subtests: Picture Completion, Block Design, Matrix Reasoning, Picture Arrangement, Digit Symbol-Coding, Symbol Search, and Object Assembly. The Verbal Comprehension Index is formed by three subtests: Vocabulary, Similarities, and Information; the Working Memory Index is constituted by Arithmetic, Digit Span, and Letter-Number Sequencing; the Perceptual Organization Index has three subtests: Picture Completion, Block Design, and Matrix Reasoning; the Processing Speed Index is formed by Digit Symbol-Coding, and Symbol Search. It is easily understandable that the verbal scale is a measure of crystallized intelligence and the performance scale a measure of fluid intelligence. Therefore, the verbal scale represents more of a measure of the actual intelligence (crystallized intelligence), while the performance scale represents a measure of the intellectual potential (fluid intelligence). When performance IQ is higher than verbal IQ it means that the individual's intellectual potential is not as developed. It could possibly depend on the subject's low educational level.

The three IQs have a mean of 100 and a standard deviation of 15. These values are independent from the age of the subject. For the same reasons, an IQ of 115 is one standard deviation above the mean independent from the subject's age.

The WAIS III (and in general all the Wechsler scales) is the most used intelligence test and it is regarded as the benchmark test of intelligence.

The *progressive matrices test* (PM; Raven, 1965) is one of the oldest and best researched intelligence tests. There are different editions of the progressive matrices able to measure intelligence from 5 years to old age (standard matrices, colored matrices and advanced matrices). The items are sequences of diagrams or patterns which require completion. The requested ability consists into finding a rule explaining the relationships between the diagrams and then to apply the rule to new cases: the subject has to select the next pattern or diagram in the sequence. The PM are called "progressive" because they are of crescent difficulty, even if it is not ever the case.

The problem presented by the progressive matrices' items are new, that is, the subjects are equally unfamiliar with them. So the PM measure fluid intelligence. In fact, the PM are considered one of the best measures of fluid intelligence.

The *Culture Fair Test* (Cattell and Cattell, 1959) has different forms. It can be used to test persons from 4 years of age to old age. This test was constructed by Cattell with the idea to realize an intelligence test independent from culture. Cattell reached only in part this aim. So his test, as its name demonstrates, could be considered more a culture fair test than a culture free one. The Culture Fair Test is a measure of fluid ability. The Culture Fair Test has four different types of non-verbal items:

1) series items: after a series of patterns is shown, subjects have to choose the next one from a selection of responses. Obviously, the subject has to find the rule specific to the series;

2) classification: they are also called "odd-man-out", because the subject has to select from a list the part that does not fit;

3) matrices: they are similar to the progressive matrices' items;

4) topological conditions: these items were invented by Cattell. Five boxes are drawn in which are squares and circles in different configurations. Subjects are asked to indicate into which of the five presented boxes a dot could be placed so that it would be outside a square and inside a circle.

THE CONCEPT OF EXECUTIVE FUNCTION

Executive functions currently represent one of the hottest topics in neuropsychological research. However, the notion of executive processes is relatively new, and can be dated back to the eighties. Historically, it has been introduced in the attempt to qualify a set of neuropsychological symptoms well known since the origins of neuropsychology, and classically labeled as "frontal lobe syndrome" (Stuss and Benson, 1986). Patients with prefrontal lesions typically show disinhibition, impulsivity and distractibility, rigidity and perseveration, apathy, and lack of response (Luria, 1966). These patients show a widespread disorganization of behavior, with a marked incapacity to successfully face common problems in their daily life, while they may be still able to score relatively well on many complex cognitive tests.

The concept of executive functions tries to account for this wide range of deficits by postulating the existence of a set of mental processes specifically devoted to organize and control cognitive functions and to coordinate the execution of goal-directed behavior. These processes enable a person to engage successfully in independent, purposive, self-serving behavior (Lezak, 1995). Such a high-level control is especially needed in daily-life or experimental situations where habitual behavior is unsatisfactory or insufficient to achieve a personal goal, for example when facing novel problems (e.g., when learning a complex motor or mental task), when the interference between two competing alternatives must be resolved (e.g., when strong habitual responses have to be inhibited), when mental planning or decision-making is needed before actual action (e.g., when looking for the best possible move in a chess game), or when multiple task goals are pursued at the same time.

Executive functions are particularly difficult to characterize and understand, and there is a good deal of theoretical debate about their nature. A fundamental question is whether any single, unified account of executive processes may explain the wide range of behaviors associated with prefrontal lesions. Several prominent theories of working memory and attention have promoted a singular view of executive functions. For example, Norman and Shallice's (1986) model of attentional control proposes a unitary "supervisory attentional system" biasing the activation of task schemas. Similarly, the framework for working memory introduced by Baddeley (1986) proposes a single "central executive" that manipulates the contents of a set of storage and rehearsal buffers in the service of some ongoing task. These and similar models all distinguish between two levels of cognitive functioning: a lower level of routine cognitive skills, including language, memory, etc., and an upper level specifically devoted to modulation and control of ongoing cognitive ability. It has been observed (Burgess, 1997) that this distinction resembles the distinction between automatic and controlled behavior in traditional cognitive psychology. Executive functions would then correspond to Fodor's (1983) central processes, which would be intrinsically non-modular and thus a difficult matter for scientific research.

By contrast, one can conceive executive functions as a set of distinct mechanisms. Unfortunately, however, there is no consensus even on the number and nature of these cognitive subprocesses. There is agreement on the fact that executive functions include at least high-level motor programming (programming and performance of complex series of movements), cognitive flexibility in shifting (inhibition of automatic programs or schemas, initiative and resistance to interference), planning, and self-monitoring. However, it has been noted that most of these hypothetical components, such as inhibition, planning, monitoring, and control, are in fact descriptions of task demands rather than of hypothetical processes (Rabbit, 1997). Furthermore, as we will review later, these distinctions have shown a very poor construct validity from the psychometric point of view.

As in other areas of psychology, double dissociations between neuropsychological patients showing different behavioral deficits might offer new insights on plausible subdivisions of the concept of executive control. Clinical and correlational studies (e.g., Miyake, Emerson, and Friedman, 2000) are in line with the idea of separate executive components: in different executive tasks patients may fail on one task but not on the other, while different patients can perform the opposite suggesting a non unitary underlying function.

Also, data from functional neuroimaging experiments may provide important information, at least if one assumes that different cognitive mechanisms are likely to be implemented in different brain systems. The prefrontal cortex is in fact a huge sector of the human brain, and is anatomically divided in different regions, thus it is probable that these different regions subserve different functions onto anatomical subdivisions of the prefrontal cortex. Systematic reviews of functional neuroimaging experiments (Duncan and Owen, 2000; Ramnani and Owen, 2004) rather point to a broad similarity of prefrontal recruitment for many different types of cognitive demand.

MEASURING EXECUTIVE FUNCTIONS

Developing instruments specifically devoted to measure executive functions have proved to be very difficult. One important point is related to the possible independent components of the executive behavior, as it is demonstrated by clinical and correlational studies (Miyake et al., 2000). Also in the "normal" population large individual differences have been observed in the same task and low correlations between different executive tests have been shown (Spitoni, Antonucci, Orsini, D'Olimpio, and Cantagallo 2002).

These data represent a convincing argument in favor of a separation of different components. Following this idea, even the historical models of executive functioning which hypothesized a unique executive controller, have been reviewed and interpreted as if formed by different units (Baddeley, 1996, 2003; Carlesimo, Perri, Turrizziani, Tomaiuolo, and

Caltagirone, 2001; Pickering, 2001; Pickering, Gathercole, Hall, and Lloyd, 2001; Klauer and Zhao, 2004). This point of view needs to find a correspondence in the tests used to assess executive behavior. As pointed out by Miyake et al. (2000), the construct validity of many common executive tasks like Wisconsin Card Sorting Test (WCST; Grant, and Berg, 1948) and Tower of London (TOL; Shallice, 1982) is not well clear. Between WCST requirements different authors have suggested the involvement of abilities such as "mental set shifting", "problem solving" or "inhibition", just to cite a few. In spite of the real difficulty to distinguish between the different capacities required to solve its demands, this test continues to be used as a measure of executive functions.

On the other hand, the relatively undefined construct of this kind of test accounts at least in part for the different methods employed by different authors to study the same executive ability. So, different approaches have been developed to have a measure of the same construct, from the study of a single, specific and relatively basic component (Goldman-Rakic, 1996; Bechar, Damasio, Tranel, and Anderson., 1998; Wagner, Maril, Bjork, and Schacter, 2001) to a more complex executive behavior (Miotto and Morris, 1998; Chevignard, Pillon, Pradat-Diehl, Taillefer, and Rousseau, Le Bras, and Dubois 2000). The consistent evidence is that also a single ability implies the involvement of more basic cognitive processes and their integration.

In order to assess executive functions, what appears to be necessary is a multidisciplinary and multi-dimensional approach; hence, more tasks aimed to detect specific executive abilities seem more adequate than a single complex test which involves different cognitive processes. A further aspect needs to be taken into account: the presence of everyday problems in dysexecutive patients may not (necessary) fit with the scores resulting from a structured testing assessment. The use of tasks more sticking to real situations may improve the measure of these behaviors.

In different neuropsychological areas an ecological approach has been recognized as an imperative issue (Burgess, Alderman, Evans, Emslie, and Wilson 1998; Norris and Tate, 2000) and possibly in the executive functions assessment this need is more and more obvious. The Behavioral Assessment of the Dysexecutive Syndrome (B.A.D.S.; Wilson, Alderman, Burgess, Emslie, and Evans 1996) was specifically developed to predict everyday problems using an ecological approach. This test has been designed as a battery that overcomes deficiencies associated with previous tests by including items that are specifically sensitive to those skills involved in problem solving, planning, and organizing behavior over an extended period of time. The battery thus assesses capacities that are normally exercised in everyday living. The battery comprises six different subtests: *the Temporal Judgment test* uses four questions to assess subject's ability to estimate how long various events last (such as a routine dental appointment). The *Rule Shift Cards* tests the ability to change an established pattern of responding by using familiar materials. In Part One a response pattern is established according to a simple rule. In Part Two, subject is asked to shift from the first rule to a new one. The *Action Program* is a test of practical problem solving. A cork has to be extracted from a tall tube, a result which can only be achieved by the planned use of various other materials provided. The *Key Search* is a test of strategy formation. In an analogue of a common problem, subjects are required to demonstrate how they would search a field for a set of lost keys, and their strategy is scored according to its functionality. The *Zoo Map* is a test of planning. It provides information about the ability to plan a route to visit six of 12 possible locations in a zoo. The *Modified Six Elements* is a test of planning, task scheduling and performance monitoring. It is a simplified version of the original Shallice and Burgess (1991) test.

The tests are constructed in order to sample the range of problems commonly associated with the dysexecutive syndrome in four broad areas: emotional or personality changes, motivational changes, behavioral changes, and cognitive changes. Norris and Tate (2000) demonstrated the ecological validity of this battery and suggested it as a valid instrument to assess different executive processes and, as a consequence, different components of the dysexecutive syndrome.

INTELLIGENCE AND EXECUTIVE FUNCTIONS: SAME OR DIFFERENT?

Following the work of Hebb and Penfield (1940), there was a general consensus that frontal lobe functions are unrelated to conventional intelligence (see also Teuber, 1972). This finding has been generally accepted because of the frequent clinical observation of normal IQ in patients suffering from frontal lesions (e.g., Damasio and Anderson, 1993; Brazzelli, Colombo, Della Sala, and Spinnler, 1994). Milner (1983), for instance, reported a normal IQ score in a patient who had undergone a dorsolateral frontal lobectomy. Similarly, Damasio and Anderson (1993) documented a consistent preservation of WAIS scores in 10 frontal patients. Boone, Ghaffarian, Lessere, Hill-Guitierrez, and Berman (1993) observed no significant differences on WCST performance across different full scale IQ groupings. This result was interpreted as the absence of a relationship among executive functions and intelligence. More recently, Ardila, Pineda, and Rosselli (2000) investigated this issue by administering a set of executive tests and the WISC to a group of adolescents. A correlation matrix between WISC scores and the executive function measures (verbal fluency, Trail Making Test; Reitan, and Wolfson, 1985) showed a significant, but poor correlation among executive and intelligence scores. Taken together, these results seem to suggest that executive functions are not related with intelligence, or at least that psychometric intelligence tests are not sensitive to frontal lobe deficits.

However, in the quoted studies the link between intelligence and frontal functioning was usually investigated by standard intelligence tests, which, as seen above, are highly sensitive to knowledge. Probably the unchanged IQ scores in frontal patients observed in many studies may simple reflect relative preservation of knowledge. Following this line of reasoning, Duncan, Burgess and Emslie (1995) submitted three patients with frontal lesions of different etiologies and five control patients with posterior cortex involvement to standard and fluid intelligence tests. They reported a selective decrements of Culture Fair IQ scores associated with no changes in WAIS IQ scores only in the frontal lobe patients. In posterior patients, they did not find any discrepancy between WAIS and Culture Fair IQs.

These results point to a specific link between *fluid* intelligence and executive functions. In particular, Duncan, Emslie, Williams, Johnson, and Freer (1996) have stressed the role of goal management ability as the fundamental key in picturing the relation between fluid intelligence and executive control. They used a complex visual switching task, in which subjects were asked to follow a specific rule coded by a cue. Subjects sometimes behaved as if they were neglecting one of the cues, even if they clearly remembered the task rules. It seemed that the neglected cue was somehow inactive in controlling behavior. This "goal neglect" is frequently observed in frontal patients, but strikingly it can also be observed in neurologically normal volunteers. Interestingly, subjects who more frequently showed goal neglect were the same who obtained low g scores at the Culture Fair. The correlation between g_f and goal neglect leads to hypothesize that both "executive" and "fluid" processes deal with a higher-level function concerning abstract action and goal selection under condition of novelty.

Working memory is another specific cognitive function which has been related to fluid intelligence. In a paper presented at the annual meeting of the American Educational Research Association in Seattle, Lohman (2001) suggested that reasoning tasks, such as Raven Advanced Progressive Matrices (RAPM), place demands on the management of attentional resources in working memory, since they require one to simultaneously remember and transform information. Specifically, fluid intelligence could be defined as "inductive reasoning" characterized by the capacity to maintain, transform, and coordinate information: these three abilities would be under control of working memory, and g_f and working memory could be interpreted as two sides of the same coin.

An elegant study by Carpenter, Just, and Shell (1990) shows the importance of both working memory and goal management in solving RAPM. They first analyzed the items composing the RAPM, and tried to figure out the different logical mental processes involved in the performance. They individuated two kinds of problems (figural and analytic), and marked five types of rules that govern the disposition of the stimuli in each matrix and allowed the subject to grasp the correct answer. The kind of problem (figural vs analytic) and the number of rules (or tokens of the same rule) determine the difficulty of the task. The authors analyzed detailed performance characteristics, such as verbal protocol (reported during the execution of the task), eye-fixation patterns, errors, and then individuated the processes distinguishing between high- and low-scoring subjects. The most important individual differences in solving the Raven test derived from the abilities to decompose the main principal goal in smaller sub-goals, to "keep in mind" traces of this process, and to proceed in solving the single sub-problems step by step In other words, the authors highlighted the important contribution of working memory and goal management in solving the most g_f representative test (Show, Kyllonen and Marshall, 1984). This was also sustained by the significant correlation found between Raven scores and the performance in a puzzle test similar to TOL.

Other arguments supporting the hypothesis of a relationship between executive functioning and fluid reasoning come from studies on normal aging. It is now well documented that aging is associated with the deterioration of the frontal lobes, earlier and more severely than other brain areas (Haug, Barmwater, Eggers, Fisher, Kuhl, and Sass, 1983). This frontal deterioration may be the substrate of age-related cognitive impairments (Daigneault and Braun,1993; Moscovitch and Winocur, 1995; West, Ergis, Winocur, and Saint-Cyr, 1996) in many tests commonly used to assess executive functions, such as letter fluency (Whelian and Lesher, 1997; Phillips, 1999), Tower of London (Allamanno, Della Sala, Laicona, Pasetti, and Spinnler, 1987; Phillips, Gillholy, Logie, Della Sala, and Winn, 1996), the Stroop test (Boon, Miller, Lessere, Hill, and D'Elia 1990), and WCST (Daigneaul, Braun, and Whitaker, 1992). Similarly, age-related deficits in carrying out intelligence test were found. As elegantly reviewed by Phillips and Della Sala (1998), the first study showing a clear age-related decline of abstract reasoning abilities was that of Yerkes (1921). Since that, much evidence has accumulated that reasoning abilities undergo a systematical decline during normal aging (for a review see Phillips and Della Sala, 1999). Given that, and in accordance with Cattel's theory of fluid vs. crystallized intelligence, it is plausible that age differences on intelligence tests particularly reflect a decline in g_f.

NEUROIMAGING AND NEUROPHYSIOLOGICAL STUDIES

The idea of uncovering the biological basis of intelligence has a long history. Intelligence scores have been correlated with brain size, localization of brain lesions, spontaneous electroencephalographic activity, event-related potentials, molecular genetics, hemodynamic changes in the brain, speed of neural transmission. It seems that there is a strong interest in studying intelligence as an expression not just of human ability, but also of the biological functioning of the nervous system. Sternberg (2000) moved important critics to this kind of research. He considered the existing intelligence tests as measures of limited aspects of intelligence. The g factor discovered by Spearman would just cover the limited abilities involved in classical intelligence tasks. Consequently, the study of the underlying biological functioning would have a limited impact. Furthermore, studies based on correlations among two or more variables do not imply any causal relation: for example, a pattern of activation in some specific areas during an intelligence test does not mean that this area is the "locus" of intelligence.

Although Sternberg's critics are worthy of value, standard intelligence tests do surely measure important components of individual differences able to predict individual performances in cognitive tests and in real life (Kline, 1991; Jensen, 1998). Furthermore, neuroimaging studies of intelligence not only consider the question of *where* but also the question of *how* the brain produces an intelligent behavior. We will focus our attention on the concept of fluid intelligence. In particular, we will consider the hypothesis that prefrontal cortex functioning has some particular properties similar to ones attributed to g_f: large involvement in many diverse cognitive processes, independence from the nature of the stimuli, and adaptability to current task demands.

Historically, Spearman's idea of g as "mental energy" was the first concept to find correspondence in a neuroimaging study. Haier, Siegel, Nuechterlein, and Hazlett, (1988) administered the RAPM, the Continuous Performance Test (CPT), a visual vigilance test, and a control task to three different groups of volunteers. They observed that people with high g scores differed from subjects with low g scores for the amount of cortical metabolism during the performance of the RAPM, measured using positron emission tomography (PET). They obtained quite a counterintuitive negative correlation between glucose metabolism and RAPM performance, suggesting that some individual differences in cognitive ability may be related to efficiency or density of neural circuits. In other words, people with high g scores seem to be more parsimonious and efficient in using Spearman's "mental energy".

Even if Haier's first hypothesis was interesting and stimulating, it was probably the result of a methodological bias. Larson, Haier, Casse and Hazen (1995) submitted 28 subjects to PET scanning while solving easy and hard backward digit-span problems tailored to participants' own ability levels. In this way, they controlled group differences in aptitude to study the effective correlation between cortical metabolism and intelligence. The data were in contrast with the previous one, showing that high aptitude, in both high g and low g groups, was associated with a high cortical glucose use. This study suggested that tasks with high demands on cognition require *broader* neural activity (or "mental energy") if compared with easy problems.

Which cortical networks are recruited during high g problems, and how do they integrate each other? Prabhakaran, Desmond, Glover, and Gabrieli (1997) used functional magnetic resonance imaging (fMRI) while subjects solved three different types of problems (figural, analytic and match) taken and adapted from the RAPM and the Standard Progressive Matrices (SPM). The figural items required mostly visual-spatial analysis to determine the correct answer, while the analytic required more abstract reasoning. Match problems were considered as the control task and required matching identical figures. Fluid reasoning yielded fMRI activation of an extensive, but specific, network of cortical regions, including regions involved in domain-dependent and domain-independent working memory systems. Specifically, figural reasoning activated regions mediating working memory for spatial and object information and for mental imagery (middle frontal gyrus, inferior and superior parietal regions, inferior and middle temporal gyrus, predominantly situated in the right hemisphere). During analytic reasoning, the same right frontal activation was observed, plus left frontal activations along the inferior and middle frontal gyrus and in premotor cortex. These regions have been shown to be involved in verbal and semantic working memory. These results demonstrate a huge recruitment of different domain dependent working memory systems in the fluid and figural reasoning. But is there a specific cortical network deputed to coordinate and direct all those systems? The authors revealed a pattern of activation in the dorsolateral and rostrolateral prefrontal areas exclusively in the analytic condition. They suggested that these regions constitute a domain-independent working memory systems and play the role of executive control on other higher-order processes. Probably these areas are also involved in maintaining active information relevant to the current task, independently from the nature of the stimuli (verbal, spatial, semantic, etc.).

Other neuroimaging studies corroborate this hypothesis. Duncan and Owen (2000) reviewed 20 separate functional imaging studies with different cognitive task demands (response conflict, task novelty, number of elements in working memory, working memory delay, perceptual difficulty) searching for common specific cortical activations. They showed clusters of activation from very different studies on the same frontal and parietal regions. On the lateral surface of both hemispheres, two major clusters were observed around the posterior part of the inferior frontal sulcus and along both banks of the intraparietal sulcus. On the medial surface of both hemispheres, a clear cluster of activations was observed in the dorsal part of the anterior cingulate and the adjacent supplementary motor area. Thus, it is evident that a fronto-parietal cortical network is recruited by diverse cognitive demands, sustaining the existence of a unique factor. Is this factor related with g_f? Duncan, Rudiger, Kolodny, Bor, Herzog, Newell, and Emslie (2000), in a PET study, directly analyzed brain activation during problem solving of high g and low g items in a sample of normal subjects. The results showed a specific recruitment, for the high g loaded task, of some frontal areas that resemble the ones individuated by Duncan and Owen (2000) in their review paper. This led the authors to conclude that general intelligence derives from a specific frontal system important in the control of diverse forms of behavior.

This purported a supervisory role of the lateral prefrontal cortex is also supported by an elegant fMRI study by Gray, Chabris, and Braver (2003). In this study, for the first time individual differences in brain activation were correlated with intelligence scores, in a vast sample of healthy subjects. The authors directly investigated whether fluid intelligence (g_f) is mediated by brain regions that support executive control, by administering a demanding working memory task which included a number of high-interference trials. From a behavioral point of view, g_f was correlated with behavioral accuracy, but only when specifically considering high-interference trials, where a correct answer requires high executive control. Taken by itself, these data suggest a very specific link between intelligence and executive functions. Furthermore, among the regions activated by the working memory task, the lateral prefrontal cortex showed a positive correlation between the amount of activation during high-interference trials and g_f, thus suggesting that this region mediates the relationship between ability (g_f) and executive performance.

Thus, neuroimaging studies clearly show that prefrontal cortex, and a specific prefrontal-parietal network, are involved in many different cognitive processes, and that their functioning is specifically related with g_f. It has been proposed that these regions constitute a domain-independent WM system that plays a role of executive control over other higher order cognitive processes. If so, we would expect activity of neurons belonging to the prefrontal cortex to be related not to specific stimuli or responses, but to more abstract processes.

Single neuron recordings from the prefrontal cortex of the behaving monkey show that prefrontal activity reflects many and different kinds of information salient to current task demands (Miller and Cohen, 2001). For example, Asaad, Rainer, and Miller (1998) found prefrontal activity selective for the current association between a cue and a saccade, with just few neurons responding to specific cues or specific saccades. Furthermore, it has been shown that lateral PFC neurons become selective for a specific stimulus only if this stimulus is salient for the task. In two different studies, Watanabe (1990, 1992) trained monkeys to associate a particular visual or auditory stimuli to reward. He observed that lateral prefrontal neurons became selective for the stimuli only if this signaled a reward. An elegant paper of Wallis, Anderson, and Miller (2001) highlighted the role of PFC neurons in abstracting ability. This ability is surely fundamental to adapt behavior to the context and to guide the ongoing actions in an efficient manner, allowing for the flexibility and adaptability that are central to intelligent behavior. The authors trained two monkeys to produce a specific behavior in response to visual stimuli, shifting between two abstract rules (match and non-match). A visual sample was presented together with a specific cue which indicated the rule to follow. A period of delay anticipated a visual stimulus that could be either identical or different from the sample. In the match condition, the monkey released a lever if the second visual stimulus was the same as the sample; in the non-match condition, the monkey released the lever if the stimulus differed from the sample. Data showed a specific neuronal activity reflecting the current rule in 41% of the recorded neurons during the sample and delay periods. Neurons were specific for the kind of rule: 50% of the rule-selective neurons responded to the match condition rule, while the other 50% to the non-match condition. Furthermore, the encoding of abstract rules was evident throughout the prefrontal cortex, in the sample and delay epochs, even if there was a greater activity of the dorsolateral prefrontal cortex, if compared to the ventrolateral and orbitofrontal prefrontal cortex, during the sample period.

In summary, single cell recordings prove some fundamental features of neurons belonging to the prefrontal cortex: they are independent from the nature of the stimuli and the kind of response to produce; their activity is highly flexible; they respond to relevant and salient inputs relative to the current task. Thus, it seems that, from a cognitive point of view, prefrontal functioning is deeply related to g_f, and plays a role in coding all the different inputs and adapting one's actions to task-related demands.

CONCLUSION

As underlined by our review, executive functions and gf are often described in similar ways and with similar properties. We have also reported an overlapping of the same underlying cortical processes and the same localizations. Therefore, are we studying the same construct or gf and executive functions must be considered two different psychological constructs? We think this is a complicated question to figure out, and that it is necessary to have a more unitary framework.

Surely, the two concepts of fluid intelligence and executive functions have a completely different historical genesis. The concept of executive functions was introduced in neuropsychology to account for a wide range of symptoms presented by frontal lobe patients, while g was mathematically developed to account for the common variance existing among a large set of cognitive tasks. Obviously, these two different approaches, clinical vs. individual differences, led to different definitions and different descriptions of probably similar underlying processes.

Important behavioral and lesion data historically led to the idea of two separated and independent constructs. The low correlation of traditional executive test scores with IQs in normal subjects, and the unchanged IQ scores observed in many frontal patients, were considered the scientific basis of this hypothesis. We previously reported the possibility, in agreement with Duncan et al. (1995), that the absence of correlation between g and executive functions was the result of the use of culture loaded intelligence tests. In fact, only fluid intelligence would be impaired in patients with frontal lesions, whenever crystallized intelligence would not be influenced. Studies of normal aging have well documented the association of the g_f decline to the deterioration of the frontal lobe (e.g., Haug et al., 1983). The same pattern happens with the executive functions (e.g., Allamanno et al., 1987). A further proof is represented by the correlation between g_f and goal neglect in normal subjects (Duncan et al., 1996). So both "executive" and "fluid" processes seem to deal with a higher-level function concerning goal selection and abstract action under condition of novelty.

Hence, we think that the general opinion that sees intelligence as independent from executive functions must be seriously reconsidered. Many neuroimaging, neurophysiological, and behavioral studies reviewed in this chapter seem to converge on the idea that a strong link between g_f and EF does exist, and it reflects executive control processes and prefrontal functioning.

Neuroimaging techniques prove the direct involvement of prefrontal regions in solving high g_f tasks, the existence of a fronto-parietal network common to very different task demands, and the correlation across subjects between g_f and the activation of this network. Single cell recordings show the high flexibility of the prefrontal neurons in coding several kinds of stimuli and behavioral responses in order to successfully adapt their activity to relevant task information. Finally, neuropsychological data remark the link between executive control, goal management, g_f scores, and the broad disorganization of "intelligent behavior" following frontal lesions.

Executive control can be seen as a supervisor process dedicated to organize and control other cognitive processes. It implies a constant on-line maintaining and selection of internal and external information to provide a reference context for the ongoing actions. It also implies maintaining of the final goal and smaller sub-goals to successfully cope with a current task. We can imagine it as a supervisor working memory system, whose main evolutionary meaning is adaptability of behavior to task demands. We have to keep in mind that this cognitive construct is fundamental in the neuropsychology of executive functions. Even in the context of a multidimensional view of executive functions as composed by specific executive abilities, we must take into account the important role of such a coordinating system.

On the other hand, it seems that executive control is deeply involved during the execution of high g task, providing the ability to decompose the main goal in small subgoals, to keep in mind traces of this process, and to proceed in solving the single subproblems step by step (Carpenter et al., 1990). So we think that the linking bridge between intelligence and executive functions lies on this adapting process being fundamental for both. Hence, we can picture it as a continuum in which we find on the two opposites of the pathological expression, namely dysexecutive symptoms, and the efficient behavior (high g score) of the same process. In fact, a disruption of the control system can spread out in a varied symptomatology, but surely expresses a disorganization of adapting and coping behavior. At the same time, subjects belonging to low g population can manifest difficulty in fitting their "normal" behavior to task demands.

We previously showed that the population of prefrontal neurons have specific properties compatible with the ones required to an executive control system (Miller and Cohen, 2001). Flexibility, independence from the kind of stimuli and the type of the required response, selectiveness for task relevant information are some of these properties. Furthermore, neuroimaging studies clearly show specific patterns of activations in high g tasks involving bilaterally the dorsolateral region of the prefrontal cortex. Therefore, lesions in the same prefrontal regions often result in a symptomatology characteristic of the desexecutive syndrome.

REFERENCES

Allamanno, N.S., Della Sala, M., Laicona, C., Pasetti, C., and Spinnler, H. (1987) Problem solving ability in aging and dementia: normative data in non-verbal test. *Italian Journal of Neurological Science 8*, 111-120

Ardila, A., Pineda, C., and Rosselli, M. (2000). Correlation between intelligence test scores and executive functions measures. *Archives of Clinical Neuropsychology*, *15*, 31–36

Asaad, W.F., Rainer, G., and Miller, E.K (1998). Neural activity in the primate prefrontal cortex during associative learning. *Neuron*, 21, 1399-1407

Baddeley, A. (1986). *Working memory*. Oxford, UK: Oxford University Press.

Baddeley, A.(1996). The fractionation of working memory. *Proceedings of the National Academy of Sciences U S A*, 93, 13468-72.

Baddeley, A. (2003). Working memory and language: An overview. *Journal of Communication Disorders*, 36, 189-208.

Bechara, A, Damasio, H, Tranel, D, and Anderson, S. W. (1998). Dissociation of working memory from decision making within the human prefrontal cortex. *Journal of Neuroscience*, 18, 428-437

Boone, K. B., Ghaffarian, S., Lesser, I. M., Hill-Guitierrez, E., and Berman, N.G. (1993). Wisconsin Card Sorting Test performance in healthy, older adults: Relationship to age, sex, education and IQ. *Journal of Clinical Psychology,*. *49*, 54-60

Boone, K.B,, Miller, B.L, Lesser, I.M., Hill, E., and D'Elia, L. (1990). Performance on frontal lobe tests in healthy older individuals. *Developmental Neuropsychology, 6*, 215-223.

Boring, E. G. (1923). Intelligence as the tests test it. *New Republic, 35*, 35-37.

Brazzelli, M., Colombo, N., Della Sala, S., and Spinnler, H. (1994). Spared and impaired abilities after bilateral frontal damage. *Cortex, 30,* 27-51.

Burgess, P. W. (1997) Theory and methodology in executive function research. In P. Rabbit (Ed.), *Methodology of frontal and executive function* (pp. 81-116). Hove, U.K.: Psychology Press.

Burgess, P. W., Alderman, N. , Evans, J., Emslie, H., and Wilson, B. A. (1998). The ecological validity of tests of executive function. *Journal of the International Neuropsychology Society*, 4, 547-558

Carlesimo, G. A., Perri, R., Turriziani, P., Tomaiuolo, F., and Caltagirone, C. (2001). Remembering what but not where: Independence of spatial and visual working memory in the human brain. *Cortex*, 37, 457-73

Carpenter, P.A., Just, M.A., and Shell, P. (1990). What one intelligence test measures: A theoretical account of the processing in the Raven Progressive Matrices Test. *Psychological Review, 97*, 404-431.

Carroll, J.B. (1993). *Human cognitive abilities: A survey of factor analytic studies.* New York, N.Y.: Cambridge University Press.

Carroll, J.B. (2003). The higher-stratum structure of cognitive abilities: Current evidence supports g and about ten broad factors. In H. Nyborg (Eds.), *The scientific study of general intelligence. Tribute to Arthur R. Jensen* (pp. 5-21). Oxford. U.K.: Elsevier Science.

Cattell, R. B., and Cattell, A. K. S. (1959). *The Culture – Fair Test.* Champaign, Ill.: IPAT.

Cattell, R. B. (1971). *Abilities: Their structure, growth and action. New York*, NY: Houghton Mifflin [Revised edition: Amsterdam, North-Holland, 1987]

Cattell, R. B. (1978). *The scientific use of factor analysis.* New York, N. Y.: Plenum.

Chevignard, M., Pillon, B., Pradat-Diehl, P., Taillefer, C., Rousseau, S., Le Bras, C., and Dubois, B. (2000). An ecological approach to planning dysfunction: Script execution. *Cortex, 36,* 649-69

Corsi, P. M. (1972). Human memory and the medial temporal region of the brain. *Dissertation Abstracts International, 34 (02),* 891B.

Daigneault, S., and Braun, C. M. J. (1993). Working memory and the Self-Ordered Pointing Task: Further evidence of early prefrontal decline in normal aging. *Journal Of Clinical And Experimental Neuropsychology*. 15, 881-95.

Daigneault, S., Braun, C. M. J., and Whitaker, H. A. (1992). Early effects of normal aging on perseverative and non-perseverative prefrontal measures. *Developmental Neuropsychology, 8*, 99–114

Damasio, A. R., and Anderson, S. W. (1993). The frontal lobes. In K. M. Heilman, and E. Valenstein (Eds.), *Clinical neuropsychology* (3rd ed., pp. 409–460). New York, N.Y.: Oxford University Press.

Deary, I.J., (2000). Looking Down on Human Intelligence. London, UK: Oxford University Press

Duncan, J. (1995). Attention, intelligence and the frontal lobes. In M. S. Gazzanica (Eds.), *The cognitive neuroscience* (pp-721-733). Cambridge, MA: MIT Press.

Duncan, J., Burgess, P. and Emslie, H. (1995). Fluid intelligence after frontal lobe lesions. *Neuropsychologia*, 33, 261-268

Duncan, J., Emslie, H., Williams, P., Johnson R., and Freer C. (1996). Intelligence and the frontal lobe: the organization of goal directed behaviour. *Cognitive Psychology*, 30, 257-303

Duncan, J., and Owen, A. M. (2000). Common regions of the human frontal lobe recruited by diverse cognitive demands. *Trends in Neurosciences, 23,* 475-483.

Duncan, J., Rudiger, J.Z, Kolodny, J, Bor, D., Herzog, A., Newell, F., and Emslie, H. (2000) A neural basis for general intelligence. *Science, 289,* 457-460,

Fodor, J.A. (1983). *The modularity of mind.* Cambridge, MA: MIT Press.

Goldman-Rakic, P.S. (1998). The prefrontal landscape: Implications of functional architecture for understanding human mentation and the central executive. In A.C. Roberts, and T.W. Robbins, (Eds.), *Prefrontal cortex: Executive and cognitive functions* (87-102). London UK: Oxford University Press.

Gray, J.R., Chabris, C.F., and Braver, T.S. (2003). Neural mechanisms of general fluid intelligence. *Nature Neuroscience, 6,* 316-322

Gustafson, J. E. (2001). On the hierarchical structure of abilities and personality. In J. M. Collis, and S. Messick (Eds.), *Intelligence and personality: Bridging the gap in theory and measurement* (pp. 25-42). Mahwah, N.J.: Erlbaum.

Haier, R.J., Siegel, B.V., Nuechterlein, K.H., and Hazlett E. Cortical glucose metabolic rate correlates of abstract reasoning and attention studied with positron emission tomography. *Intelligence*, 12, 199-217

Haug, H., Barmwater, U., Eggers, R., Fischer, D., Kuhl, S., and Sass, N. L. (1983). Anatomical changes in aging brain: Morphometric analysis of the human prosencephalon. In J. Cervo's-Navarro, and H. I. Sarkander (Eds.), *Brain aging: Neuropathology and neuropharmacology* (pp.1–12). New York, NY: Raven Press.

Hebb, D.O., and Penfield, W. (1940). Human behavior after extensive removal from the frontal lobes. *Archives of Neurology and Psychiatry, 44,* 421-438.

Horn, J.L. (1998). A basis for research on age differences in cognitive capabilities. In J. J. McArdle and R. Woodcock (Eds.), *Human cognitive abilities in theory and practice* (pp. 57-91). Mahwah, N. J.: Erlbaum.

Jensen, A. (1998). *The g factor.* Westport, CT: Praeger.

Klauer, K.C., and Zhao, Z. (2004). Double dissociations in visual and spatial short-term memory. *Journal of Experimental Psychology, 133,* 355-81

Kline, P. (1991). *Intelligence. The psychometric view.* London, U.K.: Routledge.

Kline, P. (1993). *The handbook of psychological testing.* London, U.K.: Routledge.

Kline, P. (1994). *An easy guide to factor analysis.* London, U.K.: Routledge.

Larson, G.E., Haier, R.J., LaCasse, L., and Hazen K (1995). Evaluation of a "mental effort" hypothesis for correlations between cortical metabolism and intelligence. *Intelligence*, 21, 267-278

Lezak, M. (1995). *Neuropsychological assessment.* Oxford, UK: Oxford University Press.

Lohman, D.F. (2001). Fluid intelligence, inductive reasoning, and working memory: Where the theory of multiple intelligences falls short. Paper presented at the annual meeting of the American Educational Research Association in Seattle, WA

Luria, A.R. (1966). *Higher cortical functions in man.* London,UK: Tavistock.

MacPherson, S.E., Phillips, L.H., and Della Sala S. (2002). Age, executive function, and social decision making: a dorsolateral prefrontal theory of cognitive aging. *Psychology and ageing*, 17, 598-609

Miller, E.K., and Cohen J.D. (2001). An integrate theory of prefrontal cortex function. *Annual Reviews of Neuroscience*, 24, 167-202

Milner, B. (1982). Some cognitive effects of frontal-lobe lesions in man. *Philosophical Transactions of the Royal Society of London, 298,* 211-226

Miotto, E.C., and Morris, R.G. (1998). Virtual planning in patients with frontal lobe lesions. *Cortex, 34,* 639-57.

Miyake, A., Emerson, M.J., and Friedman, N.P. (2000). Assessment of executive functions in clinical settings: Problems and recommendations. *Seminars in Speech and Language*, 21, 169-83.

Moscovitch, M., and Winocur, G. (1995). Frontal lobes, memory, and aging. *Annals of the New York Academy of Sciences, 769*, 119–150

Norman, D.A., and Shallice, T. (1986). Attention to action: Willed and automatic control of behavior. In A. D. Norman, and Shallice, T. (Eds.), *Consciousness and self regulation: Advances in research and theory* (pp. 1-18). New York, N. Y.: Plenum Press.

Norris, G., and Tate, R. (2000). The behavioral assessment of the dysexecutive syndrome (BADS): Ecological, concurrent and construct validity. *Neuropshyological Rehabilitation, 10*, 33-45.

Phillips, L.H. (1999). Age and individual differences in verbal fluency. *Developmental Neuropsychology 15*, 249-267

Phillips, L.H., and Della Sala, S. (1998) Aging, intelligence and anatomical segregation in the frontal lobes. *Learning and Individual Differences, 10*, 217-293

Phillips, L.H., Gillholy, K.J., Logie, R.H., Della Sala S., and Wynn, V. (1996) The role of memory in Tower of London Test. Paper presented at the Second International Conference on Memory, Abano (Italy)

Pickering, S.J. (2001). Cognitive approaches to the fractionation of visuo-spatial working memory. *Cortex*, 37, 457-73

Pickering, S.J., Gathercole, S.E., Hall, M., and Lloyd, S.A. (2001). Development of memory for pattern and path: Further evidence for the fractionation of visuo-spatial memory. *Quarterly Journal Of Experimental Psychology A, 54*, 397-420.

Prabhakaran, V., Smith, J.A.L., Desmond, J.E. Glover, G.H., and Gabrieli, J.D.E. (1997). Neural substrates of fluid reasoning: An fMRI study of neocortical activation during performance of the Raven's Progressive Matrices Test. *Cognitive Psychology*, 33, 43-63

Rabbit, P. (1997). Methodologies and models in the study of executive function. In P. Rabbit (Ed.), *Methodology of frontal and executive function* (pp. 1-38). Hove, UK: Psychology Press.

Rabbit, P. (2005). Frontal brain changes and cognitive performance in old age. *Cortex*, 41, 238-240

Ramnani, N., and Owen, A.M. (2004). Anterior prefrontal cortex: Insights into function from anatomy and neuroimaging. *Nature Reviews Neurosceince, 5*, 184-194.

Raven, J. C. (1965). *Progressives Matrices.* London, U.K.: H. K. Lewis.

Saggino, A., Balsamo, M., Grieco, A., Cerbone, M.R. and Raviele, N.N. (2004). Corsi's block tappino task: standardization and location in factor space with the WAIS-R for two normal samples of adults. Perceptual and Motor Skills, 98, 840-848

Reitan, R. M., and Wolfson, D. (1985). *The Halstead-Reitan Neuropsychological Battery. Theory and clinical interpretation.* Tucson, AZ: Neuropsychology Press.

Shallice, T. (1982). Specific impairments of planning. *Philosophical Transactions of the Royal Society of London, B*, 298, 199-209.

Shallice, T., and Burgess, P.W. (1991). Deficits in strategy application following frontal lobe damage in man. *Brain, 114*, 727–741.

Skinner, B. F. (1953). *The science of human behavior.* New York, N. Y.: MacMillan.

Snow, R.E., Killonen, P.C., and Marshalek, B. (1984). The topography of ability and learning correlations. In R.J. Sternberg (Eds.) *Advances in the psychology of human intelligence.* (Vol. 2, pp. 47-103). Hillsdale, NJ: Erbulam.

Spearman, S. (1904). "General intelligence": Obiectively determined and measured. *American Journal of Psychology, 15*, 201-292.

Spearman, C. (1927). *The abilities of man: Their nature and measurement.* New York, N. Y.: MacMillan.

Spitoni, G., Antonucci, A., Orsini, A., D'Olimpio, F., and Cantagallo, A. (2002). A first step to assess different components of executive processes. Paper presented at the 3rdWorldCongress in Neurological Rehabilitation, Venice, Italy, April 2-6 2002

Sternberg, R. (1977). *Intelligence, information processing and analogical reasoning: The componential analysis of human abilities.* Hillsdale, N.J.: Erlbaum.

Sternberg, R. (2000). The holey grail of general intelligence. *Science*, 289, 399-401

Stuss, D.T., and Benson, D.F. (1986). *The frontal lobes.* New York, NY.: Raven.

Teuber, H. L., (1972). Unity and diversity of frontal lobe functions. *Acta Neurobiologiae Experimentalis , 32*, 615-656

Wagner, A.D., Maril, A., Bjork, R.A., and Schacter, D.L. (2001). Prefrontal contributions to executive control: fMRI evidence for functional distinctions within lateral prefrontal cortex. *Neuroimage, 14*, 1337-47.

Wallis, J.D., Anderson, K.C., and Miller, E.K. (2001). Single neurons in prefrontal cortex encode abstract rules. *Nature*, 411, 953-956

Watanabe, M. (1990). Prefrontal unit activity during associative learning in the monkey. *Experimental Brain Research*, 80, 296-309

Watanabe, M. (1992). Frontal units of the monkey coding the associative significance of visual and auditory stimuli. *Experimental Brain Research*, 89, 233-247

Wechsler, D. (1975). Intelligence defined and undefined: A relativistic appraisal. *American Psychologist, 30,* 135-139.

Wechsler, D. (1981). *Manual for the Adult Intelligence Scale – Revised.* San Antonio, TX: The Psychological Corporation.

Wechsler, D. (1997). *Wechsler Adult Intelligence Scale III administration and scoring manual.* San Antonio, TX: The Psychological Corporation.

West, R. L., Ergis, A., Winocur, G., and Saint-Cyr, J. (1998). The contribution of impaired working memory monitoring to performance of the Self-Ordered Pointing Task in normal aging and Parkinson's disease. *Neuropsychology, 12*, 546–554.

Whelian, W.M., and Lesher, E. (1985). Neuropsychological changes in frontal functions in aging. *Developmental Neuropsychology, 1*, 371-380

Wilson, B.A., Alderman, N., Burgess, P.W., Emslie, H., and Evans, J.J (1996). *Behavioural Assessment of the Dysexecutive Syndrome (BADS).* Bury St. Edmunds, UK: Thames Valley Test Company.

Yerkes, R.M. (1921). Psychological examining in the United States Army. *Memories of the National Academy of Science, 15*, 1-8.

In: Intelligence : New Research
Editor: Lin V. Wesley, pp. 23-46
ISBN 1-59454-637-1
© 2006 Nova Science Publishers, Inc.

Chapter 2

SPECIFIC GENES FOR INTELLIGENCE

*Jon L. Karlsson**

Institute of Genetics, Reykjavik, Iceland

ABSTRACT

While the original studies in Mendelian genetics focused on unit characters, traits that could be classified as present or absent, it later became necessary to deal with quantitative attributes, such as size or intelligence, assessed by a series of measurements. Polygenic inheritance has long been accepted as the principal model applicable in that field. It now appears that sometimes a different approach may be appropriate, based on hybrid vigor as a chief force in individual variability. The present analysis is an attempt to illustrate that intellectual differences may at times be related to individual mutant genes that exist at levels much higher than would be expected on the basis of mutation pressure counteracted by natural selection. The emphasis is thus on genetic abnormalities known to remain quite frequent. The first itemized segment describes psychotic disorders, analyzing the evidence for heredity and evaluating the probable genetic mechanism. Relationship to creative forms of thinking are then discussed in detail. The second part assesses the genetic basis of myopia and its connection to learning ability. Finally the influence of these factors on personality traits is summarized. This leads to a view of the need for natural selection to ensure retention of intellectual gains achieved in the past.

INTRODUCTION

Recent well controlled investigations of twins and foster reared individuals have reinforced the conception of genetic factors being principal determinants of mental abilities. By adulthood adopted persons show no correlation with biologically unrelated associates they

---

* Address for correspondence: Jon L. Karlsson Ph.D., M.D., 1380 Thompson Ave., Napa, California , 94558, jonlk@interx.net

grew up with, but instead resemble their genetic parents or siblings. These findings demand intensive attempts to identify the responsible factors transmitted within bright families.

When Gregor Mendel discovered the basic laws of genetics his systematic studies focused on opposing homologous features that were relatively simple, easily observed, and commonly rated as present or absent. In that category are red versus white flower color in plants or curly versus straight hair in mammals. Such traits have been described as unit characters, and in the initial application in various organisms of the Mendelian principles the emphasis was generally on this type of characteristic. To be detectable and suitable for study a gene had to exist in at least two identifiable forms, one usually being the normal ancestral allele and the other the mutant counterpart.

In subsequent research most genes have been revealed through the disorder appearing in the presence of a mutant allele. Usually there is then no specific corresponding characteristic associated with the ancestral allele other than the absence of the abnormality. A state of health is obviously a desirable condition, including freedom from any specific disease, although it cannot be described as a recognizable individual trait.

QUANTITATIVE CHARACTERISTICS

Although geneticists originally focused on unit characters, the attention eventually became directed toward desirable more complex normal attributes, such as stature, strength, body mass, or mental ability, which rather than being present or absent show a continuous distribution made up of individual measurements. Often the pattern of occurrence in a population follows a bell-shaped curve, tapering in both directions from the highest peak in the center. Such characteristics are frequently found to be the product of many genes acting in concert.

While specific characteristics, other than just good health, are usually not identifiable in connection with the normal alleles of most individual mutant genes, it is thus possible to differentiate certain desirable states recognized as the preferred human condition. Good body habitus, including absence of obesity, is in this category. Athletic ability, adequate muscle strength, and superior coordination are generally admired. In some societies tallness is seen as a superior quality. A pleasant personality is always appreciated as well as good humor. Facility to socialize and impress an audience is universally worshipped. High intelligence is at least approved by some, and it is a necessary attribute for cultural advancement. All these traits are complex and dependent on multiple factors rather than being associated with single genes.

A specific polygenic hypothesis concerning inheritance of complex normal characteristics has been supported by geneticists for more than half a century. According to this thesis it is posited that there exist multiple pairs of genes, designated *AaBbCcDd* etc., each dual set contributing to the development of the biological trait in question. The alleles indicated by capital letters are postulated to be superior, so that with this hypothesis the best constitution carries all genes of that variety while the most inferior is *aabbccdd* etc. For convenience each large letter gene is claimed to provide approximately equally toward the final trait. Thus the constitutions *AaBbCcDd*, *AABBccdd*, or *aabbCCDD* are considered to be essentially equivalent, each carrying four productive alleles. A system of this nature can theoretically account for the normal type of distribution usually seen for complex traits, and hence it has enjoyed general acceptance.

Several serious objections to the details of this hypothesis can now be raised, at least in relation to inheritance of human abilities. One is that there is no independent evidence for the occurrence of the specified series of multiple genes and that no explanation exists of the maintenance of the mutant alleles at very high frequencies. Another is that no barrier is visible to the shift of the entire population toward the most favorable state in the presence of strong selective forces, yet pure breeding superior populations dont seem to arise. And a third objection is that the hypothesis fails to explain why human cultures invariably decline after reaching a peak of achievement. Over a long period there has been no real progress toward further elucidation of the basic concept, so that in that sense the classical polygenic hypothesis has been unproductive. Since it is not possible to identify the individual genes making up the hypothesized system, tests of the proposal have proven very difficult.

In view of these weaknesses explorations have been undertaken more recently of alternate possibilities [1]. The fundamental premise of a polygenic substrate is not questioned, the focus being on the details of the internal structure of the mechanism. Through proper modifications it becomes possible to amend the hypothesis to meet the multiple objections.

One significant change, suggested in particular by data on creative or gifted people, is that rather than the most desirable constitution at each locus always involving homozygosity for the ancestral gene it may in relation to certain specific loci be advantageous to maintain heterozygosity. The phenomenon of heterosis or hybrid vigor is well known to geneticists, sometimes at least revolving around heterozygosity for specific factors. Presumably in such instances the organism happens to be best served by the somewhat lower metabolic rate conditioned by one active allele where normally there should be two.

It simply was not appreciated in the beginning of genetics that a benefit could be derived from the heterozygous state. Allelic genes were seen as alternative forms, each with its own function, and when two different factors were present together, the more active one prevailed over the other. But now that it is understood that a genetic locus has just one basic action, the different alleles varying only in their degree of efficiency, it becomes apparent that sometimes an intermediate rate of the corresponding chemical reaction may be optimal, the favored state being associated with a single active allele.

Since overreproduction, with long term survival of just a fraction of the progeny, is a universal biological phenomenon, any negative effects of a heterozygous constitution are easily absorbed. Still, an organism cannot tolerate several factors each of which is required in a heterozygous state, as the fit fraction of the offspring then becomes too small. When two identical single locus heterozygotes mate, only half the progeny is of the same constitution as the parents, so that just one quarter is well suited for survival if a duplex of separate loci is involved. However, if just one or the other of the loci is required to be heterozygous in each individual, the acceptable fraction remains larger. Heterotic states can in that manner be maintained indefinitely if the species derives a significant benefit.

The new proposal, that heterozygous inheritance may in certain instances be fruitful, can help to explain the persistence of certain mutant genes at high levels, as inactive alleles always arise and selective advantage of the heterozygotes will sustain elevated frequencies. When heterozygous individuals enjoy unusual strength, selection to establish a pure superior breed is not possible. And if a hybrid system is required, genetic loss is expected when selective forces cease to operate. Only a few of the multiple loci involved in the development of a complex trait need to show heterozygote advantage, but they become the major source of diversity, as other genes that function best in the homozygous state will tend to establish themselves in an essentially pure form.

While heterozygosity at a few autosomal loci may be beneficial, there is of course also a possibility that genes on the sex chromosomes may result in positive effects limited to one gender.

GENETIC POLYMORPHISMS

It should be kept in mind that a very basic premise of the present genetic analysis is that hereditary alterations are in the majority of instances related to mutant genes which have lost their metabolic function. Most such genes result in lethal or sublethal effects in the abnormal homozygotes, while the heterozygotes may or may not be burdened with a potential weakness. The carrier states for such genes can thus range in medical terms from normal health, where the only associated abnormality is the recessive one, to total disease, the latter condition then being fully dominant. The most commonly recognized unhealthy situation is dominance with incomplete penetrance, only a portion of the heterozygotes becoming ill, usually with a delayed onset of a relatively mild or even intermittent affliction. Because of adverse effects in the carriers, in addition to the severe condition of the homozygotes, most mutant genes are ordinarily destined to remain rare.

In a few instances a partly dominant genetic disease is found to be quite common. Here it can be assumed that the heterozygotes, apart from their disease propensity, derive some benefit from their constitution. The possession of one active allele, instead of the more normal two, may in these circumstances serve the organism best due to a superiority of the slower chemical reaction rate mediated by a single gene. The resulting hybrid vigor, leading to a balanced polymorphism, then may contribute positively to a metric characteristic, and it also becomes a useful tool to point the direction of investigations of the genetic basis of favorable inherited traits, such as intelligence [2]. Frequently occurring mutant genes are thus candidates for exploration of their possible role in a polygenic system involved in mental development.

While the general impression in the early days of genetics indeed was that individuals who were homozygous for ancestral genes usually manifested the greatest stamina, geneticists soon noticed that hybrids, sometimes heterozygous only at a single locus, often exhibited unexpected competitive advantages. Originally this was interpreted as some nebulous benefit of the hybrid state as such, but later it became apparent that often the phenomenon simply illustrated an occasional merit conditioned by the slower biochemical rate associated with a heterozygous constitution.

It was not immediately realized that the principles underlying heterotic strength provided an important additional genetic mechanism through which advantage over competitors could be achieved, at least for the time being. But every species seems to harbor some loci at which one functional gene serves the organism better than the otherwise more normal two.

Persistence of a mutant factor at unusually high levels is termed a polymorphism. Maintenance of a beneficial heterozygous state requires constant ongoing selection, as loss of inactive genes is unavoidable when the abnormal homozygotes fail to reproduce. Selection can be viewed as a built-in participant in a balanced polymorphic system, and relaxation of that force leads to elimination of the gain. But under the right circumstances the hybrid vigor principle can be utilized by a species to establish superiority that otherwise is unattainable.

It is a fundamental characteristic of all organisms that they reproduce at excessive rates, mandating survival of only a fraction of the offspring. As measured by adaptation of the species the sacrifice of numerous young members is an easy price to absorb, causing no real hardship in terms of longitudinal success. Those individuals who live into adulthood have had to compete and demonstrate their superior qualities.

In a competitive world there is no tolerance of inborn weaknesses. Natural selection is commonly thought of as the process that allows for evolutionary progression, and it certainly does serve in that role. But its more immediate function is to prevent deterioration of the genetic material and preserve the gains already made. The appearance of a few new detrimental mutations and subsequent cleansing of the gene pool is only a minor inconvenience in the overall scheme. But to preserve proper balances constant rigorous selection is so fundamental in all biological systems that it is an absolutely indispensable component of the total organic machinery.

SELECTIVE FORCES

Survival of the fittest can take many forms and does not have to involve death of those unable to compete. Protection of the best suited genes is the crucial element, and this can be achieved by differential reproduction. As long as the unfit do not procreate, their maintenance may not be a great burden on the species. While with most organisms failure of survival by the weaker members is indeed the rule, systems of sexual competition are also highly developed. When a dominant male in the animal world gathers a harem and excludes the competitors from contact with the females, he is exercising his role in natural selection without demanding death of weaker members. External factors, such as climate, also enter into the total picture. Poorly fit individuals are more likely to succumb during periods of hardship often experienced in winter seasons. Only the healthy and vigorous can withstand the challenges of prolonged deprivation.

Humans have never been exempt from the principles enumerated above. Before the advent of effective contraceptive methods it was not uncommon for a married woman to give birth to as many as 20 children, although in most areas less than half the babies survived. Many nations had strict rules about breeding privileges, generally permitting only acceptably married prosperous couples to produce offspring freely.

Fertility was obviously necessary to allow for a large family, but excessive fecundity could be negative if food was limited. Hardship and disease might wipe out all the children when a harsh winter combined with insufficient food. The limiting factor in raising a family was the ability of the male provider and the female caretaker to furnish the means of livelihood. If sufficient food, clothing, and shelter were available, the family was likely to fare well. With more restricted resources the children were doomed to suffer, and diseases took their toll among the undernourished and ill clothed.

Only a few systematic studies have been published of human reproduction in past times. Data from China and India gathered more than a century ago indicated that prosperous families were able to raise to adulthood a larger group of children than those who were less well off [3]. A study of the Icelandic population born 1851-1880 similarly showed that males listed in Whos Who were unusually successful in bringing up a large family. Comparable results were seen in American IQ studies of families born early in the 20th century. Such data as are available thus support the concept that in the past the most able were reproductively the best fit.

In more recent times quite adequate information is on hand, but now it is the least intellectual groups that produce the most children. When socialistic systems guarantee the wherewithal for all those born, the unfit are invited to procreate.

It has actually been recognized for centuries, mainly in relation to agriculture and animal husbandry, that choice of the fittest individuals for breeding is necessary to attain a productive and healthy stock. No one questions the biological soundness of this principle, although conceptual mistakes have naturally sometimes been made when underlying knowledge was inadequate. The fundamental aims have been to preserve the integrity of an existing population and perhaps attempt to improve the overall quality.

DESIRABLE MUTANT GENES

Most mutant genes are kept at low levels by the forces of natural selection, but there are several human hereditary diseases that are maintained at surprisingly high frequencies. The first clear, although localized, example involved the gene responsible for sickle cell anemia in African Negroes, which follows recessive inheritance. The heterozygous carriers show resistance to malaria, being able to survive in certain regions otherwise essentially uninhabitable by humans. The very high frequency of the sickle cell gene in these areas is thus an example of a balanced polymorphism, a mutant gene being maintained at an unexpectedly high level by some favorable condition.

Other very common abnormalities, not limited to one region, include psychosis, alcoholism, diabetes, allergy, and myopia. The reason for the elevated levels of these disorders is thought to be some associated positive effect, although its precise nature may at this time be unknown. In human biology effects on intelligence are so important that any observed favorable action of a mutant gene is likely to impinge on the polygenic system involved in mental abilities. Consequently a focus on frequent mutant genes may lead to identification of some of the specific factors that influence brain action.

It should be clear from the concepts discussed here that it is now imperative for mankind to embark on a concerted effort to identify some of the specific genes that are operative in the polygenic mechanisms which determine basic mental traits. The focus must for now be primarily on mutant genes known to exist at unexpectedly high frequencies, but other factors should be considered as well, including those involved in gender differences.

Since no more than one percent of all existing genes can be identified with currently available breeding techniques, it remains possible that some obscure factors exist which result in benefits in heterozygous carriers without any disease condition being associated. Perhaps such genes are involved in the occasional appearance of highly creative individuals who tower over all others in human populations.

MENTAL ILLNESS AND CREATIVITY

Mental health problems occur in different forms and in variable degrees of severity, but only disturbances that fall into the category classified as psychoses will be considered here. Such disorders cause serious interference with the individuals capacity to meet the ordinary demands of life. A mentally ill person may be unable to reason, remember, interpret reality, communicate, or respond emotionally. He may experience sleep disturbances, delusional thinking, and hallucinations. When chaotic speech or strange and paranoid ideations are prominent, the official diagnosis may be schizophrenia. If mood depression or excessive elation are the main symptoms, the illness is likely to be considered manic depressive, now often termed affective. Pressure of speech may be prominent. Most patients with severe mental disease exhibit disorders of both thought and affect. Rates of psychosis are surprisingly high and have been reported to be similar in all regions of the world. Severe mental disorders seldom become manifest until after age 15 years.

INTERPRETATIONS AND FORMS OF TREATMENT

Because of the diversity of the symptoms psychosis has always been difficult to define. Many more individuals suffer from mild mental disorders classified as neuroses, but when the disturbance is sufficiently severe to interfere with normal activities, the diagnosis is likely to be psychosis. Some patients are considered neurotic when the symptoms are mild, only to be changed to a psychotic category as they get older.

Although mental patients do not always exhibit the entire array of signs and symptoms, there is usually a characteristic pattern of behaviors and experiences that is shared by those prone to psychotic illness. Depression is very common and probably the most universal sign, inappropriate elation being less frequent. Psychiatrists describe loosening of associative thinking as an early occurrence, although this is difficult to assess. Overt delusions, when they appear, are more definitive. They can consist of just weird ideas, or they can be paranoid or grandiose in nature. Anger and emotional lability are often prominent. Some patients commit serious crimes, but as a group the mentally ill are not a risk to society. Thought insertions may occur, the patient complaining that his mind is being influenced by external agencies. Hallucinations are experienced in more severe instances, most commonly auditory, the patient hearing internal voices which frequently are accusatory. Sometimes the experiences are visual. In untreated very ill patients catatonic symptoms may occur, with rigid posturing or so called waxy flexibility of the extremities. Hebephrenia, characterized by improper personal hygiene, silly mannerisms, and willingness to live in filth, was seen in the past in chronically ill individuals. Low energy levels are very common in mental patients although hyperactivity may also occur, the latter more likely in episodes. Confusion and disorientation are often seen. Interference with sleep is almost universal, usually lack of sleep, but occasionally hypersomnia. In the past some patients died in a chronic state of restless agitation. Individuals who become ill early in life are more likely to be diagnosed schizophrenic and show severe symptoms while those becoming sick later may experience episodic occurrences often diagnosed affective.

Psychological hypotheses proposed by Freud and others dominated the field of psychiatry during the first half of the 20th century. Mental disorders were claimed to have their roots in improper development during childhood, influenced by flawed family relationships and deviant or double-bind communication. Failure in interpersonal adjustment during the period of growth was claimed to account for abnormal behavior later in life and cause emergence of neurotic as well as psychotic behavior. Blame for inadequate upbringing fell in particular on mothers who were said to exhibit schizophrenogenic character faults.

Treatment of mental patients was governed by these conceptions for several decades. Psychotherapy could be administered not only by physicians, but by psychologists, social workers, hospital attendants, and even clergymen. Sometimes the patient's family was included in group therapy sessions, since the relatives were assumed to be in need of training to learn appropriate behavior. Individual psychological treatment was at times continued for decades, often at great expense. When improvement was observed in the patient it was attributed to the therapeutic procedures, although mental illness is known to run an episodic course.

This multifaceted professional system based on psychological concepts was shaken to its foundations when half a century ago it emerged that medications of the phenothiazine type could effectively terminate a psychotic episode and bring on normal behavior in a previously grossly disturbed individual. Authorities in psychiatry resisted this development and insisted on not only blind studies, but double-blind, where neither the patient nor the doctor knew whether a medication or a placebo was being administered. But the phenothiazines passed that test, and eventually the new reality had to be accepted. Patients could now return to living in their communities and most mental hospitals were closed. Facilities for outpatient treatment were then established or expanded, although systematic follow up often failed, leaving many sick individuals homeless roaming the streets.

Unfortunately there are many seriously ill patients who dislike the effects of the new antipsychotic drugs, even though others can see that their condition is greatly improved. Constant pressure is therefore needed to ensure continuation of the treatment regime. The disease is not cured, but rather can be kept under control by the medication, usually in a smaller dose than that needed for initial improvement. It is fortunate that the antipsychotic drugs are not habit forming, so that abuse by the patient need not be considered. They also show low toxicity, dangerous overdoses being uncommon. It is difficult to tell whether a person experiencing an initial psychotic episode may after treatment be able to manage without further therapy, but most individuals who are prone to psychosis will experience a relapse if treatment is discontinued, although this can show up months or even years later.

Because of their negative attitude towards any medication therapies psychiatrists overemphasized adverse side effects that could be blamed on the phenothiazines. Patients and their families were told that they were at great risk of developing a serious complication termed tardive dyskinesia if treatment was continued for an extended period. But the reality is that numerous individuals have stayed on the medications for almost half a century without institutions filling up with neurologically debilitated persons.

OLDER FAMILY STUDIES

The familial nature of psychotic disorders has long been recognized, particularly in northern Europe. There was a dispute in Germany a century ago about the relationship between affective and delusional disorders, Greisinger favoring a unitary hypothesis, but Kraepelin prevailing with his dual concept. He defined dementia praecox, later called schizophrenia, as having a poor prognosis, while manic depressive psychosis, now often described as bipolar affective disorder, had a more favorable outlook. Later findings have failed to confirm the validity of such a difference, but the dichotomy has become well established in psychiatric and psychological circles and is still defended vigorously. However, it is generally recognized that there is no sign or symptom that occurs in one of the major psychoses and not in the other. They also tend to occur in the same families.

Shortly after the rediscovery of the Mendelian principles a century ago systematic attempts were initiated, also in Germany, to gather data on families with psychosis and attempt to unravel the genetic mechanisms. The main effort was centered in Munich under the leadership of Rudin, but similar studies were later conducted in the Berlin area, particularly by Kallmann. These and related investigations in other countries led to voluminous family data which showed rather high risks in the closest relatives, tapering off as a move was made to more distant relations [4]. But considerable fluctuations in the rates were observed, and no success was achieved in terms of an acceptable genetic interpretation of either schizophrenia or manic depression. The German effort terminated with the start of World War II.

These older family studies were structured to assess the risk in various groups of relatives of index cases located through the records of mental hospitals. The sample sizes were quite large, although some categories were smaller than others. Full siblings are readily available while adult grandchildren are less abundant. Corrections had to be applied to make groups of different ages comparable.

One major obstacle to success was the diagnostic dichotomy. Individuals who produce offspring are unlikely to have developed early onset severe disease. Consequently parents of index cases, when they become mentally ill, have an increased probability of being diagnosed affective. This results in rates of schizophrenia being found to be low in parents. Children of schizophrenic index cases, on the other hand, arise from severely ill individuals and therefore have a higher risk of becoming ill. Since all sick children are likely to be identified while some healthy offspring of patients may be missed, such problems also tend to raise the rates found in children of index cases. Difficulties of this kind no doubt caused distortions in the assessment of risks in various relatives. In the family studies there seems to have been a trend to consider psychotic close relatives, especially the siblings and children, to suffer from the same disorder as the index case whereas more distant family members were partitioned into schizophrenic and affective categories.

While the volume of data on different kinds of relatives was quite sufficient, problems of the kind described above seem to have resulted in a great deal of variability in the reported rates. It was also difficult to attain consistency between different teams of investigators sent into the community to gather family information and try to decide which family members had suffered from specific types of illness.

The risks were found to be definitely elevated in all groups of relatives, particularly in close relations. Still, the pattern could not be shown to fit any recognized genetic hypothesis.

Many authors have subsequently tried without success to reanalyze the German data, often coming to the conclusion that no standard genetic system is operative.

NEWER FAMILY DATA

Although the old family statistics and corresponding information about twins were indeed quite impressive, emphasis on the entire subject dwindled in the postwar period, when environmental hypotheses gained preeminence. It is only in the last 40 years that revival of interest in genetics has taken hold and new data gathered by improved designs have emerged. The importance of genetic factors has now been fully established with further investigations of twins and of foster reared offspring of mentally ill mothers. The latter type of study proved that the risk remained the same regardless of the place of rearing. Although heated debates had raged for many years regarding the interpretation of findings in twins, the importance of genetics could no longer be denied.

Recent more reliable family information has in particular come from Iceland [5], where population circumstances are quite favorable for such studies. In this nation of a quarter million people it is possible to identify and locate essentially all the relatives of diagnosed mental patients. Different groups, including the general population, can be studied in a uniform manner, such as establishing the risk of ever having been treated at the single mental hospital for psychosis. The comparative rates thus ascertained can be converted to actual risks by multiplication with a factor based on the known psychosis rate for the population at large. Because of the study design there is no need for age corrections, which created a difficult problem in the older investigations. The Icelandic data are entirely in harmony with the older reports, although showing greater precision. Consequently the remainder of the present evaluation will take advantage of the improved quality of the new findings. Even though a summary of the older world data to attain a single set of risk figures has also been attempted, the resulting tabulations are unsatisfactory for a genetic analysis.

The diagnostic question is a very crucial issue in all the family investigations. Authorities in psychiatry make frequent and sweeping conceptual changes, so that it becomes impossible for a geneticist to base a meaningful analysis on the specific official diagnoses found in hospital records. For example, a quarter century ago over 90 percent of hospitalized psychotic patients in North America carried a schizophrenic label and were treated accordingly. At present only a small fraction receives this diagnosis, and older individuals are told that the previous opinion about their illness was wrong. The same patient has also often been given different diagnoses during different hospital stays. In Iceland the fluctuations have been less drastic, but no correlation is found between the category assigned to a psychotic parent and to the offspring. The only genetic studies that have turned out successful have been based on the unitary concept, combining data on the various endogenous psychoses. Many investigators have actually found the risks in different classes of relatives and in cotwins of index cases to be quite similar for manic depressive illness and schizophrenia. Both disorders also respond to the same treatments, although psychiatrists recommend only temporary use of the strong neuroleptic medications for severely ill affective patients, who are known to fail to respond to weaker drugs. Sometimes it has been a source of confusion, especially in dealing with outpatients, that disorders diagnosed as depressions can occur in other disorders, such as alcoholism or the rare Wolfram syndrome, but the severity is usually less extreme.

In Iceland it has been possible to perform longitudinal surveys of the distribution of psychosis within kindreds whose genealogy has been traced for several centuries. Although generations are often skipped, there is a pattern of continuity once psychosis appears in a particular kinship. A definite segregation occurs at times into high and low risk segments, the disorder persisting in certain family branches while it disappears in others. That pattern has been interpreted as inconsistent with polygenic inheritance, as such a model demands extremely high frequencies for genes that all must then occur together in over one percent of the people. Quite common genes would be expected to show up in all branches of a family and equally in all kinships. Since psychotic illness afflicts over five percent of all people at some time in their lives, division into several biological entities would still leave each sufficiently frequent to require some favorable associated effect. A very high frequency for several separate genes involved in psychosis is quite improbable, so that genetic heterogeneity also seems a remote possibility.

THE GENETIC MECHANISM

These considerations narrow down the plausible systems to relatively simple mechanisms. To pursue the analysis further the statistics on the risks in different classes of relatives need to be examined. The Icelandic family data are much more precise than the cumulative older information. They fall into a definite pattern and demonstrate that the lifetime risk is similar in all first degree relatives of psychotic index cases, almost 15 percent, while the rates for second and third degree relatives are progressively lower. The overall distribution demonstrates a proportionality of the risk to the degree of genetic relatedness to psychotic index cases so that the pattern can be predicted by a simple mathematical expression.

Further evaluation of these findings makes any form of recessive inheritance quite unlikely, although that mechanism was favored by some of the early German investigators. Pedigrees have been gathered in Iceland which indicate that in many families mental disorder is transmitted by one parent and not by the other. It is also possible to exclude any type of sex linked inheritance; Icelandic data show the lifetime risk to be 50 percent higher in females than in males, both for affective and delusional disorders.

This leaves some form of modified dominant transmission as the only plausible system. However, it is necessary to deal with certain objections to that mechanism which in the past have led to its rejection. A major problem has been the assumption that penetrance may be treated as a fixed parameter that can be incorporated into mathematical formulations. But it appears that the likelihood of manifestation is under the influence of secondary factors whose concentration can vary. The rate must consequently be expected to be excessive in groups with extra risk factors, such as individuals related to more than one index case or to unusually severely ill patients. The highest risk would be expected in monozygotic cotwins of mentally ill index cases. And it is the elevated rates in these very groups that have formed the basis for the conclusion that the family data disagree with a modified dominance mechanism.

When these considerations are taken into account, the family distribution can be said to be quite consistent with a system of dominance with incomplete penetrance. If it is assumed that the genotype of a normal person is *SS* and that of a psychosis-prone individual *Ss*, the expectation is that a little over 50 percent of first-degree relatives of index cases are carriers of a psychosis gene. With 25 percent penetrance the predicted illness risk is 14 percent, very close to the reported figures. An important longitudinal German study [6] indicates that the risk in the offspring of two psychotic parents is 35 percent and that such individuals exhibit no greater severity of illness than other mentally ill persons. This suggests that the *ss* genotype is lethal, probably never born. The survivors in a dual mating must then be two thirds *Ss* and one-third *SS*, so that the penetrance rate can here be set at 50 percent. That same rate has been proposed for others related to two ill index cases, such as siblings of patients who also have an affected parent. Kallmann [7] found in his Berlin study that siblings of nuclear cases, those diagnosed with hebephrenic or catatonic schizophrenia, exhibited a 20 percent risk while those related to paranoid or simple schizophrenics showed a 10 percent rate. It is thus apparent that penetrance is raised as additional risk factors come into play.

Since American psychiatrists have been thoroughly indoctrinated in the convention to separate the endogenous psychoses into delusional versus affective categories, they have refused to pay attention to the new Icelandic data which combine the two classes of disorders. But the reality is that it is the older data that are flawed. Many studies have shown that schizophrenia and manic depression occur intermingled in the same families although there is some tendency for the expression to be similar in related persons. And there is no correlation between the diagnostic categories assigned to parents and their children in studies that have been made of parent-child pairs found in the records of mental hospitals. The separation of affective from delusional psychoses may have a clinical utility, but it makes no sense in biological investigations. The fact that the family pattern follows the mathematical relationships demanded by the Mendelian laws when the psychoses are combined certainly gives support to that approach. If the major psychoses have a common biological substrate, it is obvious that a distortion will occur in the data when the sickest patients are studied separately. Severely ill individuals, perhaps with an early onset, are unlikely to raise families, and hence the rate of schizophrenia becomes artificially low in parents of index cases with application of the standard diagnostic system. Conversely, the risk in the children becomes too high when they are all the offspring only of seriously ill patients. Geneticists cannot solve the question of the hereditary mechanism using the distorted data that inevitably result from the diagnostic dichotomy.

It is well known that relatives of psychotic patients often suffer from personality disorders of a nature too mild to be considered to fall in the psychotic category, and this is not surprising in view of the postulated low penetrance. Genetic studies of that kind of material become essentially impossible because of its complexity. This problem has been avoided in the Icelandic study by application of the same criteria to all groups, including the general population, the index cases, and various relatives. The comparative risks are all based on hospitalization rates with a psychotic diagnosis. Although the interpretation of the Icelandic data has not been universally accepted, other authors have arrived at the same basic conclusion on the basis of different investigations. For example, two smaller studies done in Sweden [8] and the United States [9] produced comparable data. Holzman and his associates [10] studied eye tracking abnormalities in families with psychosis and found evidence of dominant transmission.

With the partly dominant hypothesis it is necessary to propose a frequency of 0.07 for the psychosis gene. This high rate, particularly for a dominantly transmitted factor, demands an explanation, such as a system of balanced polymorphism. Something favorable must promote an increase in the psychosis gene which occurs even though some of the carriers are prone to mental disease.

It is evident that the family statistics on psychotic illness are indeed entirely compatible with a model based on a single inactive mutant gene which recurs in all human populations. Presumably there is at a certain chromosomal locus a gene which is involved in the regulation of dopamine activity in the brain. One hypothesis is that the ancestral gene functions in reabsorption of the neurohormone after the latter has been released into the interneuronal cleft following nerve stimulation, thus terminating the activity. It so happens that the constitution with only one active gene, where normally there should be two, is favored, and thus the frequency of the mutant factor is maintained quite high. Although heterozygous individuals usually benefit from that constitution, they also harbor a potential weakness, since one active factor is only marginally sufficient, and thus one fourth of them is destined to suffer at some time from a psychotic disorder. Most often the illness is mild and intermittent, but occasionally severe and chronic. The risk in carriers is increased above 25 percent in persons who are related to more than one sick individual or to an unusually severely ill one as well as in monozygotic cotwins. With this model it is possible to predict the risks in various classes of relatives of psychotic index cases. The fact that the family data follow a pattern consistent with an established genetic mechanism when all the so-called functional or endogenous psychoses are treated as a unit gives strong support to that approach. Although authorities in psychiatry still reject the partly dominant hypothesis, there is no valid scientific reason for that negative attitude. The single gene hypothesis receives additional support from the rather common existence of pedigrees showing persistence of psychosis for several generations, most often transmitted through individuals who themselves are unaffected. Other branches of these kinships may be free of the disorder, consistent with a segregation of a dominant gene and inconsistent with a polygenic interpretation. In view of the high frequency of psychosis in all human populations, demanding some favorable concomitant presumably limited to one major factor, genetic heterogeneity also seems ruled out except possibly as a rare occurrence outweighed by one major gene maintained at a high level.

Some relatives of psychotic patients suffer from milder disorders, variously diagnosed as schizoid, neurotic, or Tourette syndromes. For some reason females are excessively prone to have such complaints. Treatment with sedative or calming medications may be helpful.

RELATION TO CREATIVITY

The surprisingly high frequency of psychosis in all human populations leads to the conclusion that a balanced polymorphism must be operative. The detrimental effect of mental illness is obvious, but greater complexity is encountered in attempts to explain positive influences of the heterozygous constitution.

It is now accepted in academic circles that a connection exists between psychotic tendency and creative thinking. For centuries it has been reported that men of genius exhibit an elevated risk of mental illness, which also occurs in their families. This association is seen in all fields of novel contributions, whether it be art, literature, or science. Most of the older information is anecdotal, but several systematic investigations have been reported.

A century ago Lombroso [11] reviewed biographies of creative individuals, concluding that mental abnormalities were in fact frequent in their ranks. His book received considerable attention, but eventually the opinions were dismissed and considered misdirected.

Lange Eichbaum [12] published a very extensive survey of world famous persons in 1928, followed by a smaller volume dealing with the characteristics of highly creative men. He concluded that there indeed existed a relationship between psychotic tendency and creativity, especially when the focus was on the most important contributors. Thus he found a 40 percent rate of psychosis among the greatest men of genius. Kretschmer also wrote a book on creative individuals, expressing similar views. Other studies include those of Ellis, Nisbet, and Juda.

It is impressive that all these authors have arrived at corresponding conclusions, although questions have been raised about their validity. The main skepticism has revolved around the representativeness of the material. It obviously is difficult to assemble reliable medical information about people who lived a long time ago, and fame often comes only after the person is deceased.

In recent years several differently designed studies have appeared, comparing rates of mental disease in contemporary creative and randomly selected groups. Andreasen [13] evaluated well known writers affiliated with the University of Iowa, concluding that an increase in psychosis existed in them and their families. Jamison [14] published a similar study of English authors. In Iceland a comparison was made of the general population with fiction writers and poets, once more showing a significant increase in psychotic disorders in creative individuals and their relatives. These studies, while better controlled than the older ones, do not deal with creative persons of as high a caliber, but they all demonstrate the same findings.

In a different approach Barron and associates [15] at the University of California subjected outstanding living architects and writers to a battery of psychological tests in a controlled setting. To their surprise these studies revealed that the responses favored by these people were similar to those seen in groups of mental patients.

Still another kind of association has been investigated in Iceland. Instead of focusing only on writers and artists these studies evaluated also the characteristics of top graduates of the Icelandic schools [16]. With the excellent available records a comparison was possible of the psychosis rates of intelligent individuals and their families with those of random segments of the general population. The risk of psychosis turned out to be twice the expectation in the accomplished groups. An even more definitive relation to psychosis was found among high performers in mathematics and their relatives, suggesting that good reasoning ability often develops in carriers of the psychosis gene.

A particularly impressive study deals with mathematicians in the population born 1911-1940. During that interval 70 thousand individuals arose and survived past age 15. Reykjavik College was long the only institution graduating high performing students who went on to a university career. At age 20 those attending the mathematics and science section had to pass a rigorous written examination covering difficult problems in algebra, geometry, analytical geometry, trigonometry, and calculus. For the purposes of the investigation the top six performers each year 1931-1960 were defined as a group of 180 good mathematicians, constituting 0.25 percent of the total population. This material could then be used as a yardstick for measurement of success of various groups. If mathematical ability is assumed to be evenly distributed the expectation would be that 1 person in 400 of any population segment must fall into the high achievement category. The procedure was applied to formerly collected information on families with psychosis, showing rather surprising results. The 544 individuals who at some time had been hospitalized for mental disease showed a 4-fold increase in mathematical achievement while the 3283 first-degree relatives had a 2-fold rate. Success was even seen in more distant relatives. Mathematicians were found equally in material dealing with schizophrenic and affectively ill patients [17].

All these findings can now be tied together in terms of an established physiological mechanism. The reticular activating system in the brain stem is known to be responsible for arousal and mental alertness, and dopamine is the principal chemical vector in this process. Enhancement of dopamine action can be induced by agents like amphetamine pep pills. Excessive chemically induced stimulation over a period of time often leads to temporary amphetamine psychosis, which clinically is indistinguishable from paranoid schizophrenia. Psychotic patients are also thought to suffer from overactivity of dopaminergic neurons in the brain. In either case amelioration of the symptoms is achieved by treatment with antipsychotic medications such as phenothiazines, which reduce the activity of dopamine.

Increased arousal, linked to the *Ss* constitution, appears to result in creative forms of thinking in persons who can tolerate the overstimulation. But some individuals are unable to withstand the excessive pressure and develop psychotic illness. Frequently the disorder is episodic, interspersed with healthy periods. Families with psychosis can take comfort in the concept that they are paying the price for mans inventiveness. Sir Isaac Newton, the greatest scientist of all times, suffered from psychosis, and Albert Einstein had a schizophrenic son. Carriers of the psychosis gene thus seem to have contributed fully to mankinds cultural advancement.

ISOLATION OF A PSYCHOSIS GENE

When procedures were developed for localization amd isolation of individual genes, several groups of investigators started attempts to establish the chromosomal position of the proposed psychosis gene. The research turned out to be difficult, fraught with many obstacles. As a starting point a search was needed for large families with multiple instances of mental disease. The various members needed to be located and induced to donate blood samples for analysis. These had to be properly processed and shipped to the central laboratory. Using multiple radioactive probes the biochemists then attempted to find evidence of linkage to a specific region on one of the 23 human chromosomes. The work was hampered not only by diagnostic questions, but also by the fact that many of the healthy family members must be assumed to carry the psychosis gene without showing evidence of it. Since mental illness tends to show up rather late in life, members of the older generations are often deceased while the younger relatives have not as yet developed overt mental illness.

In view of such problems it is not surprising that little success has as yet been achieved in this laborious search. One group of investigators reported evidence of an affective illness gene located on chromosome 11, creating considerable excitement and encouraging others to join in the effort. Unfortunately this finding did not hold up and had to be dismissed. Another team claimed to have found signs of a schizophrenia factor on chromosome 5, but this also turned out to be wrong. Some have suggested that a psychosis gene may be located on chromosomes 1, 6, 8, 10, or 22. The current methods for isolation of genes may not be suitable for low penetrance factors existing at high frequencies.

Despite the lack of success up to now it seems certain that eventually the work will bear fruit, when better procedures become available. The evidence for existence of a major factor as a cause of psychosis is so compelling that it must just be a matter of time till it is found. One possible explanation of the difficulties is that the basic factor involved in psychosis may be multicentric, various parts located on separate chromosomes, but leading to synthesis of one enzyme. This would be analogous to the experience with hemoglobin, where the component alpha and beta chains are dependent on different DNA segments although the final protein is a single entity. With this kind of system the currently used methods to detect the position of proposed gene(s) can be unsuitable, especially when the disease is hard to diagnose and only a fraction of the carriers affected. Further progress in understanding and treating psychosis is bound to follow if a major factor can be isolated and its structure determined. Its function in relation to creative forms of thought will be a challenging subject for future exploration.

Although some authors have concluded that failure to locate a major gene suggests that it does not exist, it seems more likely that the presently available methods are somehow deficient.

MYOPIA AND MENTAL TRAITS

Vision is often seen as the most important of the five major senses. Light perception guides most organisms in their daily activities. Good eyesight is essential for location of food, search for shelter, avoidance of dangers, and engagement in reproduction. Man has the benefit of both color vision and three dimensional sight, which are not shared by all mammals.

DEVELOPMENT OF VISION

The human eye is essentially fully formed at birth, although the newborn child tends to be somewhat farsighted. In the process of embryonic differentiation the anterior portion of the organ develops from the tissues of the skin while the posterior part originates as an outcropping from the brain. The two components unite into a well integrated structure, capable of processing images and transmitting them to the rear of the brain, where the visual cortex is located.

The eyeball resembles a camera, with an adjustable lens assembly in the front and the retina in the back, the latter corresponding to the film. Receptors in the rear part of the eye respond to the image, which arrives placed upside down, and convert the stimuli into electrical impulses ready to travel through the optic nerves to the visual cortex. The pupil can contract or expand to adjust the amount of light admitted, and the flexible lens can accommodate to correct for variations in distance. In older people the lens becomes rigid, creating a need for reading glasses.

Most of the eye is surrounded by the rather firm white scleral coat while the front is covered by the transparent cornea. The latter is responsible for a major part of the refraction of the incoming light. The interior of the organ is divided into the anterior chamber, which contains the aqueous humor, and the posterior chamber harboring the jelly like vitreous. Between them is the crystalline lens, all of these portions being transparent. The pupil, which appears black, is surrounded by the iris capable of regulating the size of the aperture, as well as a circular muscle to alter the shape of the lens and thus adjust the total refractive power to take distance into account.

Each eyeball has attached to it six small muscles to aim the organ toward objects of interest. The bony orbit helps to give protection from external injuries. The lacrymal and other small glands provide moisture and lubrication. Coordinated use of the two eyes is regulated by the brain.

VISUAL FUNCTIONS

Light rays entering the eye are refracted first by the cornea and then by the lens to bring them into the proper relationship. In the normal emmetropic eye the image is in good focus at the level of the retina, the fovea being the region of sharpest sight. Anomalies can upset this mechanism and interfere with the acuity of vision, requiring corrective measures.

The physiology of vision is rather complex, involving specialized cells called rods and cones. The former are more sensitive and serve well at night in limited light, but the latter are responsible for color perception. The biochemical mechanism utilizes certain pigments related to vitamin A.

Some individuals see clearly only things at a close range, more distant objects being blurred. They are thus nearsighted or myopic. As young children they usually enjoy normal vision, eye problems developing mostly during the maturing years [18]. With concave lenses myopic vision can be corrected, overcoming what otherwise would be a serious handicap. Degrees of myopia range from very mild to quite severe. Women tend to exhibit more extreme forms of myopia than men, sometimes associated with an earlier onset. Certain studies suggest that the overall rate of myopia may be higher in females than in males. This can result from the observed fact that for some unknown reason nearsightedness develops earlier in girls than in boys. If this leads to a higher fraction of males ending up in the very mild category, their total rate becomes somewhat lower. Other than this there is no indication of a gender difference in myopia.

Historical accounts of nearsightedness date back to antiquity. It is said to have been illegal in Rome to sell a myopic slave without revealing his condition. Postmortem measurements of the eyeball were carried out in the 17th century. Still, the actual frequency of the disorder was not known until quite recently. Corrective lenses came into use during the middle ages both in Europe and in China.

Nearsightedness can result from several abnormalities in the anatomy of the eyeball. Variations in the thickness of the cornea can influence the total refractive power. The shape of the lens is critical, and if it is too convex this may cause a deviation in the light pattern. Even the internal media of the eye sometimes alter the position of the image. The most frequent etiology of nearsightedness is axial myopia, which changes the structural relationships and shifts the focus forward in relation to the retina.

It is well established that axial myopia results from elongation of the eyeball. Measurements of the physical dimensions can be made during life with sonograms or more directly later by postmortem examination. When the retina is displaced further back, the sharp image falls in front of it unless correction is made by proper lenses. There is also thinning of the supportive tissues, the weakened structures rendering myopes susceptible to retinal detachment, especially in higher degrees of the disorder. This can occasionally lead to blindness, although such a development is rare. Myopia is not considered to be a disease, rather being seen as an anatomical variation of the organ of vision. Still, parents often become quite concerned when their children start to show signs of nearsightedness and even seek unorthodox treatment, which is futile.

CAUSES OF MYOPIA

Population rates of myopia vary greatly. Studies from Taiwan report a 90 percent frequency [19] while older data from Japan, Israel, and Germany suggest a figure close to 50 percent. In the United States approximately 15 percent of the population is nearsighted. Some areas of Africa have rates below one percent.

Because nearsightedness usually develops during the years that children attend school, some authors have attempted to explain its occurrence through environmental mechanisms, blaming intensive close use of the eyes for adverse effects on vision. Several specific hypotheses have been proposed, such as improper posture during reading, inadequate lighting, altered muscle contraction around the lens of the eye, or excessive visual strain.

Nearsightedness has always been known to run in families, with some kinships manifesting very high risks and others low. Heredity is consequently seen by most scientists as the main etiologic factor, and studies of twins have confirmed the importance of genetics. Among monozygotic pairs the rate of concordance is close to 100 percent if each index twin requires a correction of more than two diopters and the pairs are past age twenty [20]. Even when they have been separated at birth and reared without contact with each other, identical twins have been found to be concordant for myopia. Dizygotic twins are frequently discordant.

Despite this convincing scientific evidence the belief persists that myopia may be caused by environmental influences. This view is held not only by lay persons, but by many of the authorities who control research activities in this field. Rather than appropriating funds for further exploration of the genetic basis these leaders continue to channel support to perceived mechanisms related to external causes of the disorder.

Excessive reading has long held the center stage in the hypothetical schemes claimed to explain the emergence of myopia during the school years. Despite the popularity of this view the actual evidence has failed to show a correlation between near work and the eye disorder. It is not uncommon for people to be avid readers without any adverse effect on vision.

Some time ago the report surfaced that Eskimo children in northern Alaska exhibited a very high rate of myopia although their parents were mostly nonmyopic. Liberal amounts of research funds were allocated for an extensive exploration of the reasons for this discrepancy.

The hypothesis was promulgated that improper lighting might be the main adverse factor, forcing pupils of the local schools to strain their eyes and become nearsighted. No actual support for this thesis emerged from the investigation, but one finding was that even among Eskimos there was a family concentration of the disorder, siblings often being concordant. But the genetic aspect was not explored in greater detail.

The first systematic family investigation was carried out by Jablonski [21] in Germany in the early days of human genetics and was aimed at establishing the mode of inheritance. When a nonmyopic set of parents had produced a nearsighted child, the risk in subsequent children was found to be approximately 25 percent, but if one of the parents was myopic the rate rose to almost 50 percent. This suggested recessive transmission. However, the interpretation of these and other family data became controversial, although all investigators agreed that certain families exhibited recessive inheritance. Some authors saw the high risk occasionally observed in children of one myope as consistent with dominant transmission and proposed that there were two biologically different kinds of myopia. Still, the results can just as well represent pseudodominance, produced by the mating of an affected homozygous recessive individual with a nonmyopic heterozygous carrier, which would not be infrequent where the myopia rate is high.

Another good family study was done in Japan over 40 years ago by Furusho [22]. His data were fairly systematic, but since the investigation was centered around a school population, many of the subjects were relatively young. The premise was accepted that myopia is fully developed by age 16 years, but unfortunately this is not entirely correct. Sophisticated statistical procedures were employed, leading to the conclusion that the data fit best a hypothesis of recessive inheritance, although incomplete penetrance had to be invoked. While scientifically this is perhaps the best study reported in the literature, it suffers from inadequacies inherent in data dealing with a school age sample.

Few attempts have been made in recent years to resolve further the question of the genetic mechanism. The fact that mild and severe myopia occur in the same families is consistent with a single disorder. And the high rate of nearsightedness in some nations requires a very elevated gene frequency, which is unlikely to exist for more than one gene affecting vision. A third argument in favor of a single factor is the reported 100 percent risk of myopia in children of two myopes who both require corrections of more than two diopters. No mechanism other than recessive inheritance, with two homozygotes mating, leads to all the offspring being affected. The proposed myopia gene has not as yet been located on one of the human chromosomes.

The general population distribution curve for visual acuity where the myopia rate is low shows the standard bell shaped pattern with a high peak at zero correction, tapering off to +2D and -2D on either side of the mean. Thus a genetically normal individual does not automatically have entirely perfect vision, but rather can be mildly hyperopic or myopic. In nations with a very high frequency of myopia the distribution has been reported to be bimodal, one peak centering around zero and the other at about 4 diopters. Several authors have described findings of this type in Japan, and an observation on students in Hong Kong, where the myopia rate is 60 percent, is even more convincing [23]. It shows well separated peaks, one representing the group with normal vision and the other the myopes. The two populations overlap, myopic persons seeming to generally range from almost 0 to 6 diopters and occasionally as high as 20D. This is why it is necessary to select individuals with corrections above 2D to determine the risk in children of two genetic myopes. The cutoff point of 2D is also supported by data gathered on military recruits in Denmark.

RELATION OF MYOPIA TO MENTAL ABILITY

The occurrence of a bimodal curve for the distribution of nearsightedness when the myopia rate is high gives further support to a genetic etiology and excludes polygenic inheritance. The latter mechanism would lead to a single curve rather than two separate peaks. If the hypothesis of recessive inheritance is accepted, it becomes necessary to explain the extremely high frequency of the myopia gene in many populations. Mutant genes are ordinarily kept at low levels by the forces of natural selection. A balanced polymorphism requires some favorable concomitant to maintain the elevated gene frequency.

In populations dependent on hunting and gathering the handicap of myopia is quite evident, and the rate of the disorder remains low. An exception to this has been seen both in Eskimos and in northern tribes of American Indians, where the older generation has been reported to be almost free of myopia while the children show a high frequency of the disorder. One proposed explanation has been that the severe conditions under which these people have lived allowed survival of mostly heterozygous individuals, both the normal and abnormal homozygotes tending to perish before maturity. This would be analogous to the findings in sickle cell anemia in heavily infested malaria regions, where only the heterozygotes are protected. Other proposals ignore the genetic factor, contending that young individuals have in recent times been forced to read under adverse conditions, thus becoming nearsighted from eye strain which their forebears did not experience.

The proposed favorable effect of the myopia gene appears to be linked to its influences on mentality. This is not entirely unexpected since the retina of the eye is developmentally a part of the brain. It has long been known that myopic individuals outperform their peers in academic or IQ test competitions. Three separate studies have shown a gain for myopes of 7 IQ points over the general population.

One large investigation [24] was conducted on high school students in an affluent community in northern California. Among 2500 graduating seniors an overall myopia rate of 15 percent was established. They all had been rated on IQ tests, the average score for the entire student body being 106. The myopic subgroup achieved an IQ of 113. Ten years earlier, when most of the incipient myopes still had normal vision, corresponding tests had yielded essentially the same scores for the two groups.

Another study, also done in California, confirmed the finding of an IQ advantage for myopic students, interestingly arriving at the same figure of a 7 point gain over the general population. Although the authors presented no data on that claim, they disputed the likelihood of recessive inheritance for myopia.

A third investigation was conducted on military recruits in Denmark [25], taking advantage of health records carefully collected over a period of time and covering all young males. Once more the myopes achieved a score 7 points higher than the total group. In this material progressive rise in intelligence was demonstrated for different groups as myopia increased from zero to 2.5 diopters, but the ability leveled off at that point. This finding is consistent with the thesis that individuals below 2.5D represent a mixture of genetic myopes and nonmyopes, while above that figure only true myopes are found. The degree of myopia is thus unrelated to the brain effect, only presence of the proper genes being required to enhance mentality. The mental effect and the exact eye influence are then independent although basically related to the same fundamental gene. The IQ gain of 7 points over the general score or 8 points over the nonmyopes is highly significant.

The finding in the original California study that the intellectual advantage precedes the development of nearsightedness was confirmed in a previously mentioned report from England. That study also demonstrated that children destined to become myopic engaged just as much in play or sports as their nonmyopic peers.

Besides the more direct academic evaluations of myopes versus nonmyopes there are voluminous data on the performance of nearsighted individuals in various forms of achievement. A high percentage of physics graduate students at major universities wears myopia glasses. Even law school graduates have been found to show elevated rates. In Iceland the population frequency of myopia is approximately 10 percent, but the honors graduates in the mathematics section of the university preparatory college in Reykjavik exhibit a 50 percent rate. While the frequency of myopia in the United States is approximately 15 percent, students at the University of California show a 50 percent rate. Throughout the world myopic individuals seem to be people of success.

Some nations show an exceedingly high rate of myopia, and all ethnic groups exhibit frequencies far above that expected for a detrimental recessive disorder. This indicates that there may indeed be a moderate favorable mental effect in heterozygotes, although it must be lower than that seen in the homozygous myopes. Thus the myopia gene may originally have been in the same category as other frequent mutant factors which exert their benefits through heterozygotes. But while most abnormal homozygotes with other conditions are severely handicapped, the myopes only suffer from an eye defect that can be remedied. And then it turns out that the brain benefit is greatest in the homozygous myopes.

The cerebral stimulus linked to the myopia factor is so powerful that there exists no advanced industrial society without a high rate of myopia. And it seems to be predictable that any nation with an elevated myopia rate is capable of adapting to an industrial life when the opportunity presents itself. The Chinese were long considered a backward people, but the potential for progress was evidently there, presumably because of the high rate of myopia.

Direct studies of myopia heterozygotes to demonstrate their favorable brain influence is difficult, as the groups available for comparison with them are a mixture of noncarriers and carriers. One study was performed in Iceland where families of myopic women could be classified in terms of the intellectual status of their nonmyopic husbands. When the fathers in these family units were quite intelligent, the risk of myopia in the children was close to 50 percent, but it was lower in groups of less accomplishment. While a larger study is needed, the findings agree with the hypothesis that myopia carriers indeed derive some benefit from that constitution. The result is thus in harmony with the genetic interpretation of the data on Eskimos discussed above.

Despite all the evidence to the contrary the preferred explanation of the high rate of nearsightedness seen in educated persons has for many years been that excessive reading or other near work is detrimental to the eyes, resulting somehow in elongation of the organ. But ophthalmologists have not found this hypothesis to be sound. Many people engage in reading without developing myopia, and many myopes are nonreaders. The fit of the family risks to a genetic mechanism, giving the expected mathematical relationships, has no environmental explanation. It is now generally accepted among research scientists that myopia is a hereditary condition, although the mode of transmission is still debated, some authors still favoring genetic heterogeneity or polygenic inheritance.

To explain the well documented relationship of myopia to scholastic performance the most commonly heard argument is that myopes, because of their visual problems, stay indoors and read while other children are outdoors playing. This is then claimed to account for the higher IQ and academic scores among myopes. But studies have shown that premyopes, while their vision is still normal, already attain the same elevated scores on tests that distinguish them later from nonmyopes. If the intellectual gain precedes the eye disorder, it is difficult to see that it can be secondary to it. The British study referred to earlier [18] demonstrated that myopic pupils engaged just as much in play as other children. But it is still hard to satisfy the skeptics who are unwilling to accept the scientific data.

The nature of the relationship to mental ability has also been controversial, although that association is so universal that there is no possibility of it being fortuitous. All studies of ability groups have demonstrated a high rate of nearsightedness. For example, the Terman Study of gifted Californians revealed a high rate of myopia as the students matured, although the investigators chose to dismiss that finding and consider it to be a result of excessive reading and above average attention to eye problems. Icelandic honor students were also found to exhibit a high rate of myopia. Benbow and Stanley encountered a great excess of myopia in mathematically precocious boys.

CONCLUSION

The evidence for operation of hybrid vigor systems in human intellectual differences can now be said to be quite substantial. The proposed gene that can result in psychosis seems to be involved in creative thinking while the myopia gene in a single dose appears to influence learning ability. In a homozygous state the latter gene is even more effective.

It is an interesting fact that individuals who themselves have become mentally ill have contributed to human endeavors far in excess of the expectation in terms of their proportion in the population. Those who at some time in their lives develop symptoms of psychosis constitute approximately five percent of the people, but that fraction includes scholars like Isaac Newton, Michael Faraday, Charles Darwin, and Gregor Mendel. Many of the most creative men of genius in literature, music, or art have similarly come from the ranks of mental patients. Relatives of psychotic individuals have also distinguished themselves in all areas of artistic or scholarly accomplishment.

Metabolically active mentality genes that are fully productive in the normal homozygous state probably will be found to have established themselves in essentially pure form so that most individuals will possess them in duplicate sets. However, persons endowed only with these basic genes are perhaps of marginal ability. They lack the combinations involving mutant genes discussed in this chapter. Only limited diversity and low overall ability can be expected in a population devoid of the latter genes.

The factors that are most effective in heterozygous situations are by their nature the principal source of human variation. The largest group of carrier individuals will possess just one type or another of these genes, but some will have received two or more. Since mathematicians appear to arise mainly in areas of the world with elevated rates of myopia, it seems possible that highly logical reasoning requires a psychosis factor and at least one myopia gene. Thus there may be an interaction of these entities when they exist together. This notion is further supported by the finding that the highest performers in mathematics and science in the Icelandic schools show a 5-fold rate of myopia in addition to being burdened with psychosis genes.

The chief reason for the currently claimed acceleration of mental decline in the developed countries may be the natural effect resulting from recently altered social conditions. It simply is not possible to eliminate selective forces and invite people of low mentality to reproduce freely without suffering adverse influences. Dire results are inevitable when all decisions are left to leaders who have no comprehension of biological necessities.

As was stated previously, natural selection can be said to serve three vital functions, all biologically important and intimately integrated to maintain proper balances in the organic world. The most fundamental role is that of guiding evolutionary progression. When random changes occur in the genetic material, selection determines what is preserved as survival of the fittest leads to gradual adaptation and advance. In terms of human experiences this function has little effect, since the process is so slow that nothing changes perceptively even in thousands of years. A more immediate contribution of selective forces to mans biology is the weeding out of deleterious mutations, which threaten continued health if the genetic legacy is allowed to deteriorate. Inactivated genes arise constantly, albeit at relatively low rates, and selection is necessary to guard against increases in hereditary abnormalities. The third function of selection is the most important one for survival of mankind. Creative intelligence is mandatory for continuance of advanced cultures, which human life is now entirely dependent on. Since creativity is linked to hybrid states, which can only be preserved by constant rigorous selection, longitudinal human existence demands removal of unfit individuals from the breeding pool and promotion of heterozygous persons capable of intellectual efforts. Creative mentality cannot be stabilized and must constantly be protected through selection.

REFERENCES

[1]   Karlsson JL: Genetic basis of intellectual variation in Iceland. *Hereditas* 95:283-288, 1981

[2]   Karlsson JL: *Inheritance of Creative Intelligence*. Nelson-Hall, Chicago, 1978

[3]   Osborn F: *The Future of Human Heredity*. Weybright and Talley, New York, 1968

[4]   Zerbin-Rudin E: Genetic research and the theory of schizophrenia. *International Journal of Mental Health* 1:42-62, 1972

[5]   Karlsson JL: Partly dominant transmission of schizophrenia in Iceland. *British Journal of Psychiatry* 152:324-329, 1988

[6]   Elsasser G, Lehmann H, Pohlen M, and Scheid T: Die Nachkommen geisteskranker Elternpaare. Fortschritte der Neurologie, *Psychiatrie und ihrer Grenzgebiete* 39:495-522, 1971

[7]   Kallmann F: *The Genetics of Schizophrenia*. Augustin, New York, 1938

[8]   Book JA, Wetterberg L, and Modrzewska K: Schizophrenia in a north-Swedish geographical isolate 1900-1977. *Clinical Genetics* 14:373-394, 1978

[9]   Reed SC, Hartley C, Phillips VP, and Johnson NA: *The Psychoses: Family Studies.* Saunders, Philadelphia, 1973

[10] Holzman PS, Kringlen E, Matthysse S, Flanagan SD, Lipton RB, Cramer G, Levin S, Lange K, and Levy DL: A single dominant gene can account for eyetracking dysfunctions and schizophrenia in offspring of discordant twins. *Archives of General Psychiatry* 45:641-647, 1988

[11] Lombroso C: *The Man of Genius.* Walter Scott, London, 1891

[12] Lange-Eichbaum W: Genie, *Irrsinn und Ruhm.* Reinhardt, Munich, 1928

[13] Andreasen NJC and Canter A: The creative writer: psychiatric symptoms and family history. *Comprehensive Psychiatry* 15:123-131, 1974

[14] Goodwin FK and Jamison KR: *Manic Depressive Illness.* Oxford University Press, Oxford, 1990

[15] Barron FX: *Creative Person and Creative Process.* Holt, Rinehart and Winston, New York, 1969

[16] Karlsson JL: Mental abilities of male relatives of psychotic patients. *Acta Psychiatric Scandinavica* 104:466-468, 2001

[17] Karlsson JL: Relation of mathematical ability to psychosis in Iceland. *Clinical Genetics* 56:447-449, 1990

[18] Peckham CS, Gardiner PA, and Goldstein H: Acquired myopia in 11-year old children. *British Medical Journal* 1:542-545, 1977

[19] Lin LLK, Chen CJ, Hung PT, and Ko LS: Nation-wide survey of myopia among school children in Taiwan 1986. *Acta Ophthalmologia* (Supplement 185) 66:29-33, 1988

[20] Karlsson JL: Concordance rates for myopia in twins. *Clinical Genetics* 6:142-146, 1974

[21] Jablonski W: Zur Vererbung der Myopie. *Klinische Monatsblatter fur Augenheikunde* 68:560-573, 1922

[22] Furusho T: Studies on the genetic mechanism of short-sightedness. *Japanese Journal of Ophthalmology* 1:185-190, 1957 23.

[23] Wallman J: Nature and nurture of myopia. *Nature* 371:201-202, 1994

[24] Karlsson JL: Influence of the myopia gene on brain development. *Clinical Genetics* 8:314-318, 1975

[25] Teasdale TW, Fuchs J, and Goldschmidt E: Degree of myopia in relation to intelligence and educational level. *The Lancet* 2:1351-1354, 1988

In: Intelligence : New Research
Editor: Lin V. Wesley, pp. 47-81

ISBN 1-59454-637-1
© 2006 Nova Science Publishers, Inc.

Chapter 3

THE NEUROPSYCHOLOGY OF INDIVIDUAL DIFFERENCES IN ABILITY AND PERSONALITY

Norbert Jaušovec*, Zlatka Cugmas,
Ljubica Marjanovič Umek and Maja Zupančič
University of Maribor
University of Ljubljana

ABSTRACT

The neurophysiological research of ability has mainly focused on the verbal and performance components of intelligence, and has, only recently paid some attention to emotional intelligence. The explanation of individual differences in ability was an efficiency theory. Neuroscientists have, despite the acceptance of the 'Big 5' model of personality including extraversion (E), neuroticism (N), openness to experience (O), agreeableness (A) and conscientiousness (C), been mainly interested in extraversion. It was suggested that extraverts have relatively low levels of cortical arousal, by contrast, introverts are assumed to display comparatively high levels of cortical activity.

The present study investigated neuropsychological differences in verbal/ performance intelligence (IQ – measured with WISC-R), and emotional intelligence (EIQ – measured with MSCEIT), as well as the 'Big 5' personality traits (measured with BFQ). For that purpose the EEG of 70 individuals (38 females and 32 males) was analyzed in two conditions: resting with eyes closed, and while solving a figural task. The EEG was analyzed in the time and frequency domain. Correlations between EEG parameters and behavioral measures were obtained. The findings can be summarized as follows:

The major finding of the study is that males and females differed in resting brain activity related to their level of general intelligence. Brain activity in females increased with the level of intelligence, whereas an opposite pattern of brain activity was observed in males. In males an even more pronounced correlation between EIQ and EEG power measures was observed. High emotional intelligent males in all three alpha bands showed more synchronous oscillations equally distributed over both hemispheres and three brain

---
* Corresponding Author, Univerza v Mariboru, Koroška 160, 2000 Maribor,norbert.jausovec@uni-mb.si

areas. Females showed no significant correlations between EIQ and EEG power measures, however the trend of correlations was opposite to the one observed for males.

The correlation patterns between EEG parameters and personality factors differed between males and females mainly for the factor N, whereas for the factor E similar patterns of brain activity between males and females could be observed. This differences were mainly observed for the resting condition.

Comparing the correlations between EEG parameters, on the one hand and EIQ, IQ and personality factors, on the other, suggests that emotional intelligence represents a construct being distinct from general intelligence and personality factors. It can be also concluded that males and females achieve similar IQ results with different brain regions, suggesting that there is no singular underlying neuroanatomical structure to general intelligence and that different types of brain designs may manifest comparable intellectual performance

1. INTRODUCTION

Individual differences in abilities, personality traits, and many other human behaviors have been of interest to psychologists for as long as psychology has been a field of scientific investigation. Furthermore, some of the earliest researchers who examined individual differences tried to explain them in terms of underlying biological mechanisms. Gall and Spurzheim (after Olin, 1910) almost two centuries ago considered that gross anatomical features of the brain are related to personality traits such as wit, causality, self esteem and many others. Some of these traits can be related to intelligence (Detterman, 1994, Kolb and Whishaw, 1996The idea was that the shape of the skull – bumps and depressions – indicate the size of the underlying brain area, and in that way point to a more or less developed trait. To measure these bumps they developed a device called cranioscopy. Today methods used to measure brain activity and ability have become much more accurate, and sophisticated. Yet, knowing about the immense controversies in psychology concerning intelligence, emotional intelligence and personality, and similar debates in neuroscience on the use of EEG and other techniques, one can realize how difficult it is to give a more definite answer to the question of the relationship between brain activity, ability and personality.

1.1. Intelligence and Emotional Intelligence

Intelligence represents the individual's overall level of intellectual ability. It serves as a general concept that includes several groups of mental abilities. One of the most influential divisions of intelligence splits it into verbal, performance and social intelligence (Thorndike, 1920). In recent years the term social intelligence has been replaced by emotional intelligence – the ability to recognize emotion, reason with emotion and emotion-related information, and process emotional information as part of general problem-solving (Mayer, et al., 2000). Neurophysiological research has been mainly interested in the verbal and performance components of intelligence (Anokhin, et al., 1999; O'Boyle, et al., 1995; Haier, and Benbow, 1995; Haier, et al., 1988; Haier, et al., 1992 Jaušovec, 1996, 1998, 2000; Jaušovec and Jaušovec 2000 a, 2000 b, 2001; Lutzenberger, et al., 1992; Neubauer, et al., 1995; Neubauer,

Table 1. Overview of studies investigating the relationship between brain activity and intelligence

Author	Method	Tasks used	NET*
Anokhin, et al., 1999	EEG coherence, and dimensional complexity. Broad band: theta, alpha and beta	Verbal (naming of categories); and visuo-spatial (mental rotation) tasks	Y
Doppelmayr, et al., 2002	Log-transformed EEG power values, in 3 narrow alpha frequency bands	resting (correlation with different intelligence tasks – LGT-3 and IST-70)	N
Gevins and Smith, 2000	ERP, EEG power values, theta, lower alpha band	Working memory tasks ('n-back')	Y/N
Haier, et al., 1988	PET – fluor-2-deoxyglucose	Raven's Advanced progressive matrices	Y
Haier, et al., 1992	PET – fluor-2-deoxyglucose	Computer game "Tetris"	Y
Haier and Benbow, 1995	PET - deoxyglucose	Mathematical reasoning	Y
Haier, 2003	PET – fluor-2-deoxyglucose	Raven's Advanced progressive matrices, viewing emotional video tapes	Y
Jaušovec, 1996	EEG spectral power. Broad alpha band.	Resting, solving of closed and open problems, free-recall tasks	Y
Jaušovec, 1998	EEG spectral power, and entropy measures. Broad alpha band.	Resting, Stroop tasks, reasoning tasks, numerical tasks	Y
Jaušovec, 2000	EEG spectral power and coherence. Lower (7.9 – 10.0 Hz) and upper alpha band (10.1 – 12.9 Hz)	Solving of closed and open problems	Y
Jaušovec and Jaušovec, 2000 a	ERP – approximated entropy measures	Visual and auditory oddball tasks	Y
Jaušovec and Jaušovec, 2000 b	Induced and event-related ERD, theta (4-7 Hz) and upper alpha (10-13)	Auditory oddball task	Y
Jaušovec and Jaušovec, 2001	EEG current density – LORETA	Auditory oddball task	Y
Jaušovec, et al., 2001	Induced and event-related ERD, theta (4.4-6.4 Hz), lower-2 alpha (8.4-10.4 Hz), upper alpha (10.4-12.4)	Emotional intelligence tasks	Y
Jaušovec and Jaušovec, 2003	EEG current density – LORETA	Raven's Advanced progressive matrices, Emotional intelligence tasks	Y
Jaušovec and Jaušovec, 2004a	EEG current density – LORETA, induced ERD, theta (4.4-6.3 Hz), lower-1 alpha (6.4-8.3) lower-2 alpha (8.4-10.3 Hz), upper alpha (10.4-12.3)	Memory tasks	N
Jaušovec and Jaušovec, 2004b	Induced ERD, theta (4.17-6.16 Hz), lower-1 alpha (6.17-8.16) lower-2 alpha (8.17-10.16 Hz), upper alpha (10.17-12.16)	Working memory and learning tasks	Y/N
Jaušovec and Jaušovec, (in press)	Induced ERD and upper alpha (10.17-12.16 Hz) and gamma (31-49 Hz)	Raven's Advanced progressive matrices, identifying emotions in pictures	Y/N
Klimesch, 1999	ERD, theta, upper alpha band	semantic and episodic memory tasks	N
Klimesch and Doppelmayr, 2001	Log-transformed EEG power values, in 3 narrow alpha frequency bands	resting (correlation with different intelligence tasks – LGT-3 and IST-70)	N
Lutzenberger, et al., 1992	EEG dimensional complexity. Broad band: 2 – 35 Hz	Resting, emotional imagery	N
Neubauer et al., 1995	ERD, upper alpha	sentence verification test	Y
Neubauer et al., 1999	ERD, narrow alpha bands (8-10 Hz, 10-12 Hz)	Posner's letter matching task	Y
Neubauer et al., 2002	ERD, upper alpha (10.70-12.69 Hz)	Posner's matching tasks (verbal, numerical, figural)	Y
Neubauer and Fink, 2003	ERD, upper alpha (10.10-12.09 Hz)	Stankov's Triplet Number test	Y
O'Boyle, et al., 1995	EEG spectral power. Broad alpha band.	Chimerical face processing, word processing	Y

* NET – Neural Efficiency Theory (Y = supporting NET; N = not supporting NET)

et al., 1999; Neubauer, et al., 2002; Neubauer and Fink, 2003 – for a detailed overview see Table 1) and has, only recently paid some attention to emotional intelligence (Jaušovec, et al. 2001; Jaušovec and Jaušovec, in press). Most of these studies have demonstrated a negative correlation between brain activity under cognitive load and intelligence. The explanation of these findings was an efficiency theory. This efficiency may derive from the non-use of many brain areas irrelevant for good task performance as well as the more focused use of specific task-relevant areas in high intelligent individuals. It was even suggested that high and low intelligent individuals preferentially activate different neural circuits even though no reasoning or problem solving was required (Haier, White and Michael, 2003; Jaušovec and Jaušovec, 2003

Studies which have used memory and learning tasks, requiring encoding of information have produced some inconsistent results, opposite to what would be predicted by the neural efficiency hypothesis (Klimesch, 1999; Klimesch, and Doppelmayr, 2001Doppelmayr, et al., 2002Jaušovec and Jaušovec, 2004a Some studies have shown a specific topographic pattern of differences related to the level of intelligence. High-ability subjects made relatively greater use of parietal regions, whereas low-ability subjects relied more exclusively on frontal regions. (Gevins and Smith, 2000; Jaušovecand Jaušovec, 2004a). More generally these results suggest that higher-ability subjects tend to better identify strategies needed for the solution of the task at hand. It was further reported that high intelligent subjects displayed more brain activity in the early stages of task performance, while average individuals showed a reverse pattern. This temporal distribution of brain activity suggests that cognitive processes in high intelligent individuals are faster than in average intelligent individuals (Jaušovecand Jaušovec, 2004b).

A second characteristic of the reported studies employing the EEG methodology was that they have almost exclusively based their findings on analyzing the alpha (7-12 Hz) and theta (4-6 Hz) bands. Probably because the relationship of activity in these bands with mental effort is well documented. Alpha amplitude tends to decrease (desynchronization) with increases in mental effort, while theta band amplitude tends to increase (synchronization) (Nunez, Wingeier, and Silberstein, 2001; Klimesch, 1996, 1997, 1999). Recent research has revealed that the gamma band (>30 Hz) may be of particular relevance to cognition – e.g., attention and arousal, basic acoustic and visual perception, perception of gestalt and language, music perception (for review, see Pulvermüller et al., 1997; Tallon-Baudry and Bertrand 1999, Başar, et al., 2001, Bhattacharya et al., 2001Of special relevance for high level cognitive processes is the induced gamma band activity. In contrast to evoked gamma responses which are strictly phase-locked, induced gamma activity consists of oscillatory bursts whose latency jitters from trial to trial and its temporal relationship with stimulus onset is fairly loose (Tallon-Baudry and Bertrand 1999). It has been suggested that induced gamma activity reflects a binding mechanism which is enhanced when a coherent percept is created in response to a given stimulus. Neuronal activity is expressed in spatially separate areas of the cortex, which requires processes for linking the separate nodes of activity, thereby allowing identification of the object as a whole. The linking mechanism is provided by the oscillations in the gamma-band (Singer and Gray, 1995). To our knowledge there are only few studies relating gamma-band activity to the level of intelligence. Some indirect conclusions on the relationship between gamma band oscillations and intelligence can be made based on the research of Strüber (Strüber, et al., 2000), and Bhattacharya (Bhattacharya et al., 2001). Using visual motion tasks, Strüber showed that better task performance was associated with higher gamma band activity. Bhattacharya showed that while listening to music, degrees of the gamma band synchrony over distributed cortical areas were found to be significantly higher in musicians than non-musicians. In a recent study (Jaušovec and Jaušovec, in press) students, who could be clustered as high-average verbal/performance intelligent (HIQ/AIQ), or emotionally intelligent (HEIQ/AEIQ), were performing the Raven's advanced progressive matrices (RAPM), and identifying emotions in pictures (IDEM). Significant differences in event-related desynchronization/synchronization (ERD/ERS) related to verbal/performance intelligence were only observed while respondents solved the RAPM. The HIQ and AIQ groups displayed temporal and spatial differently induced gamma band activity. Significant differences in ERD/ERS related to emotional intelligence were only observed for the IDEM task. HEIQ individuals displayed more gamma band ERS and less upper alpha band ERD than did AEIQ individuals. It can be concluded that HIQ and HEIQ individuals employed more adequate strategies for solving the problems at hand. The results further suggest that emotional intelligence and verbal/performance intelligence represent distinct components of the cognitive architecture.

Another approach to studying salient brain areas involved in intelligence is to examine how individual differences in intelligence among subjects correlate with brain functioning while subjects are at rest. However, the comparison between studies is difficult because different measures were used to investigate brain activity. In general, two categories of EEG variables are correlated with IQ and neuropsychological performance: (1) Power or amplitude measures and, (2) network connection measures such as coherence, phase delays and non-linear dynamical models of network complexity. Studied were mainly oscillations in the alpha band (7-12 Hz) because it is believed that they represent oscillations of postsynaptic potentials in the neocortex, and are reduced in amplitude by eye opening, drowsiness, and moderate to difficult mental tasks (Nunez et al., 2001). It is further assumed that the amplitude of the EEG is mainly influenced by the number of synchronous synaptic generators and much less by asynchronous generators, or the total number of generators. EEG coherence is a somewhat different measure than EEG synchrony . It is a measure of phase angle consistency or phase "variability" between pairs of signals in each frequency band. Thus, it provides an estimate of functional interactions between oscillating systems and may yield information about network formation and brain binding – coupling/decoupling of brain areas (Nunez et al., 2001). The relation between EEG coherence and synchrony is rather complex. Sources that are synchronous will also tend to be coherent, however the converse need not be true; e.g., desynchronization is associated with amplitude reduction, but may still be coherent if the sources are 180 degrees out of phase, so their individual contributions to EEG amplitude tend to cancel. The measure of dimensional complexity reflects the complexity of neural generators – the relative number of concurrently oscillating neuronal assemblies and degrees of freedom in the competitive interaction between them. It appears to be relatively independent of EEG spectral power, and inversely related to coherence (Anokhin et al., 1999).

It was suggested that a faster oscillating brain reflects rapid information processing associated with high intelligence (Anokhin and Vogel, 1996; Klimesch, 1997. Support for this theory is provided by the studies of Giannitrapani, (1969), who reported a significant correlation between IQ and the average EEG frequency in a group of 18 adults; of Anokhin and Vogel (1996) who obtained a correlation of 0.35 between alpha peak frequency and verbal abilities; and of Klimesch (1997), who found that the alpha peak frequency of good working memory performers lies about 1 Hz higher than that of poor working memory performers. Further, a study by Lehtovirta et al., (1996), comparing Alzheimer's patients with controls, found that the alpha peak frequency of Alzheimer's patients was significantly lower than that of controls. All these studies suggested that high intelligence is associated with a faster oscillating brain, however, some recent large-scale studies could not replicate these findings (Jaušovec and Jaušovec, 2000c; Posthuma et al., 2001).

Using a non-linear dynamical analysis of the multichannel EEG, Lutzenberger et al. (1992) showed that during resting conditions subjects with high IQs demonstrated higher dimensional complexity in the EEG pattern than subjects with low IQs. Yet, in a follow up study (Anokhin et al., 1999), a negative correlation between the level of IQ and dimensional complexity was obtained. Yet, in another study (Jaušovec, 1998) no correlation between the complexity of oscillations in the resting brain and IQ could be observed.

Similarly inconsistent are the findings using EEG power measures. Several studies by Jaušovec have shown positive (Jaušovec, 1996), negative (Jaušovec, 1997), and no significant correlations (Jaušovec, 1998; Jaušovec and Jaušovec, 2000a), between resting alpha power and IQ. Contradictory are also the findings of other researchers. Doppelmayr, et al., (2002 reported significant positive correlations between resting power measures in three individually determined narrow alpha frequency bands and scores on two German intelligence tests measuring semantic memory and the ability to learn new material. In contrast, Razoumnikova (2003) reported a negative correlation between lower alpha power and intelligence. Razoumnikova further showed that high intelligent individuals displayed higher coherence (coupling of brain areas) than did low intelligent individuals. A similar finding was also reported by Jaušovec and Jaušovec (2000c), but only for the eyes-open relaxed state, whereas for the eyes-closed resting condition no significant correlations were obtained. The explanation for the diversity of results was usually ascribed to methodological differences. However, in our opinion the main reason for the diversity is that most of the studies neglected gender related differences in abilities. Despite the fact that robust sex differences on the behavioral level in spatial (McGee, 1979and verbal abilities (Garai and Scheinfield,1968 as well as emotional intelligence (Mayer, et al., 2000, 2002), and intelligence (Colom and Lynn, 2004) have been observed, many of the reported studies generalized the relationship between intelligence and brain activity on only male samples (Anokhin and Vogel, 1996; Lutzenberger et al., 1992; Razoumnikova, 2003), or on predominantly female samples (Jaušovec, 1996, 1997, 1998; Jaušovec and Jaušovec, 2000a; Doppelmayr et al., 2002). Some recent EEG studies relating intelligence with brain activity under cognitive load have shown that males while solving numerical and figural tasks are more likely to produce cortical activation patterns which are in line with the neural efficiency hypothesis (i.e. less activation in brighter individuals), whereas in females for the same tasks no significant differences could be observed (Neubauer et al., 2002; Neubauer and Fink, 2003). Sex related differences were also observed in EEG coherence and global field power studies. The results of Corsi-Cabera et al., (1997) and Rescher and Rappelsberger (1999) indicate different intra- and interhemispheric correlations of EEG activity in males and females, a finding commonly related to sex differences in certain brain structures (e.g., the posterior corpus callosum). Skrandies et al., (1999) found a consistently larger global field power in females suggesting that during visual information processing different neural assemblies are activated in males and females. Empirical evidence favoring sex differences in physiological parameters of cortical activation comes also from PET, fMRI, and brain nerve conduction velocity (NCV) studies. It was found that for figural tasks males show significantly stronger parietal activation, while females show significantly greater frontal activation (Weiss et al., 2003). A similar greater left frontal brain activation in females was also observed in relation to verbal intelligence scores (Pfleiderer et al., (2004). Nyberg et al., (2000 observed sex differences in brain activation during memory retrieval, while Haier and Benbow (1995 reported a positive relationship in glucose metabolic rate in temporal lobe regions and mathematical reasoning ability only in men. A similar finding was also reported by Mansour et al., (1996). In a recent study by Reed, et al., (2004) NCV, the speed at which impulses travel along nerves, was compared in the visual nerve pathway of males and females. It was found that the mean NCV of males was about 4% faster than in females.

Summarizing these findings suggests that gender related differences in intelligence can be observed in relation to the type of task (verbal/figural), and activated brain regions (frontal versus temporal-occipital and parieto-occipital areas). A tentative conceptual framework for the differences observed could be provided by age changes in white matter in the brain. It is now established that during childhood and adolescence the volume of white matter (WM: nerve axons, myelin around the axons, and glial cells) in the brain steadily increases. In males this volume probably increases faster than in females (De Bellis et al., 2001). This would also explain the finding, that among adults, males have an advantage of approximately 4 IQ points (Colom and Lynn, 2004). The increase in WM could be due to increased myelination, increased axon size, glial proliferation, or a combination of these (De Bellis et al., 2001). Miller (1994) proposed that myelination could also be an explanation of the neural efficiency theory of intelligence – the more focused use of specific task-relevant brain areas in high intelligent individuals could be the result of less leakage and cross-talk between neurons.

1.2. PERSONALITY

Hans Eysenck has been among the foremost exponents of the hypothesis that personality traits provide a window on individual differences in brain functioning. Eysenck (Eysenck, 1967 Eysenck and Eysenck, 1985) identifies two key components of his conceptual nervous system: reticulo-cortical and reticulo-limbic circuits. The reticulo-cortical circuit controls the cortical arousal generated by incoming stimuli, whereas the reticulo-limbic circuit controls response to emotional stimuli. Under strong emotional stimulation, limbic system activity may spread to the cortex. Extraversion-introversion (E) relates to arousability of the reticulo-cortical circuit, so that introverts are typically more aroused than extraverts. However, methodological analyses of extraversion studies (Gale, 1973) have illuminated two basic problems for theory testing. First, people actively seek a moderate level of arousal, so that relationships between personality and arousal may also reflect individual differences in strategies for seeking or avoiding stimulation. Second, according to Eysenck (1994), increasing stimulation provokes increasing central nervous system (c.n.s.) reactivity until an optimal point is reached, beyond which inhibition and decreasing reactivity set in. Hence, introverts may be higher, lower or equal to the arousal level of extraverts according to complex interactions of personality type and environmental manipulation. Neuroticism (N) is associated with arousability of the limbic circuit, such that neurotics become more aroused than stable individuals as a consequence of emotion-inducing stimulation. Therefore, individual differences in N may only be evident in emotional contexts. The neuropsychology of Eysenck's third dimension of Psychoticism (P) has not been worked out in detail.

There exist several reviews of the relationship between raw EEG measures and E (Gale, 1983, O'Gorman, 1984; Zuckerman, 1991; Eysenck, 1994; Matthews and Gilliland, 1999). According to Gale, several studies supported the hypothesis that introverts are higher in cortical arousal than extraverts. However, a similar number found no differences, and three studies found results that contradicted the theory. Gale argued that moderate arousal-inducing environments were the most amenable to testing predictions of Eysenck's (1967) theory. Low arousal-inducing environments resulted in paradoxical arousal, especially in extraverts. Similar to high arousal-inducing environments (e.g., task performance demands) which resulted in possible over-arousal, again especially in extraverts. Some recent studies (Fink, et al., 2002; Fink and Neubauer, 2004) lend some support to Gale's theory. In contrast, O'Gorman's (1984) analysis of the EEG studies found that use of Eysenck's original E scales or similar measures, was a more important influence on outcome than arousal level . On the other hand, Matthews and Gilliland, (1999) and Zuckerman (1991) have been less enthusiastic about the level of support that past EEG studies have provided for the cortical arousal hypothesis of extraversion. Although Zuckerman (1991) has pointed out that studies using female subjects or equal numbers of both sexes seem to more often support Eysenck's theory.

There have been a few more recent studies that are noteworthy. Matthews and Amelang (1993) reported correlations (.19) between EEG power measures and extraversion, which largely match the hypothesis that extraverts display a lower cortical arousal as compared to introverts. Smith et al. (1995) reported that introverts were generally found to produce lower levels of alpha activity reflecting higher levels of arousal, but there were also complex hemisphere by gender interactions. These findings suggest again that concerns about the sex of subjects may be important.

Evidence in line with Eysenck's arousal theory comes also from measures of regional cerebral blood flow (rCBF) quantified with positron emission tomography (PET). In a study by Mathew, Weinman, and Barr (1984) rCBF during a resting state was inversely related to extraversion in all brain regions, suggesting that extraversion is associated with a lower rCBF (i.e., lower arousal). A decreased cerebral blood flow among extraverts during a resting state was also reported by Ebermeier et al. (1994) for the anterior and posterior cingulate cortex, and for the secondary visual cortex by Fischer, Wik, and Fredrikson (1997).

Much less material is available in the field of psychopathological dimensions of neuroticism and psychoticism. N is an extremely robust personality trait that has been associated with an increased sensitivity to fear, anxiety, and distress. Not surprisingly, neuroticism (N) and negative affectivity (NA) have been shown to correlate highly across numerous samples (Hagemann et al., 1999; Watson and Clark, 1992). In addition, a great body of literature exists on the relationship between positive/negative emotions and brain activity. Positive emotions, as well as negative yet approach-related emotions, are typically associated with relative left-frontal and anterior-temporal activity, while negative, withdrawal-related emotion has been associated with higher relative activity of the right frontal and anterior-temporal regions (Ahern and Schwartz, 1985; Davidson, 1995; Harmon-Jones and Allen, 1997; Heller, 1990; Tomarken, Davidson, and Henriques, 1990). Based on the linking of N with NA, one might predict that N would also be associated with relative right-frontal activation. However, investigators have reported inconsistent results in this area.

In general, studies within the normal population have not been particularly successful in linking N with psychophysiological measures of activation (see Eysenck, 1990, for a review).

From a psychometric perspective there has been a growing acceptance of a five-factor model of personality incorporating two of Eysenck's dimensions E and N together with Openness to Experience (O) , Agreeableness (A) and Conscientiousness (C). Despite the growing acceptance of the 'Big 5' model of personality there have been very few studies that have examined the biological basis of O, A and C. In a preliminary study Stough et al., (2001) showed that O was moderately and positively correlated with photic driving at a frequency in the theta band across all cortical regions; A was moderately and negatively correlated with photic driving at frequencies in the beta-1 band in the left central-temporal region; and C was moderately and negatively correlated with photic driving at frequencies in the theta band frontally, and moderately and positively correlated with photic driving at frequencies in the beta-1 band in the occipito-parietal and left and right central-temporal regions. The most pertinent finding was that individuals with higher scores in O tend to have a greater amount of theta production. Because theta activity decreases with age, the interpretation of the authors was that respondents high on O may have retained a somewhat childlike wonderment and open-mindedness about their world with a willingness to explore alternative views about issues.

2. METHOD

2.1. Aims of the Study

The aim of the present study was to investigate if differences in personality structure, general and emotional intelligence are reflected in brain activity. As pointed out in the introduction it seems that these relationships to a great extent depend on gender. Therefore in the present study differences in brain activity related to personality, general and emotional intelligence were analyzed separately for males and females. As stressed by Eysenck (1994) we never measure any dimension of personality in isolation; we are always dealing with individuals that differ from others not only in E but also in intelligence, or emotional intelligence as well as thousands of other variables. Therefore an additional goal of the study was to investigate how the combination of personality and ability variables is reflected in brain activity. Of special interest was the relationship between emotional intelligence personality and general intelligence. Some recent studies have suggested that emotional intelligence is not much more than general intelligence and personality (De Raad, 2005). On the other hand, studies employing physiological parameters have suggested that emotional intelligence and verbal/performance intelligence represent distinct components of the cognitive architecture (Jaušovec, et al. 2001; Jaušovec and Jaušovec, in press). To achieve these goals we analyzed the raw EEG and event-related data in several different ways employing frequency and time dependent measures, as well as power measures and measures of connectivity between brain areas.

2.2. Subjects

The sample included 70 right-handed student-teachers (mean age 21 years and 2 months; 32 male and 38 female students) taking a course in Psychology. The students' performance/verbal intelligence – which we will refer to as general intelligence (WAIS-R), emotional intelligence (MSCEIT), and personality structure (BFQ) was determined. The test results are summarized in Table 2.

Table 2. Behavioral results: IQ, WIQ, PIQ (WAIS-R); EIQ, EEIQ, SEIQ (MSCEIT);O,C,E,A,N (BFQ)

	MALE				FEMALE			
	M	SD	Min.	Max.	M	SD	Min.	Max.
IQ	104	8.95	85	130	101	9.79	86	126
WIQ	105	6.57	81	128	105	4.70	92	122
PIQ	102	4.42	83	125	100	3.53	83	135
EIQ	96	13.78	65	128	103	12.30	69	124
EEIQ	96	15.87	53	125	102	11.35	74	121
SEIQ	97	15.57	65	128	103	13.60	69	128
O	48	10.36	29	73	41	6.73	28	58
C	49	7.90	34	62	43	9.40	16	60
E	46	7.49	32	63	39	8.94	20	65
A	50	9.96	27	72	46	6.32	29	58
N	45	9.19	25	61	41	6.48	30	56

2.3. Material and Procedure

The individuals were tested with emotional intelligence tests MSCEIT (Mayer-Salovey-Caruso Emotional Intelligence Test, Mayer, et al., 2002), with 9 WAIS-R subtests (6 verbal: Information, Digit Span, Vocabulary, Arithmetic, Comprehension, and Similarities; and 3 performance: Picture Completion, Picture Arrangement, and Digit Symbol), and with the Slovene version of the personality questionnaire BFQ (Caprara, et al., 2002). For each person the level of general intelligence (IQ), verbal intelligence (VIQ), performance intelligence (PIQ), emotional intelligence (EIQ), experiential emotional intelligence (EEIQ), strategic emotional intelligence (SEIQ), extraversion (E), neuroticism (N), openness (O), conscientiousness (C) and agreeableness (A) was determined.

Emotional intelligence was defined as the ability to recognize emotion, reason with emotion and emotion-related information, and process emotional information as part of general problem-solving (Mayer, et al., 2000). The EEIQ assesses a respondent's ability to perceive, respond, and manipulate emotional information without necessarily understanding it. Whereas the SEIQ assesses a respondent's ability to understand and manage emotions without necessarily perceiving feelings well or fully experiencing them. The scoring of the emotional tasks was not based on a 'correct' answer, but on general consensus. A respondent's general consensus score on each task compares that individual's performance to the more than 1000 people in the Slovene normative database (corrected for age) who have taken the test.

The BFQ consists of 132 items rated on a fivepoint Likert scale ranging from ''strongly agree'' to ''strongly disagree.'' Reliability coefficients for the major traits have been reported to range from 0.67 to 0.85. In Table 3 are summarized the main characteristics of the five personality factors.

Table 3. Description of the Big 5 personality factors – Extraversion-E, Neuroticism-N, Openness-O, Conscientiousness-C, and Agreeableness-A

FACTOR	DESCRIPTION
E	Energetic, dynamic, talkative, able to show enthusiasm, able to influence others
A	Empathic, helpful, able to cooperate and work in groups, trustful
C	Reliable, orderly, persistent, exact
N	Able to control emotions, relaxed, balanced, able to cope with stress
O	Creative, original, intelligent, open for new ideas

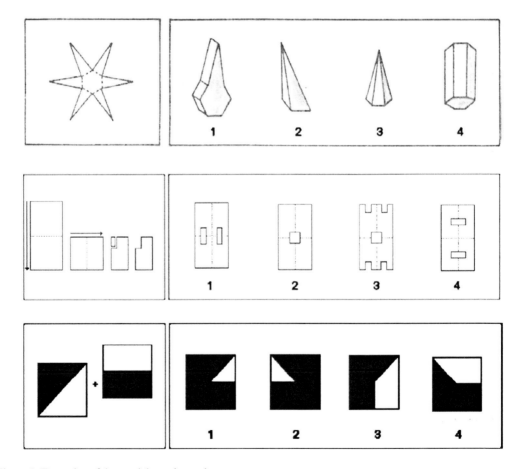

Figure 1. Examples of the spatial rotation tasks.

Subjects were told that they would be participating in a study which aims to find electrophysiological correlates of personality, general and emotional intelligence. After they had been asked to completely relax in a reclining chair, their resting EEG was recorded for a period of 10 min with eyes closed. Then they solved a test battery which consisted of 50 spatial rotation tasks. The tasks were based on a well established Slovene intelligence test (BTI test, Mihelič, 1972), on the Spatial-Temporal Animation Reasoning tasks (S.T.A.R.) designed by Peterson (2000), and on the PFandC subtest of the Stanford-Binet IQ measure (Rideout and Laubach, 1996). In Figure 1 examples of the spatial rotation task types are shown. Respondents had to judge which of the four figures on the right corresponded to the figure in the left frame. The tasks were presented on a computer screen positioned about 100 cm in front of the respondent. The tasks were presented at fixed 11 s interstimulus intervals. They were exposed for 5 s following a 2 s interval, when a cross was presented. During this time the students were instructed to press a button (1-4) which indicated their answer. All pictures were generated by the STIM stimulator.

The WAIS-R, BFQ and MSCEIT tests were administered in two sessions, individually and in small groups of 2-3 students.

2.4. EEG Recording and Quantification

EEG was recorded using a Quick-Cap with sintered (Silver/Silver Chloride; 8mm diameter) electrodes. Using the Ten-twenty Electrode Placement System of the International Federation, the EEG activity was monitored over nineteen scalp locations (Fp1, Fp2, F3, F4, F7, F8, T3,T4, T5, T6, C3, C4, P3, P4, O1, O2, Fz, Cz and Pz). All leads were referenced to linked mastoids (A1 and A2), and a ground electrode was applied to the forehead. Additionally, vertical eye movements were recorded with electrodes placed above and below the left eye. Electrode impedance was maintained below 5 kΩ. The digital EEG data acquisition and analysis system (SynAmps) had a bandpass of 0.15-50.0 Hz. At cutoff frequencies the voltage gain was approximately –6dB. The 19 EEG traces were digitized online at 1000 Hz with a gain of 1000 (resolution of .084 μV/bit in a 16 bit A to D conversion), and stored on a hard disk.

2.4.1. Task EEG Analysis

Epochs were comprised from the 4000 ms preceding and 7000 ms following the stimulus presentation and automatically screened for artifacts. Excluded were all epochs showing amplitudes above ± 50 μV (less than 2%).The analysis was performed with the Scan 4.3 software.

The frequency bands (alpha and theta) were individually determined, based on the mean alpha peak frequency (IAF = 10.13 Hz, $\underline{SD}$ = 1.13) (Klimesch,1999; Burgess and Gruzelier, 1999). On average, this method resulted in a band of 10.13 – 12.12 Hz for the upper alpha band, a band of 8.13 – 10.12 Hz for the lower-2 alpha, a band of 6.13 – 8.12 Hz for the lower-1 alpha, and a band of 4.13 – 6.12 Hz for the theta band. The broad gamma band had a range from 31 to 49 Hz. These bands were chosen because research has identified their relationship to different cognitive functions. Episodic memory processes and working memory performance seem to be reflected as oscillations in the EEG theta (4-6 Hz) frequencies

(Klimesch, 1996), whereas upper alpha (10-12 Hz) activity is modulated by semantic memory processes (Klimesch, 1997). The lower-1 and lower-2 alpha (6-10 Hz) bands are related to attentional task demands. The lower-1 alpha band is mainly related to the level of alertness, whereas the lower-2 alpha band is more related to expectancy (Klimesch, 1999). The role of the gamma band (>30 Hz) is associated with the binding hypothesis (Tallon-Baudry and Bertrand 1999).

The ERD/ERS were determined using the method of complex demodulation with a simultaneous signal envelope computation (Andrew, 1999; Otnes, and Enochson, 1978; Thatcher, Toro, Pflieger, and Hallet, 1994). In this method the raw data for each channel are multiplied, point by point, by a pure cosine based on the selected center frequency, as well as by a pure sine having the same center frequency. Both time series are then lowpass filtered (zero-phase digital filter –48 dB/octave rolloff) by the half-bandwidth. The quantification of induced ERD was done using the intertrial variance method (ERD (IV) – induced, non-phase-locked activity). Variance is computed at each time sample across trials, and the power spectrum is computed based on the variance measures, within the selected frequency band. The formulas used were as follows (Pfurtscheller, 1999)**Error! Bookmark not defined.**:

$$IV_{(j)} = \frac{1}{N-1} \sum_{i=1}^{N} \left\{ x_{f(i,j)} - \bar{x}_{f(j)} \right\}^2 \qquad (1)$$

In equation (1) N is the total number of trials, $x_{f(i,j)}$ is the j-th sample of i-th trial data, and $\bar{x}_{f(j)}$ is the mean of the j-th sample over all trials. The ERD (IV) data were used to calculate the ERD/ERS values which were defined as the percentage change of the power at each sample point (A_j), relative to the average power in the resting 1000 ms reference interval (R) preceding the stimulus onset (–1500 ms to –500 ms):

$$ERD_{(j)}\% = \frac{R - Aj}{R} \qquad (2)$$

A positive ERD indicates a power decrease, and a negative ERD a power increase (Pfurtscheller, 1999). The ERD/ERS values were determined from stimulus onset till 4000 ms. The ERD/ERS values were collapsed for different electrode locations, distinguishing the hemispheres as well as frontal, central and parietal brain areas. The electrode positions were aggregated as following: frontal left (Fp1, F3, F7), frontal right (Fp2, F4, F8), central left (T3, C3), central right (T4, C4), parietal left (T5, P3, O1), and parietal right (T6, P4, O2).

The ERCoh was determined from the same time series: $y_{i,n}^{(r)}$. The time-dependent complex correlation between each pairwise combination of channels, i and k, was then computed as:

$$\hat{\rho} = \frac{\sum\limits_{r=1}^{R}\left[y_{i,n}^{(r)} - \overline{y}_{i,n}\right]\left[y_{k,n}^{(r)} - \overline{y}_{k,n}\right]^{*}}{\sqrt{\sum\limits_{r=1}^{R}\left|y_{i,n}^{(r)} - \overline{y}_{i,n}\right|^{2}\sum\limits_{r=1}^{R}\left|y_{k,n}^{(r)} - \overline{y}_{k,n}\right|^{2}}} \tag{3}$$

In equation (3) * denotes complex conjugation and $\overline{y}_{i,n}$ are the complex average potentials calculated by averaging the complex time series for channel i across all trials. To reduce the large data set the ERCoh measures were averaged from stimulus onset till 4000 ms. They were Fisher-z-transformed and collapsed with respect to the hemispheres into left, right and interhemispheric Z-ERCohs. These ERD/ERS power values and Z-Coherence values were correlated with behavioral data.

Approximate entropy (ApEn) has been recently introduced as a quantification of regularity in time-series data. It has been shown that ApEn can distinguish a wide variety of systems ranging from multi periodic, to stochastic and mixed systems; furthermore, it is applicable to noisy, medium-sized data sets (Pincus, 1994, 1995). Mathematically, ApEn measures the likelihood that runs of patterns which are close in one observation remain close on the following incremental comparisons. The ApEn analysis was performed using the program Simulnet-Pro. Given N data points (4000 – from stimulus onset till 4000 ms), the statistic ApEn was determined for $m = 2$, and $r = .15$ SD $u(i)$ data using the formula:

$$\text{ApEn } (m,r,N) = \Phi^{m}(r) - \Phi^{m+1}(r), \tag{4}$$

where m is the length of compared runs of data, and r specifies a de facto filtering level. ApEn measures the logarithmic frequency with which blocks of length m that are close together remain close together for blocks augmented by one position. The ApEn was calculated for each electrode separately for the lower frequency band (1-30 Hz) and for the gamma band (31-49 Hz). The data were collapsed with respect to both hemispheres and three brain areas (in the same way as for the ERD/ERS measures).

The low resolution brain electromagnetic tomography (LORETA) analysis was performed by CURRY 4.5 software. For that purpose the averaged event-related data in the time window between –1500 till 4000 ms from stimulus onset were read into the computer. Current density methods are commonly applied to single time-point evaluations (Fuchs et al., 1999). In order to allow for comparison of the time course of intelligence and personality related differences in stimulus processing, four individually assessed time points were chosen for the LORETA analysis. The time points were taken in each of the 4 s following stimulus presentations. In each time segment the reference point was the highest peak amplitude – the most positive point in the mean global field power (MGFP). Prior to the LORETA analysis for each subject the SNR was estimated from prestimulus latencies (–500 to –1500 ms). These SNR values were used for the regularization parameter λ. The optimum value of λ was determined using the χ^2 criterion. This criterion was implemented by iteratively calling the LORETA method. A three-spherical-shells volume conductor model was applied (radii: 75, 82 and 88 mm; conductivities: 0.33, 0.0042, and 0.33 1/Ωm). The LORETA reconstruction was performed on a surface net constrained to the cortex, using surface Laplacians (Fuchs et al., 1999). The cortical gray matter layers were segmented from the grand average magnetic resonance image data set (CURRY – Neuroscan, Sterling, VA, U.S.A.). They consisted of 6618 vertices and 13934 triangles (mean edge length 3.6 mm). The cortex normals, which define the orientation perpendicular to the cortical sheet – the net orientation of the synapses of the pyramidal cells – were also calculated (Wagner, 1998). To account for the undesired depth dependency of all current density algorithms, and thus achieve an unbiased lead-field distribution, a locationwise singular value decomposition lead-field normalization was performed, followed by a gain determination using the infinity norm and an auto-adapted componentwise depth weighting. The quantitative evaluation of the reconstruction parameters was done by calculating the full width at half maximum (FWHM) volume (ml): that is, all current positions with strengths above 50% of the maximum current were counted and then multiplied by the cell-volume. Also determined was the maximum current density (μAmm^{-2}) and the source locations at the maximum current density. The source locations were given as (X,Y,Z) coordinates: X from left to right; Y from posterior to anterior; Z from inferior to superior. The data were analyzed for the lower frequency bands (1-30 Hz).

The ApEn and LORETA measures were correlated with behavioral data.

2.4.2. Resting EEG Analysis

The data were divided into 11-second epochs (11132 data points), and automatically screened for artifacts. Excluded were all epochs showing amplitudes above ± 50 μV. A Fast Fourier Transformation (FFT) was performed on artifact-free 11-second chunks of data in order to derive estimates of absolute spectral power (μV). Power estimates were obtained for frequency steps of 0.05 Hz. The narrow frequency bands were determined in the same way as in the task condition. To obtain Gaussian distributed data, the log power values for each lead, subject, and the five bands were calculated. These log-transformed power values were collapsed for different electrode locations, distinguishing the hemispheres as well as frontal, central and parietal brain areas. The electrode positions were aggregated in the same way as for the task condition.

Coherence was defined as:

$$R_{xy} = \frac{\sum_i (x_i - \overline{x})(y_i - \overline{y})^*}{\sqrt{\sum_i (x_i - \overline{x})(x_i - \overline{x})^* \sum_i (y_i - \overline{y})(y_i - \overline{y})^*}} \tag{5}$$

In equation (5) * denotes complex conjugation, and x_i and y_i are EEG values recorded at electrode x on sweep i at time t. Coherence values in the 5 power bands were estimated for all electrode pairs. In that way, 171 coherence measures were computed for each frequency band. They were Fisher-z-transformed and collapsed with respect to distances and location into frontal, parieto-occipital, and long distance (connecting frontal with parietal, or occipital electrode locations) Z-Coherence.

The log-transformed power and Z-Coherence values were correlated with the behavioral data.

LOWER-1 ALPHA

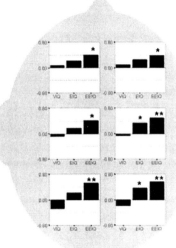

MALE

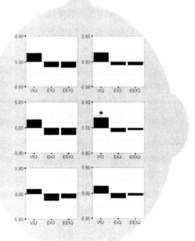

FEMALE

LOWER-2 ALPHA

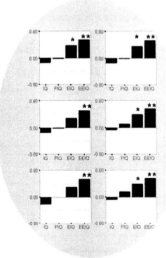

MALE

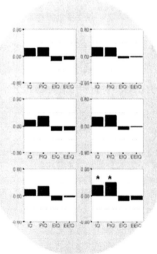

FEMALE

Figure continued on next page

UPPER ALPHA

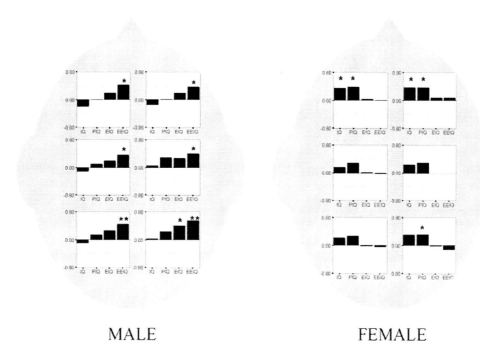

MALE   FEMALE

Figures 2-4.The six bar charts arranged in two columns (left/right hemisphere) and three rows (from top to bottom: frontal, central and parietal brain areas) in each shape (symbolizing the head, seen from above) represent correlation coefficients (y-axes) between log-transformed power measures in three alpha sub-bands and general and emotional intelligence in the resting eyes closed condition. The level of significance is indicated by one asterisk (p<.05), and two asterisks (p<.01).

3. RESULTS

3.1. Intelligence and Emotional Intelligence

3.1.1. Resting EEG

Significant correlations between behavioral data (IQ and EIQ) and the EEG power measures have been obtained in the lower-1, lower-2 and upper alpha bands. Males scoring high on EIQ and the area score EEIQ displayed increased EEG alpha power (less brain activity). No significant correlation for general intelligence was observed. On the other hand, high intelligent females scoring high on the verbal and performance intelligent tasks displayed increased alpha power (less brain activity). No significant correlations for emotional intelligence and the two area scores EEIQ and SEIQ were observed. The correlation patterns (EEG power measures with behavioral data – IQ and EIQ), differed significantly between males and females. High emotional intelligent males displayed less brain activity, whereas high emotional intelligent females displayed more brain activity, while resting with eyes closed. For general intelligence a reverse pattern of correlations was observed.

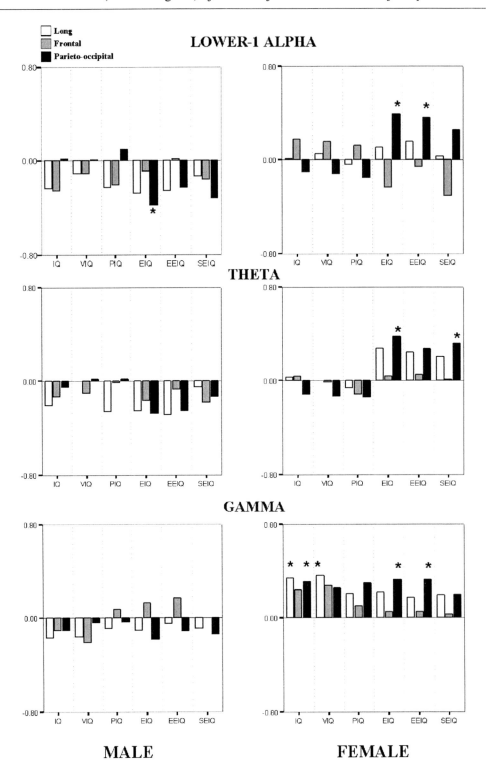

Figure 5.The bar charts represent correlation coefficients (y-axes) between Z-coherence measures (collapsed with respect to distances and location into frontal, parieto-occipital, and long distance), in the lower-1 alpha, theta and gamma band, and general and emotional intelligence in the resting eyes closed condition. The level of significance is indicated by one asterisk (p<.05), and two asterisks (p<.01).

Significant correlations between coherence in the lower-1 alpha, theta and gamma bands, and performance scores were also observed. As can be seen in figure 5, females scoring high on EIQ and EEIQ displayed increased coherence in the parieto-occipital areas in the lower-1 alpha band, whereas males scoring high on EIQ displayed less coherent brain activity. A similar pattern was also observed in the theta band. In the gamma band, high intelligent and emotional intelligent females displayed higher coherence in the parieto-occipital brain areas, as well as greater coupling of long distance (frontal with parieto-occipital) brain areas. Males displayed decreased coherence between brain areas.

3.1.2. Task EEG

In the task condition fewer significant correlations between ERD/ERS and behavioral measures were observed. Males scoring high on the PIQ subtests displayed more ERD (more brain activity) in the lower-1 alpha band only in the left and right central brain areas. High intelligent females (also scoring high on VIQ and PIQ) in the lower-1 alpha band displayed more ERD especially in the parieto-occipital and central brain areas; a similar pattern was also observed in the lower-2 alpha band (see figures 6 and 7).

In the gamma band, high EIQ females displayed more ERS (more brain activity) mainly over the left frontal and central brain areas, while high intelligent females (scoring high on PIQ tests) displayed more ERD over the right central areas. For males only a significant correlation between gamma band ERS and EEIQ in the left parieto occipital area was observed (see figure 8).

LOWER-1 ALPHA

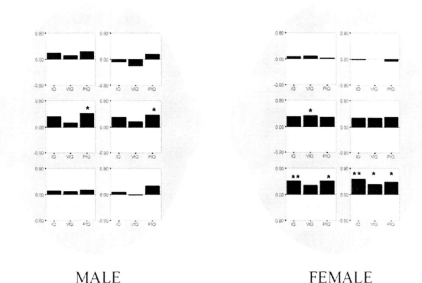

MALE   FEMALE

Figure continued on next page

LOWER-2 ALPHA

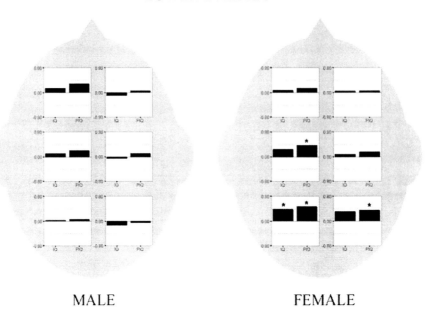

MALE   FEMALE

GAMMA

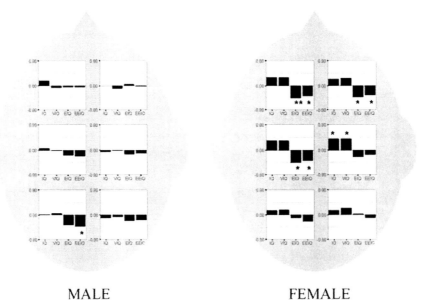

MALE   FEMALE

Figures 6-8.The six bar charts arranged in two columns (left/right hemisphere) and three rows (from top to bottom: frontal, central and parietal brain areas) in each shape (symbolizing the head, seen from above) represent correlation coefficients (y-axes) between ERD/ERS measures in two lower alpha and gamma bands, and general and emotional intelligence while respondents were solving the mental rotation tasks. The level of significance is indicated by one asterisk (p<.05), and two asterisks (p<.01).

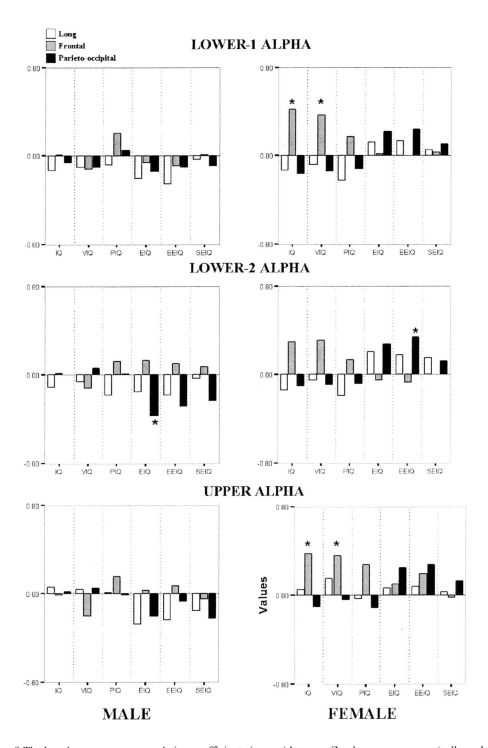

Figure 9.The bar charts represent correlation coefficients (y-axes) between Z-coherence measures (collapsed with respect to distances and location into frontal, parieto-occipital, and long distance), in the three alpha bands, and general and emotional intelligence while respondents were solving the mental rotation tasks. The level of significance is indicated by one asterisk (p<.05), and two asterisks (p<.01).

The patterns of correlations between ERD/ERS and IQ/EIQ for males and females in the task condition are more similar than in the resting condition. Differences were only observed in relation to brain areas. Intelligent males showed a greater involvement of the central and frontal brain areas in both alpha bands, whereas females displayed more activity in the parieto-occipital brain areas. In the gamma band for the EIQ scores a reverse pattern was observed, males showing more ERS in the parieto-occipital areas and females showing more ERS in the central and frontal brain areas.

LORETA PARAMETERS - MALES 1-30 Hz

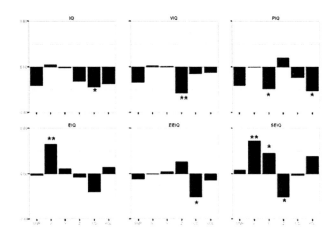

LORETA PARAMETERS - FEMALES 1-30 Hz

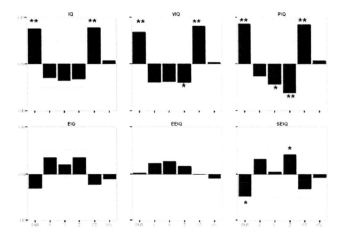

Figures 10-11.The bar charts represent correlation coefficients (y-axes) between LORETA parameters (SNR – signal to noise ratio; X – location left-right; Y – location anterior-posterior; Z – location superior-inferior; CD – current density and VOL – volume of activated gray matter), and general and emotional intelligence factors in the 1-30 Hz frequency range.

Significant correlations between coherence in the lower-1, lower-2 and upper alpha bands, and performance scores were also observed. High intelligent females displayed more coupling between frontal brain areas. For males no significant correlations between intelligence measures and coherence were observed. For the EIQ measure a significant correlation with coherence in the lower-2 alpha band was observed – males showed less coupling of parieto-occipital brain areas, whereas females scoring high on EEIQ showed more coupling of parieto-occipital brain areas.

The analysis of LORETA parameters showed that high IQ males displayed a lower volume of activated cortical gray matter, accompanied by a lower current density, with the source positioned in the inferior anterior brain area. High EIQ males also displayed a lower current density, with a source in the inferior left posterior brain region. For intelligent females a reverse pattern of current density was observed. The source was located in the inferior anterior brain region. The correlations with EIQ were not significant.

3.2. Personality Factors

3.2.1. Resting EEG

In the resting conditions with eyes closed, most pronounced correlations between the big five personality factors and synchronous/asynchronous brain oscillations for both sexes were found for the factor N. Females who are emotionally balanced (high N) tend to display more asynchronous brain oscillations in the three alpha bands and the gamma band. These asynchronous oscillations (more brain activity) displayed a more left hemispheric topography (see figures 12-15).

In contrast, males scoring high on the factor N, showed more synchronous brain oscillations mainly in the three alpha bands. However, the significant correlations were only those in the lower-1 alpha band (see figure 12) for the left and right frontal brain areas.

Significant correlations with the factor E were only observed in the two lower alpha frequency bands. This could be expected, because the lower alpha bands are assumed to be related to attention and arousal. Male and female extraverts displayed more asynchronous brain oscillations predominantly in the left parieto-occipital brain areas.

For males scoring high on the factor O (creativity, intelligence) significant correlations in the lower-2 and upper alpha bands were observed (see figure 13 and 14). The correlations were negative, indicating that more creative and intelligent males displayed more brain activity (asynchronous oscillations) in the resting states. This tendency is similar to the one observed for correlations between brain oscillations and general intelligence scores.

The correlations between coherence measures and the Big 5 personality factors showed only few significant correlations for males in the lower 1 and 2 alpha and theta bands, mainly for the factors C and N. For females only in the gamma band were more pronounced correlations observed. It seems that females scoring high on the factors N (emotional balance) and O (creativity) displayed greater decoupling of brain areas – between the short and long-range brain areas (see figure 16).

LOWER-1 ALPHA

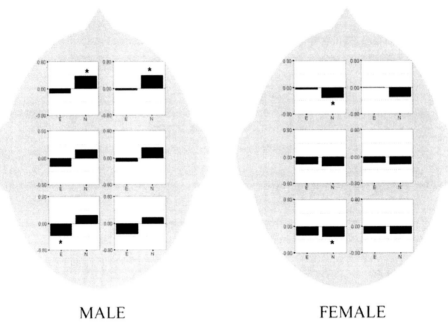

MALE   FEMALE

LOWER-2 ALPHA

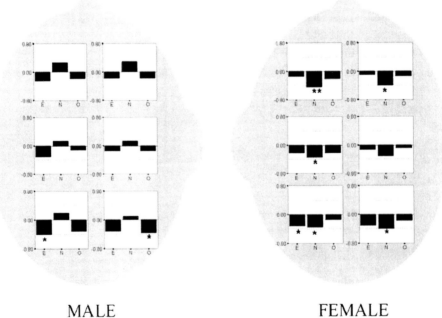

MALE   FEMALE

Figure continued on next page

UPPER ALPHA

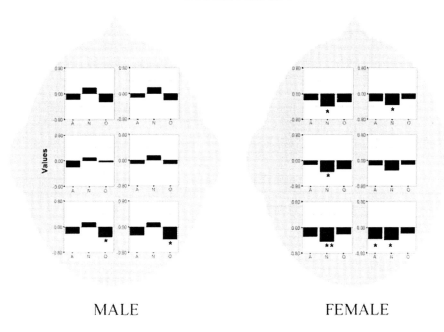

MALE   FEMALE

GAMMA

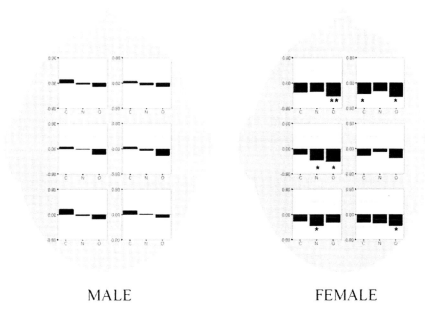

MALE   FEMALE

Figures 12-15.The six bar charts arranged in two columns (left/right hemisphere) and three rows (from top to bottom: frontal, central and parietal brain areas) in each shape (symbolizing the head, seen from above) represent correlation coefficients (y-axes) between log-transformed power measures in three alpha and gamma bands, and the five personality factors (extraversion-E, neuroticism-N, openness-O, conscientiousness-C, and agreeableness-A) in the eyes closed resting condition. The level of significance is indicated by one asterisk ($p<.05$), and two asterisks ($p<.01$).

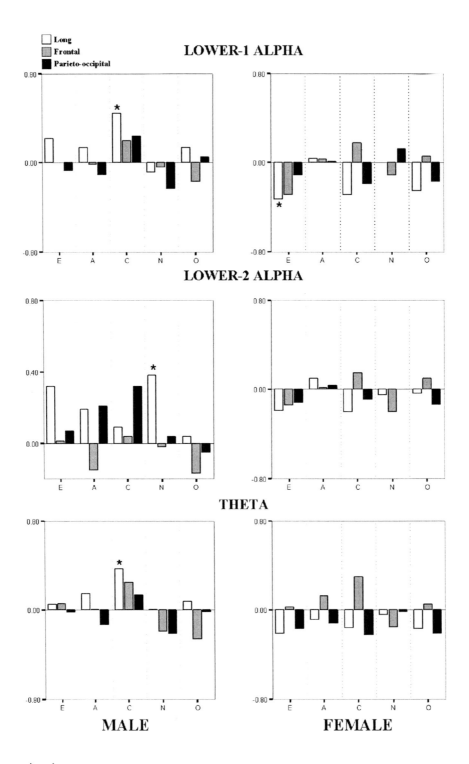

Figure continued on next page

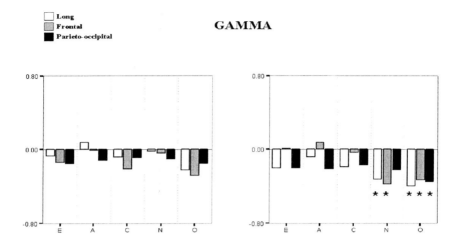

MALE   FEMALE

Figure 16. The bar charts represent correlation coefficients (*y*-axes) between Z-coherence measures (collapsed with respect to distances and location into frontal, parieto-occipital, and long distance), in the lower-1 and lower-2 alpha, theta and gamma bands, and the five personality factors (extraversion-E, neuroticism-N, openness-O, conscientiousness-C, and agreeableness-A) in the resting eyes closed condition. The level of significance is indicated by one asterisk ($p<.05$), and two asterisks ($p<.01$).

3.2.2. Task EEG

Significant correlations between the five personality factors and EEG measures were only observed for the ApEn statistic. More energetic and dynamic males displayed more regular, less chaotic EEG patterns (1-30 Hz frequency range) mainly over the left hemisphere. A reverse pattern of correlations was observed for females scoring high on factor E (more chaotic and less regular patterns of EEG). For both sexes being high on the factor N a more regular EEG pattern was observed. The difference between males and females was only that, for males this regularity was more pronounced in the right frontal regions, whereas for females a negative correlation between ApEn and N was observed in the right parieto-occipital brain area (see figure 17).

4. DISCUSSION

The major finding of the study is that males and females differed in resting brain activity related to their level of general intelligence. Brain activity in females increased with the level of intelligence, whereas an opposite pattern of brain activity was observed in males. This difference was most pronounced in the upper-alpha band, lending support to the assumption that the upper alpha band is related to semantic memory processes (Klimesch, 1997, 1999). In the upper alpha band females showed more synchronous oscillations in the frontal brain areas, whereas for males no significant correlations between brain activity and IQ were observed. Similar findings were reported by studies employing imaging techniques like PET, proton magnetic resonance spectroscopy and fMRI (Weiss et al., 2003; Pfleiderer et al., 2004; Haier, 2005).

In males an even more pronounced correlation between EIQ and EEG power measures was observed. High emotional intelligent males in all three alpha bands showed more synchronous oscillations equally distributed over both hemispheres and three brain areas. Females showed no significant correlations between EIQ and EEG power measures, however the trend of correlations was opposite to the one observed for males.

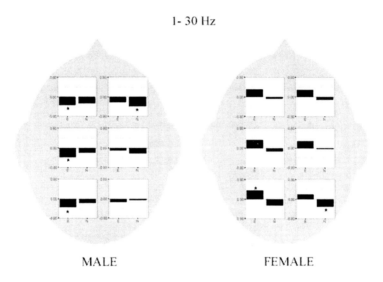

1- 30 Hz

MALE   FEMALE

Figure 17.The six bar charts arranged in two columns (left/right hemisphere) and three rows (from top to bottom: frontal, central and parietal brain areas) in each shape (symbolizing the head, seen from above) represent correlation coefficients (*y*-axes) between ApEn measures in the 1-30 Hz frequency band and the personality factors of E and N, intelligence while respondents were solving the mental rotation tasks. The level of significance is indicated by one asterisk (*p*<.05), and two asterisks (*p*<.01).

Not only did the patterns of correlations between EIQ and IQ measures differ between sexes, they also differed within males and females. This was especially pronounced for females while solving the mental rotation tasks. In the gamma band, high EIQ females displayed increased gamma band ERS (more brain activity) whereas high IQ females displayed increased gamma band ERD (less brain activity). This would suggest that the construct of EIQ can not be explained just as being a part of general intelligence. It should be further pointed out that individual variations in the EEG are determined almost exclusively by genetic differences (Vogel, 2000Together with our findings this suggests that variations in intelligence related to gender are significantly determined by genetic factors. It appears that males and females achieve similar IQ results with different brain regions, suggesting that there is no singular underlying neuroanatomical structure to general intelligence and that different types of brain designs may manifest comparable intellectual performance. However, for some types of tasks (numerical, spatial) the "male" brain design is advantageous, whereas for other task types (verbal, social) the "female" design seems to be beneficial. Consequently, research into the relationship between brain activity and ability should to a greater extent focus on gender influences.

The correlation patterns between EEG parameters and personality factors differed between males and females mainly for the factor N, whereas for the factor E similar patterns of brain activity between males and females could be observed. This relationship was mainly observed for the resting condition. Male and female extraverts showed more lower alpha-1 and alpha-2 brain activity while resting with eyes closed. According to Eysenck's (Eysenck, 1967; Eysenck and Eysenck, 1985) the personality factor E relates to arousability of the reticulo-cortical circuit. Our finding that significant correlations between E and brain oscillations were only observed in the two lower alpha bands is in line with Eysenck arousability theory. The lower-1 and lower-2 alpha (6-10 Hz) bands are related to attentional task demands. The lower-1 alpha band is mainly related to the level of alertness, whereas the lower-2 alpha band is more related to expectancy (Klimesch, 1999). However, the trend of relations was opposite to that which would be predicted by Eysenck's arousability theory, namely that introverts are typically more aroused than extraverts. An explanation for this paradox was provided by Gale (1983). He argued that moderate arousal-inducing environments were the most amenable to testing predictions of Eysenck's (1967) theory, whereas low arousal-inducing (as in our study, the eyes closed condition) environments resulted in paradoxical arousal, especially in extraverts. The reason could be, first, because people actively seek a moderate level of arousal; and second, because stimulation provokes c.n.s. reactivity until an optimal point is reached beyond which inhibition sets in.

The finding that females scoring high on N (emotional stability) displayed more left hemispheric brain activity in all three alpha bands is also in concordance with some theoretical explanations suggesting that persons low on N would also be associated with relative right hemispheric brain activation. As outlined in the introduction, positive emotions, as well as negative yet approach-related emotions, are typically associated with relative left-frontal and anterior-temporal activity, while negative, withdrawal-related emotion has been associated with higher relative activity of the right frontal and anterior-temporal regions (Ahern and Schwartz, 1985; Davidson, 1995; Harmon-Jones and Allen, 1997; Heller, 1990; Tomarken, Davidson, and Henriques, 1990).

The correlations with the other three factors A,C, and O were less clear-cut. Only the correlations with O for males in the lower-1 and lower-2 alpha band showed a trend similar to the one observed for correlations between IQ and brain activity. This could be expected because O is usually related to intelligence and creativity. Our findings further suggest that the personality factors E and N seem to be the most robust personality traits having also a specific physiological origin.

Analysis of the relationship between personality factors and emotional intelligence have mainly found similarities for the factors emotional stability (N) and Agreeableness (A). Comparison of the correlations for EIQ and N in the resting conditions indicated some similarities only for the male sample. Males high on EIQ and N displayed more synchronous brain oscillations in the three alpha bands. For females an opposite pattern was observed. Together with the results obtained for general intelligence this would suggest that emotional intelligence represents a construct which is distinct from general intelligence and personality factors.

5. REFERENCES

Ahern, G. L., and Schwartz, G. E. (1985). Differential lateralization for positive and negative emotion in the human brain: EEG spectral analysis. *Neuropsychologia, 23*, 745–755.

Andrev, C. (1999). Quantification of event-related coherence (ERCoh). In G. Pfurtscheller and F.H. Lopes da Silva (Eds). *Handbook of Electroencephalography and Clinical Neuropsychology, Event-Related Desynchronization, Vol. 6* (pp. 119-137). Amsterdam: Elsevier.

Anokhin, A., and Vogel, F. (1996). EEG alpha rhythm frequency and intelligence in normal adults. *Intelligence, 23*, 1-14.

Anokhin, A.P., Lutzenberger, W., and Birbaumer, N. (1999). Spatiotemporal organization of brain dynamics and intelligence: an EEG study in adolescents. *International Journal of Psychophysiology, 33*, 259-273.

Başar, E., Başar-Eroglu, C., Krakaş, S., and Schürmann, M. (2001). Gamma, alpha delta, and theta oscillations govern cognitive processes. *International Journal of Psychophysiology, 39*, 241-248.

Bhattacharya, J., Petsche, H. and Pereda, E. (2001). Long-range synchrony in the γ band:Role in music perception. *The Journal of Neuroscience, 21*, 6329-6337.

Burgess, A.P. and Gruzelier, J.H. (1999). Methodological advances in the analysis of event-related desynchronization data: reliability and robust analysis. In G. Pfurtscheller and F.H. Lopes da Silva (Eds). *Handbook of Electroencephalography and Clinical Neuropsychology, Event-Related Desynchronization, Vol. 6* (pp. 139-158). Amsterdam: Elsevier.

Caprara, G.V., Barbaranelli, C., Borgogni, L., Bucik, V., and Boben, D. (2002). *Model "velikih pet" Priročnik za merjenje strukture osebnosti.* Ljubljana, Center za psihodiagnostična sredstva.

Colom, R., and Lynn, R. (2004). Testing the developmental theory of sex differences in intelligence on 12–18 year olds. *Personality and Individual Differences, 36*, 75-82.

Corsi-Cabrera, M., Arce, C., Ramos, J., and Guevara, M. A. (1997). Effect of spatial abilityand sex on inter- and intrahemispheric correlation of EEG activity. *Electroencephalography and Clinical, Neurophysiology, 102*, 5–11.

Davidson, R. J. (1995). Cerebral asymmetry, emotion, and affective style. In R. J. Davidson, and K. Hugdahl (Eds.), *Brain asymmetry* (pp. 361–387). Cambridge, MA: MIT Press.

De Bellis, M. D., Keshavan, M. S., Beers, S. R., Hall, J., Frustaci, K., and Masalehdan, A. et al., (2001). Sex differences in brain maturation during childhood and adolescence. *Cerebral Cortex, 11*, 552–557.

De Raad, B. (2005). The trait-coverage of emotional intelligence. *Personality and Individual Differences, 38*, 673-687.

Detterman, D.K. (1994). Intelligence and the brain. In P. A. Vernon (Ed.) *The neuropsychology of individual differences.* (pp. 35-57). London: Academic Press INC.

Doppelmayr, M., Klimesch, W., Stadler, W., Pöllhuber, D. and Heine, C. (2002). EEG alpha power and intelligence. *Intelligence, 30*, 289-302.

Ebermeier, K. B., Deary, I. J., O'Carrol, R. E., Prentice, N., Moffoot, A. P. R., and Goodwin, G. M. (1994). Personality associations with the uptake of the cerebral blood flow marker

99mTc-Exametazime estimated with single photon emission tomography. *Personality and Individual Differences, 17,* 587–595.

Eysenck, H.J. (1967). *The biological basis of personality.* Springfield, IL: Thomas

Eysenck, H. J. (1990). Biological dimensions of personality. In L. A. Pervin (Ed.), *Handbook of personality: theory and research* (pp. 244–270). New York: Guilford Press.

Eysenck, H. J. (1994). Personality: Biological foundations. In P. A. Vernon (Ed.), The neuropsychology of individual differences.London: Academic Press.

Eysenck, H. J., and Eysenck, M. W. (1985). Personality and individual di€erences. New York: Plenum.

Fink, A., Schrausser, D. G., and Neubauer, A. C. (2002). The moderating influence of extraversion on the relationship between IQ and cortical activation. *Personality and Individual Differences, 33,* 311–326.

Fink, A. and Neubauer, A.C. (2004). Extraversion and cortical activation: Effects of task complexity. *Personality and Individual Differences, 36,* 333-347.

Fischer, H., Wik, G., and Fredrikson, M. (1997). Extraversion, neuroticism and brain function: a PET study of personality. Personality and Individual Differences, 23, 345–352.

Fuchs, M., Wagner, M., Köhler, T., and Wischmann, H.A. (1999). Linear and nonlinear current density reconstructions. *Journal of Clinical Neurophysiology, 16,* 267-295.

Gale, A. (1973). The psychophysiology of individual differences: studies of extraversion and the EEG. In P. Kline (Ed.), *New approaches in psychological measurement* (pp. 211–256). London: Wiley.

Gale, A. (1983). Electroencephalographic studies of extraversion-introversion: A case study in the psychophysiology of individual differences. Personality and Individual Differences, 4, 371-380.

Garai, J., and Scheinfeld, A. (1968). Sex differences in mental and behavioral traits. *Genetic Psychology Monographs, 77,* 169-299.

Gevins, A., and Smith, M.E. (2000). Neurophysiological measures of working memory and individual differences in cognitive ability and cognitive style. *Cerebral Cortex, 10,* 830-839.

Giannitrapani, D. (1969). EEG average frequency and intelligence. *Electroencephalography and Clinical Neurophysiology, 27,* 480-486.

Hagemann, D., Naumann, E., Luerken, A., Bartussek, D., 1999. EEG trait asymmetry and affective style I: latent state and trait structure of resting asymmetry scores, *Psychophysiology, S57.*

Haier, R.J., Neuchterlein, K.H., Hazlett, E., Wu, J.C. Paek, J., Browning, H.,L., and Buchsbaum, M.S. (1988). Cortical glucose metabolic rate correlates of abstract reasoning and attention studied with positron emission tomography. *Intelligence, 12,* 199-217

Haier, R.J., Siegel, B., Tang, C. Abel, L., and Buchsbaum, M.S., (1992). Intelligence and changes in regional cerebral glucose mezabolic rate following learning. *Intelligence, 16,* 415-426

Haier, R.J., Benbow, C.P. (1995). Sex differences and lateralization in temporal lobe glucose metabolism during mathematical reasoning. *Developmental Neuropsychology, 4,* 405-414

Haier, R.J., White, N.S., and Alkire, M.T. (2003). Individual differences in general intelligence correlate with brain function during nonreasoning tasks. *Intelligence, 31,* 429-441.

Haier, R.J., Jung, R.E., Yeo, R.A., Head, K, and Alkire, M.T. (2005). The neuroanatomy of general intelligence: sex matters. *Neuroimage, 25*, 320-327.

Harmon-Jones, E., Allen, J.J.B., 1997. Behavioral activation sensitivity and resting frontal EEG asymmetry: covariation of putative indicators related to risk for mood disorders. *Journal of Abnormal Psychology, 106*, 159–163.

Heller, W. (1990). The neuropsychology of emotion: developmental patterns and implications for psychopathology. In N. Stein, B. L. Leventhal, and T. Trabasso (Eds.), *Psychological and biological approaches to emotion* (pp. 167–211). Hillsdale, NJ: Lawrence Erlbaum.

Jaušovec, N. (1996). Differences in EEG alpha activity related to giftedness. *Intelligence, 23*, 159-173.

Jaušovec, N. (1997). Differences in EEG alpha activity between gifted and non-identified individuals: Insights into problem solving. *Gifted Child Quarterly, 41*, 26-32.

Jaušovec, N. (1998). Are gifted individuals less chaotic thinkers? *Personality and Individual Differences, 25*, 253-267.

Jaušovec, N. (2000). Differences in cognitive processes between gifted, intelligent, creative and average individuals while solving complex problems: An EEG study. *Intelligence,28*, 213-237.

Jaušovec, N. and Jaušovec, K. (2000a). Correlations between ERP parameters and intelligence: a reconsideration. *Biological Psychology, 50,* 137-154.

Jaušovec, N. and Jaušovec, K. (2000b). Differences in event-related and induced brain oscillations in the theta and alpha frequency bands related to human intelligence. *Neuroscience Letters, 293*, 191-194.

Jaušovec, N. and Jaušovec, K. (2000c) .Differences in resting EEG related to ability. *Brain Topography,12*, 229-240.

Jaušovec, N. and Jaušovec, K. (2001). Differences in EEG current density related to intelligence. *Cognitive Brain Research, 12*, 55-60.

Jaušovec, N., Jaušovec, K. and Gerlič, I. (2001). Differences in event related and induced EEG patterns in the theta and alpha frequency bands related to human emotional intelligence. *Neuroscience Letters, 311*, 93-96.

Jaušovec, N. and Jaušovec, K. (2003). Spatiotemporal brain activity related to intelligence: a low resolution brain electromagnetic tomography study. *Cognitive Brain Research, 16*, 267-272.

Jaušovec, N. and Jaušovec, K. (in press). Differences in induced gamma and upper alpha oscillations in the human brain related to verbal/performance and emotional intelligence. *International Journal of Psychophysiology.*

Jaušovec, N. and Jaušovec, K. (2004a). Intelligence related differences in induced brain activity during the performance of memory tasks. *Personality and Individual Differences,* 36, 597-612.

Jaušovec, N. and Jaušovec, K. (2004b). Differences in induced brain activity during the performance of learning and working-memory tasks related to intelligence. *Brain and Cognition*, 54, 65-74.

Klimesch, W. (1996). Memory processes, brain oscillations and EEG synchronization. *International Journal of Psychophysiology, 24,* 61-100.

Klimesch, W. (1997). EEG-alpha rhythms and memory processes. *International Journal of Psychophysiology, 26,* 319-340.

Klimesch, W. (1999). EEG alpha and theta oscillations reflect cognitive and memory performance: a review and analysis. *Brain Research Reviews, 29*, 169-195.

Klimesch, W., Doppelmayr, M. (2001). High frequency alpha and intelligence. Paper presented at the tenth biennial meeting of ISSID, Edinburgh.

Kolb, B., and Whishaw, I.Q. (1996). *Fundamentals of human neuropsychology.* New York: W. H. Freeman and Company.

Lehtovirta, M., Partanen, J., Kononen, M., Soininen, H., Helisalmi, S., Mannermaa, A., Ryynanen, M., Hartikainen, P., and Riekkinen, P. (1996). Spectral analysis of EEG in Alzheimer's disease: Relation to apolipoprotein E polymorphism. *Neurobiology of Aging,17,* 523–526.

Lutzenberger, W., Birbaumer, N., Flor, H., Rockstroh, B. and Elbert, T. (1992). Dimensional analysis of the human EEG and intelligence. *Neuroscience Letteres, 143,* 10-14.

Mansour, C.S., Haier, R.J., and Buchsbaum, M.S. (1996). Gender comparison of cerebral glucose metabolic rate in healthy adults during a cognitive task. *Personality and Individual Differences, 20,* 183-191.

Mathew, R. J., Weinman, M. L., and Barr, D. L. (1984). Personality and regional cerebral blood flow. *British Journal of Psychiatry, 144*, 529–532.

Matthews, G., and Amelang, M. (1993). Extraversion, arousal theory and performance: a study of individual differences in the EEG. *Personality and Individual Differences, 14,* 347–363.

Matthews, G., and Gilliland, K. (1999). The personality theories of H. J. Eysenck and J. A. Gray: a comparative review. *Personality and Individual Differences, 26*, 583–626.

Mayer, J.D., Caruso, D.R. and Salovey, P. (2000). Emotional intelligence meets traditional standards for an intelligence. *Intelligence, 27, 267-298.*

Mayer, J.D., Salovey, P., and Caruso, D.R. (2002). *Mayer-Salovey-Caruso emotional intelligence test (MSCEIT).* Toronto: MHS.

McGee, M. (1979). Human spatial abilities: Psychometric studies and environmental, generic, hormonal, and neurological influences. *Psychological Bulletin, 86*, 889-917.

Miller, E.,M. (1994). Intelligence and brain myelination: A hypothesis. *Personality and individual differences, 17,* 803-833.

Mihelič, A. Baterija testov sposobnosti BTI Priročnik. Zavod SR Slovenije za produktivnost dela, Ljubljana: 1972.

Neubauer, V., Freudenthaler, H.H., and Pfurtscheller, G. (1995). Intelligence and spatiotemporal patterns of event-related desynchronization. *Intelligence, 3,* 249-266

Neubauer, A.C., Sange, G., and Pfurtscheller, G. Psychometric intelligence and event-related desynchronization during performance of a letter matching task. In G. Pfurtscheller and F.H. Lopes da Silva (Ed.) *Handbook of electroencephalography and clinical neuropsychology, Vol. 6: Event-related desynchronization.* Amsterdam: Elsevier, 1999, pp. 219-232.

Neubauer A.C., Fink, A., and Schrausser, D.G. (2002). Intelligence and neural efficiency: The influence of task content and sex on the brain – IQ relationship. *Intelligence,* 30, 515-536.

Neubauer, A.C., and Fink, A. (2003). Fluid intelligence and neural efficiency: effects of task complexity and sex. *Personality and Individual Differences, 35*, 811-827.

Nunez, P.L., Wingeier, B.M., and Silberstein, R.B. (2001). Spatial-temporal structuresof human alpha rhythms: Theory, microcurrent sources, multiscale measurements, and global binding of local networks. *Human Brain Mapping, 13*, 125-164.

Nyberg, L., Habib, R., and Herlitz, A. (2000). Brain activation during episodic memory retrieval: sex differences. *Acta Psychologica, 105,* 181-194.

O'Boyle, M.W., Benbow, C.P., and Alexander, J.E. (1995). Sex differences, hemispheric laterality, and associated brain activity in the intellectually gifted. *Developmental Neuropsychology, 4,* 415-443

O'Gorman, J. G. (1984). Extraversion and the EEG: I. An evaluation of Gale's hypothesis. *Biological Psychology, 19,* 95-112.

Olin, C.H. (1910). *Phrenology.* Ohiladelphia: Penn Publishing Co.

Otnes, R.K., and Enochson, L. (1978). *Applied time series analysis.* New York: John Wiley.

Peterson, M. (2000). *S.T.A.R. Spatial-Temporal Animation Reasoning.* New York: Academic Press.

Pfleiderer,B., Ohrmann,A,P., Suslow,B.T., Wolgast,B.M., Gerlach,B.A.L., Heindela,C.W., and Michael, N. (2004). N-acetylaspartate levels of left frontal cortex are associated with verbal intelligence in women but not in men: a proton magnetic resonance spectroscopy study. *Neuroscience,123,* 1053-1058

Pfurtscheller, G. Quantification of ERD and ERS in the time domain. In G. Pfurtscheller and F.H. Lopes da Silva (Ed.) *Handbook of electroencephalography and clinical neuropsychology, Vol. 6: Event-related desynchronization.* Amsterdam: Elsevier, 1999, pp. 89-105.

Pincus, S. (1994). Approximate entropy (ApEn) as a complexity measure. *Chaos, 5,* 110-117.

Pincus. M.S. (1995). Quantifying complexity and regularity of neurobiological systems. *Methods in Neurosciences, 28,* 336-363.

Posthuma, D., Neale, M.C., Boomsma, D.I., and de Geus, E. J. C. (2000). Are smarter brains running faster? heritability of alpha peak frequency, iq, and their interrelation. *Behavior Genetics, 3,* 567-579.

Pulvermüller, F., Birbaumer, N., Lutzenberger, W., and Mohr, B.(1997). High frequency brain activity: Its possible role in attention, perception and language processing. *Progress in Neurobiology, 52,* 427-445.

Razoumnikova, O. (2003). Interaction of personality and intelligence factors in cortex activity modulation. *Personality and Individual Differences, 35,* 135–162

Reed, T.E., Vernon, P.A., and Johnson, A.M. (2004). Sex difference in brain nerve conduction velocity in normal humans. *Neuropsychologia, 42,* 1709–1714.

Rescher, B., and Rappelsberger, P. (1999). Gender dependent EEG-changes during a menatl rotation task. *International Journal of Psychophysiology, 33,* 209-222.

Rideout, B.E. and Laubach, C.M. EEG correlates of enhanced spatial performance following exposure to music. Percept. Motor Skill., 1996, 82: 427-432.

Schulte, M.J., Ree, M.J., and Carretta, T.R. (2004). Emotional intelligence: not much more than g and personality. *Personality and Individual Differences, 37,* 1059-1068.

Singer, W. and Gray, C.M. (1995).Visual feature integration and the temporal correlation hypothesis. *Annual Review of Neuroscience,* 18, 555-586.

Skrandies, W., Reik, P., and Kunze, Ch. (1999). Topography of evoked brain activity during mental arithmetic and language tasks: sex differences. *Neuropsychologia, 37,* 421-430.

Smith, B. D., Kline, R., Lindgren, K., Ferro, M., Smith, D. A., and Nespor, A. (1995). The lateralized processing of affect in emotion-ally labile extraverts and introverts: central and autonomic effects. *Biological Psychology, 39,* 143-157.

Strüber, D., Basar-Eroglu, C., Hoff, E., and Stadler, M. (2000). Reversal-rate dependent differences in the EEG gamma-band during multistable visual perception. *Int. J. Psychophysiol. 38,* 243-252.

Stough,C., Donaldson, C., Scarlata, B., and Ciorciari, J. (2001) Psychophysiological correlates of the NEO PI-R Openness, Agreeableness and Conscientiousness: preliminary results. *International Journal of Psychophysiology, 41,* 87-91

Tallon-Baudry, C. and Bertrand, O. (1999) Oscillatory γ activity in humans and its role in object representation. *Trends in Neuroscience, 19,* 151-162.

Thatcher, R.W., Toro, C., Pflieger, M.E., and Hallet, M. (1994). Human neural network dynamics using multimodal registration of EEG, PET and MRI. In: R.W. Thatcher, M. Hallet, and T. Zeffiro (Ed.). *Functional neuroimaging: Technical foundations* (pp. 259-267). Orlando FL: Academic Press.

Thorndike, E.,L. (1920). Intelligence and its use. *Harper's Magazine, 140,* 227-235.

Tomarken, A. J., Davidson, R. J., and Henriques, J. B. (1990). Resting frontal brain asymmetry predicts affective responses to films. *Journal of Personality and Social Psychology, 59,* 791–801.

Vogel, F. (2000). *Genetics and the electroencephalogram.* Berlin: Springer.

Wagner, M. (1998). *Rekonstruktion neuronaler Ströme aus bioelektrischen und biomagnetischen Messungen auf der aus MR-Bildern egmentierten Hirnrinde.* Aachen: Shaker Verlag.

Watson, D., and Clark, L. A. (1992). On traits and temperament: general and specific factors of emotional experience and their relation to the five-factor model. *Journal of Personality, 60,* 441–446.

Weiss E, Siedentopf C.M., Hofer A., Deisenhammer E.A., Hoptman M.J., Kremser C., Golaszewski S., Felber S., and Fleischhacker W.W. (2003). Sex differences in brain activation pattern during a visuospatial cognitive task: a functional magnetic resonance imaging study in healthy volunteers. *Neuroscience Letters, 344,* 169-172

Zuckerman, M., Kuhlman, D. M., Joireman, J., Teta, P., and Kraft, M. (1993). A comparison of three structural models for personality: the big three, the big five, and the alternative five. *Journal of Personality and Social Psychology, 4,* 757–768.
Agreeableness-A.

In: Intelligence : New Research
Editor: Lin V. Wesley, pp. 83-94

ISBN 1-59454-637-1
© 2006 Nova Science Publishers, Inc.

Chapter 4

INFLUENCE OF VIRTUAL AFFECTIVE INPUT ON HEART-BRAIN SYNCHRONIZATION AND COGNITIVE PERFORMANCE

*Ioannis Tarnanas**

Kozani University of Applied Science - Peopleware, Kozani, 50100

ABSTRACT

The M.I.N.D project expects to explore the best combinations of sensory stimuli that create emotional connectivity, create techniques to evoke more effective emotional links and measure these stimuli and techniques for validity and develop guidelines for future emotionally encoded training scenarios. Just as the VRML97 standard advanced virtual environment development by creating a guideline to unify the work done in dozens of individually developed virtual reality team training systems, neuroergonomics standards can help us develop systems that are compatible with natural human behavior for creating safe and comfortable training environments. In addition, methodologies and tools for measuring human behavior, understanding and accumulation of measured behavior, and assisting human behavior, will be developed. This study investigated the relationship between virtual training, physiological coherence, heart-brain synchronization, and cognitive performance in 36 healthy individuals. Subjects performed explosive ordnance disposal (EOD) task with an enhanced VE intended to instill a positive emotional state and increase physiological coherence inside a virtual incident exercise scenario of EOD Training. One VE was using the explicit biocybernetic interface that challenged the self-efficacy and team decision making of the operators in an EOD scenario by linking their heart rates (ECG), electrodermal activity (EDA) and electromyogram measurements of facial muscle tensions (EMG) with a Force Feedback Joystick of controlled "ease" of movements while engaged in a joint task. The second VE was the same EOD situation environment as the above, but without the introduction of the advanced biocybernetic interface. In both the scenarios the operators had the freedom to communicate verbally while engaged in the common task. Two performance measures were computed: (a) RMS error, and (b) number of groundings. Analyses of RMS error scores indicate that

---

* Phone: +302310580907, E-mail: ioannist@auth.gr, gtarnanas@gmail.com

performance improved over the three repeated runs with each VE, as evidence of specific-channel learning. Similarly, performance improved on the first run from Day 1 to Day 2, as evidence of near-transfer learning. However, the advanced biocybernetic interface provided to the first experimental group, provided an additional important statistical performance improvement relative to the "simple" VE group and the control groups. The mapping between the type of user - operator state and the type of medium response also had an influence on the level of presence. This project suggests that social-psychophysiological measures and team biocybernetics merit further investigation in sociotechnical systems that demand high proficiency and self-efficacy.

Keywords: Biocybernetics; Presence; Situational Awareness; Virtual Reality; Training.

1. INTRODUCTION

Symbiosis is "a relationship of mutual benefit or dependence", according to Bartleby's Dictionary. In 1960, J. C. R. Licklider predicted that human-computer "symbiotic partnership will perform intellectual operations much more effectively than man alone can perform them." This prediction was largely true: our intellectual achievements have indeed been greatly enhanced by technology. But have we reached true symbiosis? Since computers are not a separate *species* obtaining essential relational benefits (they are yet only complex tools), it is not strictly correct to classify us as symbionts in the sense of biology. If artificial consciousness is ever generated, this situation might well change, but for the foreseeable future, computer technology will simply be indispensable to life as we know it. As societies and individuals, we will become ever more deeply dependent on IT, to the point that we must honestly rename ourselves *homo sapiens cyborg*.

When using virtual reality technology people often experience a feeling of being in the computer generated environment (Kalawsky, 1993), this feeling is described in literature as presence. Presence as been more explicitly be defined by Lombard and Ditton's (1997) as experiencing the illusion of non-mediation. Virtual reality systems range from fully immersive systems to virtual environments called desktop VR, in which the user interacts with a computer-generated simulation. Many researchers argue that virtual environments represent an extension of previous simulation technology and differ from previous human-computer systems only in a matter of degree. Harmon and Kenney (1994) state that "VR technology has much in common with simulation technology, for at its simplest level it is a simulation of some aspect of reality" (p. 228). According to this view, virtual environments represent a type of simulation technology that embodies certain unique features, such as immersion and interactivity, that may lead to enhanced training.

User's feeling a high level of presence can develop fear in response to simulated anxiety-provoking stimuli (Kenyon et al, 1995). These results suggest that virtual environments could be a viable tool to the treatment of phobia, where patients could experience in a controlled environment the stimuli they fear. Although VE technology may offer the *potential* to deliver more effective training more cheaply, research has only just begun to examine the application of VE technology for training applications. An overriding question that must be addressed is under what conditions can this technology enhance training? Without a strong foundation of empirical training research, training developers run the risk of creating an impressive technology of questionable training utility. To date, there have been a relative handful of empirical studies that have examined VE training effectiveness (see Kenyon and Afenya, 1995; Kozak, Hancock, Arthur, and Chrysler, 1993; Regian, Shebilske, and Monk, 1992). Regian, Shebilske, and Monk (1992) conducted an exploratory study to examine the use of virtual environments to train procedural tasks requiring the performance of motor sequences and spatial navigation. Results indicated that subjects who were taught in the virtual environments performed to a benchmark level during subsequent testing, indicating that the VE training was effective in imparting skills; however, there were no control groups or standard-training groups for comparison. Kozak et al. (1993) conducted a study to compare VE training, real-world training and no-training groups performing a pick and place motor task. The results of this study revealed no significant difference between the VE-training group and the no-training group on a transfer task. Both groups were outperformed by the real-world training group. The authors concluded that the VE training environment may not have provided adequate training for this type of motor task, and especially noted the paucity of tactile and acoustic feedback in the virtual environment. Kenyon and Afenya (1995) replicated the Kozak et al. (1993) study using a projection-based virtual environment (Cave system) rather than the head mounted display (HMD) VE system used in the original study. Kenyon and Afenya argued that in the Cave system, the trainee can see the floor and other real objects in the environment simultaneously with the synthetic objects, thus enhancing the spatial relationship of the virtual objects with the real world. The primary comparison made was between one group trained in the virtual environment and tested in the real world and a second group trained in the real world and tested in the virtual world. The authors claimed a small improvement in performance for the VE-trained group relative to the second group, although the use of the second group as an untrained control group for comparison purposes is questionable. Witmer, Bailey, and Knerr (1994) conducted research to examine the use of a virtual environment to train route learning (navigation within an office building). Three groups, a VE-trained group, a group that physically rehearsed routes in the building, and a group that rehearsed symbolically (i.e., rehearsed the routes out loud but without any physical rehearsal, were tested on the transfer of route learning to the actual building). Results indicated that VE trained subjects outperformed those who trained symbolically, but did more poorly than those who physically rehearsed routes.

When interacting with a VE two mental models will be activated and shaped (Kozak et al, 1993):

1. The model of the Real World (RW)
2. The model of the Virtual World (VW)

Presence refers to the sense of "being in" a world, a state where these two models begin to overlap. It therefore only makes sense to speak about the degree of presence in one environment (the virtual environment) *relative to* another (the real environment). In other words: presence refers to the distinction made by the user between the RW and the VW. For each lower level model a specific type of presence can be defined:

- Personal presence is related to the 'Self'. It is a measure of the extent to which one feels like one is in a virtual world.

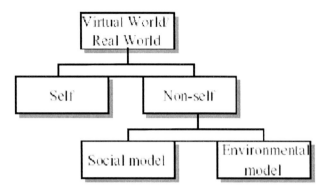

Figure 1. mental models in a VR

- Social presence relates to the social model as part of the 'Non-self'. It is sometimes defined as the extent to which a medium is perceived as sociable, warm, sensitive, personal or intimate when it is used to interact with other people. However, it is also possible that social presence is achieved using synthetic beings, for example using a creature that keeps coming back to you, asking you to pick it up and throw it away.
- Environmental presence refers to the environment model and indicates the extent to which the environment itself appears to know that you are there and to react to you.

It is perhaps inevitable that we will continue to be transformed by our technologies. This new technology was realized in systems we call *team biocybernetic*. A *biocybernetic system* is a person or group assisted by computational and sensor systems that must be able to sense human characteristics and behavior. With greater sensor power, computational resources will then be able to assist and enable human performance in novel ways. A personal assistance technology could know when we are sick, distracted, or too tired to carry out a critical team role in our workplace or at home. Based on long-term observation and automated modeling, it could notify us that we are talking too much in a mission, or that our blood pressure rises whenever we have to use a weapon in a virtual environment training.

This level of assistive technology will require fundamental advances in sensor hardware and software, and will require an understanding of both neurophysiology and social processes that elude us. In summary, at the current stage of VE training research, empirical studies of VE training effectiveness as *team biocybernetics* are few. The studies conducted to-date address the basic question of "Does VE training work?" Further research is needed to identify the conditions under which VE training is effective, to identify what aspects of the virtual environment lead to more effective training, and to empirically evaluate VE training applications.

2. PROJECT BACKGROUND

The Fully Immersive Biocybernetics Team Trainer (FIBTT) supports experiments using virtual environment (VE) technology for team training. The Peopleware Creative Assistive

Technologies Laboratory from the Kozani University of Applied Science (CATLab) developed the functional requirements to meet its research goals and has conducted research using the system. Peopleware SME designed and implemented all software, hardware and modeling components under contract to CATLab. CATLab's primary research objective is to develop and evaluate different ways to use VE technology to train leaders, teams and units. Ancillary goals include investigating the psychological effects of VEs, possible effects of VE-based distributed biocybernetics team training and rehearsal on performance, and the ergonomic aspects of proposed training systems. It also evaluates the development of Virtual Extreme Team Training Experiences for soldiers and their equipment, adapting participants' expectations to match the current capabilities and limitations of VE systems in representing locomotion, vision, audition, olfactory and haptic factors. This enhances, rather than detracts from the sense of presence in the synthetic environment.

Multisensory environments are environments that occupy more than one sense at the same time. One of the greatest outcomes and side effect of the 21st century technological advancement is the radical development and expansion of multisensory environments. To create living and social environments in which humans are able to attain more comfortable and fulfilling lifestyles, enhancement of the compatibility between environments, products, and machines with human senses is necessary. An evaluation procedure that could measure and evaluate human sensations quantitatively and an application technology, which enhances the use of data on human sensations in the design of consumer devices and environments by addressing emotional ergonomics or neuroergonomics, is nowadays essential more than ever. Are there things beyond sensory inputs we can take advantage of? *Can we provide certain cues that will enable the trainee to construct a story? Prime people to pay attention to certain things? Have parts of the environment exist in subjective time and space? Adapt techniques of other media (such as film) or create our own? Tap into people's memories? Learn from recent advances in cognitive science?*

On top of that, one of the latest World Health Organization reports, written by a Nobel Prize winner, stated that by the year 2050, the medical science would find a way to cure most of today's and future diseases, except from heart problems and depression. These two causes will be the most frequent causes of death by the year 2050 and beyond. Although the many advances of biological and computer sciences in the field of medicine, genomic research, neuroscience, biotechnology and bioinformatics the emotional interplay between multisensory environments and human behavior is largely unexplored.

As an outcome, by the development of such standards, not only will we be able to develop safe and comfortable multisensory environments, but also assist human behavior, augment cognition, prevent mental illness, adapt to novel and extreme situations and create really effective training scenarios. This can be achieved by integrating scientific knowledge on various human characteristics, including body shapes, physical movements, sensations, cognition, emotion and behavior, into the design process. Consequently, human life multisensory environments evaluation, which is a study of human beings in relation to the design of products, environments, and social systems, is becoming the center of attention.

Among the many approaches available within the field of sensory environments evaluation, this project adopts as its basis, virtual reality therapy and ergonomics, and arms to bring light to the significance of human emotional connections. In particular virtual reality therapy and ergonomics can, create emotionally evocative environments of different intensities and set up testing and evaluation environments with specific combinations of sensory stimuli.

3. RESEARCH DESIGN

The ultimate effectiveness of VE training relies on the effectiveness of the instructional features incorporated into the virtual environment. Instructional features are the instructional events leading to and accompanying the VE experience. Without the incorporation of effective instructional procedures within the virtual environment, the virtual environment remains simply a representation of reality.

A primary goal of this project is to explore the potential benefits of employing advanced training techniques in a VE-based training program. There are unique training capabilities enabled by VE technology that differentiate this technology from previous simulation approaches. Prominent among these features are artificial perceptual cues that take advantage of the wide field of view 3-D visual environment, 3-D acoustic environments, the ability to provide a variety of haptic cues and *biocybernetics.*

Objectives

The emotional connection is proven enhance learning and retention. We are going to look at the role our senses play in providing an emotional connection. Among the questions that we are going to try to answer are:

- What threshold levels of each sense are necessary to stimulate emotional connectivity?
- Can we determine the most effective combinations of these levels?
- What else can we do to create environments with more emotional links?

The M.I.N.D project is creating rich, multi-sensory virtual environments in order to investigate how environments themselves can evoke a range of emotional responses from participants who experience them. Research indicates that we become more involved with emotionally charged situations and remember them better than emotionally neutral ones. Thus, more effective training scenarios can be designed by incorporating key emotional cues.

Just as so many years of research in Cognitive Science and HCI have recently produce ergonomic guidelines and the GOMS model (1997) in order to capture the complex cognitive interactions between a user and it's environment, with M.I.N.D we aim to develop an *emotional GOMS model* to index and capture the feelings and sensations existing in a multisensory human-centered environment. These heuristics will be used the same way that we use computer language to construct and evolve multisensory experiences that encode specific situations. The data captured can be used to develop multi-agent mission critical systems, artificial emotional intelligent agents, affective computing appliances, safe and comfortable human environments, mission rehearsal exercises and next generation virtual reality simulations with somatic feedback.

Apparatus

It is an effective instructional practice to "cue" or highlight critical events during training that are perceptually indistinct or subtle. Mann and Decker (1984) argued that effective learning depends on the contrastive value of the stimulus to be learned (i.e., its distinctiveness) and the meaningfulness of that item. Distinctiveness can be created in several ways: (a) by displaying the behavior out of context, (b) by exaggerating the behavior, (c) by repeating the behavior frequently, and (d) by using learning points or instructional cueing to identify the key behavior. Mann and Decker cautioned that approaches A-C may enhance distinctiveness but detract from meaningfulness because they alter the context in which the behavior is typically encountered. On the other hand, they argue that by cueing or highlighting the key behavior to be learned, distinctiveness as well as meaningfulness is enhanced.

Therefore, the instructional approach chosen to exploit VE technology is the use of a sensor *biocybernetics* system that was noninvasive in order to observe and coach people engaged in complex collaborative activities and enhance VE training effectiveness. In a *biocybernetics* virtual environment, it is possible to record the activities of four people as they work together. The prototype was built with off the shelf components and custom software by Dr. Ioannis Tarnanas and his *Peopleware* team, based on an inexpensive networked PC platform. Each person was equipped with a sensor suite for recording electro-cardiogram, breathing, blood pulse volume/oxygenation, electromyelography of facial muscle tensions (EMG), electrodermal activity (EDA) and galvanic skin response. Accelerometers on the head and hands record movement.

Task

Following a three-month process of group study in the CATLab, we developed the concept for a task to provide an extreme team training for the implementation of VE training. An explosive ordnance disposal (EOD) task was investigated by site visits at the EOD school and evaluation of training curriculum. The environment depicted four participant avatars wearing protective gear and masks, each with the ability to communicate freely using verbal communication with the others thus adapting participants' expectations to match the current capabilities and limitations of VE systems in representing locomotion, vision, audition and haptic factors for a team training explosive ordnance disposal (EOD).

The system was monitoring the four person's stress activity and performance at the critical events during training. At those events we looked at coherence within the heart-rate (HR) time series of each participant as well as between the four participants' respiration and HR. If one of the participants was particularly stressed, then all other team members-participants were experiencing "difficulties" at their controls as a result of one member's irregular HR coherence. In terms of *biocybernetics* research inside VE, we call those difficulties "virtual pain". We used LifeShirt's VivoLogic software for the HR coherence analysis, which contained several HRV analysis capabilities and Immersion's Touch Force Desktop SDK to provide force feedback in the form of a Joystick getting harder to control. Also, for measuring RSA as a parasympathetic HRV measure, we've shown in several studies that adjustment for respiration factors is necessary, so the LifeShirt proved to be a good choice as well.

Training Effectiveness Experiment

The objective of the experiment was to test the effectiveness of a selected training intervention enabled by *biocybernetics* and VE technology. The training intervention that was selected was the use of *biocybernetic* cueing to enhance VE training effectiveness compared to a stand alone VE training environment. Specifically, this experiment tested the effects of the environments, the explicit display of VE and the display of a VE mision showing "vitrual pain", on the ability of the trainee to handle critical events in explosive ordnance disposal. A virtual explosive ordnance disposal inside ten (10) rooms for eight (8) missions training activity allowed us to track the performance of both individuals and groups quantitatively. We measured the number of rooms that each team successfully cleared according to the safe and proper operation of explosive ordnance disposal in a given time, gradually increasing the difficulty of the VE scenario in order to shift team stress inside the group.

The primary skill to be trained was the ability of the trainee to handle critical events inside as many rooms as possible of a virtual building, according to the moment-to-moment responsibility for the safe and proper operation of explosive ordnance disposal. Performance was assessed by two measures: (a) Root-mean-square (rms) deviation of the participant's performance and HR coherence from safe and proper operation, and (b) number of groundings.

Subjects

Subjects were thirty six trained personnel from the Greek Special Forces School in Athens, Greece. Eighteen subjects were placed in the Cues Group that received "virtual pain" cues on two thirds of the practice trials, and eighteen subjects were placed in the No Cues group that received no enhanced *biocybernetics* features.

Procedure

On day 1 of the study, subjects received classroom training and familiarization training with the simulation. Both groups of subjects then trained on eight missions. For each mission, subjects had free trails or runs (for a total of 12 rooms with explosives). For the No Cues group, these trials were undertaken with no *biocybernetics* enhancements. For the Cues Group, the second trial of each 3-trial included instructional cueing. Thus, the Cues Group navigated each mission on an initial trial with cueing, the second trial with no cueing, and the third trial with cueing again. On day 1, subjects completed half of the practice missions.

On day 2 of the study, subjects completed the remaining practice missions. The design of the study allowed the assessment of three indices of learning:

- *Specific-mission learning*: assessed by the improvement from Trial 1 to Trial 3 (averaged across rooms).
- *Near-transfer or general learning*: assessed by the average performance on Trial 1 of the practice rooms on Day 1 compared to the average performance on Trial 1 of the practice rooms on Day 2.
- *Far-transfer learning*: assessed by performance on the practice rooms compared to performance on the transfer rooms.

4. RESULTS

RMS Error

Analyses of RMS error scores indicate that performance on the number of rooms cleared improved over the three repeated runs with each mission, as evidence of specific-channel learning. Similarly, performance improved on the first run from Day 1 to Day 2, as evidence of near-transfer learning. However, the *biocybernetics* cues provided to the experimental group "pain" did provide a significant performance improvement relative to the control groups (see figure 2).

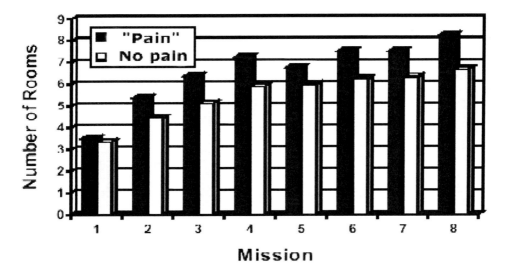

Figure 2. Number of rooms cleared by distributed and local teams over a series of eight mission.

Number of Groundings

Both groups showed an improvement over the course of training. Again, however, there was a significant performance improvement for the experimental groups relative to the control groups.

5. DISCUSSION

The results of this study indicate that practice in the *biocybernetics* VE training simulation resulted in improved performance both within a specific mission and in transferring to a new mission. The apparent links we saw between sensor data and human performance suggest to us that personal sensing in a team setting is an incredibly promising technology.

However, there we will need to invent self-programming and adaptive software that does not actually get written, but will have to evolve in response to its sensor inputs, just like the human brain develops in early childhood, as populations of neurons compete, align, merge, and grow to cognitive maturity. We might even need to develop a new kind of nanotechnology-based neuromorphic circuitry to support this software.

Leading neuroscientists tell us emphatically that the human brain is not a computer: its physical basis, its dynamics, and its modes of information processing are utterly dissimilar to those that take place in the static binary realms of explicit software architectures and integrated circuitry. Even with what little we know about the brain, we already are certain that "a wet computer" is possibly the worst analogy we can devise to understand the brain. The future of human-machine systems can be a bright one, if we develop technology that enables us to be more fully human instead of clever cyborgs!

6. FUTURE WORK

Our research involves the role sensory and emotional stimuli provide in the overall virtual experience effect. Our efforts examine detailed computer graphics, secondary sound cues, olfactory stimuli, and lighting effects, as well as associative memories to create heightened realism and believability in psychosocial systems. Secondary sounds, like distant convoys, barking dogs, fired rounds and other peripheral noises require the trainee to make order and sense out of potentially distracting environments. Enhanced graphics, including transparency and layered renders to simulate fog, rain, sleet, dust, and heat distortion, along with Hollywood-type effects techniques are incorporated into the simulation world for more "photo-realism". The addition of smells (olfactory cues) will incorporate researching the state and usefulness of current scent delivery systems. The role of memories and associative reasoning in training scenarios will also be investigated for their contribution for overall emotional content.

We are now exploring design techniques to create worlds that take advantage of expectations, interest and natural world interactions to help structure a "narrative" both within and after participation in an open-ended Multisensory Virtual Environment (VE). Future research might take advantage of a participants' natural tendency to prefer interaction when possible, resulting in worlds that form their meaning out of intention and interaction – of the author as well as the participant – in a mutual form of authorship.

Issues to be resolved concerning advanced instructional cueing include:

- Skills, Processes, and Behaviors to be Enhanced. Determination of what skill, process, or behavior is to be enhanced by the artificial cueing environment.

- Selection of Artificial Cues. Selection of the artificial cues that will enhance the selected skills/processes/behaviors.
- Presentation of Artificial Cues. Determining how to provide these cues so that they enhance long-term performance in operational situations in which the cues are no longer present.

The mission sounds innocuous enough: "to see how information technology can be diffused into standards and indices for everyday objects and settings, leading to new ways of supporting and enhancing people's lives". However, one of the risk elements that exist in this project is the process for discovering biological and emotional signal signatures for group interactions or single user interactions. Since even in single user scenarios, there is still a lot of difficulty in identifying these signatures, due to intrinsic causes (e.g. non linearity of relationships) and extrinsic causes (e.g. sweating has an effect on GSR). The challenge of this project is not to rig up the set up but find a system configuration and use a plethora of statistical tools and "*biocybernetics*" in order to discover the relationships/signatures.

The knowledge gained from the M.I.N.D project could contribute to the advancement of a highly complex and realistic Experience Learning System, providing a heightened sense of awareness for the users who use it. Context-aware and proactive systems will hide overall system complexity, and preserve human attention, by delivering to us only information, which is rich with meanings and contexts. Now maybe we are missing something, but to us this translates as: build systems that are too complicated to understand and then, after they are deployed, find ways to master their complexity.

One of the problems with "open, unbound, dynamic and intelligent systems", says Greger Linden, a Finnish expert in "psychosocial computing", is that when direct brain-computer interfaces are implemented, "people will be the problem. Rather than concentrate on one thing at a time, which suits the software, people tend to think about other things. M.I.N.D plans to develop models for "disambiguating" users' vague commands, and anticipating their actions.

It may be a long way before we find a method or a tool to try to map the unconscious, however the development of standards and indices that can guide us to monitor the users and provide them with learning, and gracefully evolving capabilities, as well as self-diagnosis, self-adaptation and self-organization capabilities, maybe a step to the right direction. The M.I.N.D can impact the creation of a mental health knowledge base that can help greatly in mental disease prevention and have an enormous social and economical impact.

Serious dangers are often created by individuals who try to carry out critical activity when they are "not in a fit state to". The M.I.N.D project could develop agents that will monitor these users and decide on behalf of them for their welfare. We mention Space Exploration and Crisis Management Situations as some examples of critical activities. We have a reason to invest a lot of money into Deep Space or even Earth terra-forming projects and activities, we see no reason why shouldn't we invest the same amount in finding out some mind terra-forming techniques and activities, that all of the above activities are depended from.

7. References

Harmon, S. W., and Kenney, P. J. (1994). Virtual reality training environments. Contexts and concerns. *Educational Media International, 31*, 228-237.

Kalawsky, R. S. (1993). *The Science of Virtual Reality and Virtual Environments*, Addison-Wesley Publishers, New York.

Kenyon, R.V., and Afenya, M.B. (1995). Training in virtual and real environments. *Annals of Biomedical Engineering, 23* (4), 445.

Kozak, J. J., Hancock, P. A., Arthur, E. J., and Chrysler, S. T. (1993). Transfer of training from virtual reality. *Ergonomics, 36,* 777-784.

Lombard, M, Ditton, T. (1997). At the Heart of it all: The Concept of Telepresence. *Journal of Computer Mediated Communication*, 3, 2. On-line: http://www.ascusc.org/jcmc/vol3/issue2/lombard.html

Mann, R. B. and Decker, P. J. (1984). The effect of key behavior distinctiveness on generalization and recall in behavior modeling training. *Academy of Management Journal, 27,* 900-910.

Regian, J. W., Shebilske, W. L., and Monk, J. M. (1992). Virtual reality: An instructional medium for visual-spatial tasks. *Journal of Communication, 42* (4), p. 136-149.

Tarnanas Ioannis and Katerina Tsirgogianni MD. Virtual Reality as a Stress Inoculation Environment for high demanding Emergency Planning and Preparedness. In *2nd International Workshop on Virtual Rehabilitation*, IWVR 2003, New Jersey.

Witmer, B.G., and Singer, M.J. (1994). *Measuring immersion in virtual environments* (Technical report 1014). Alexandria, VA: U.S. Army Research Institute for the Behavioral and Social Sciences.

In: Intelligence : New Research
Editor: Lin V. Wesley, pp. 95-113

ISBN 1-59454-637-1
© 2006 Nova Science Publishers, Inc.

Chapter 5

EMOTIONAL INTELLIGENCE: A CRITICAL REVIEW

Guo-hua Huang, Kenneth S. Law and Chi-Sum Wong[*]
Department of Management of Organizations
Hong Kong University of Science and Technology
Clear Water Bay Road, Kowloon, Hong Kong
Department of Management
The Chinese University of Hong Kong
Shatin, N.T., Hong Kong

ABSTRACT

Emotional intelligence (EI) has been one of the most controversial topics in both practitioner and academic communities since its first introduction by Salovey, Mayer and their collaborators in the early 1990s (Salovey and Mayer, 1990; Mayer, Dipaolo, and Salovey, 1990). Fervent discussions and severe debates have been raised on the meaning and domain of this concept and its validity and utility to the academic field. Proponents of the EI construct claim that it affects important individual life outcomes and has utility in various areas, such as education and organizational behavior. Empirical evidence has accumulated in support of these claims (Mayer, Salovey and Caruso, 2004; Law, Wong and Song, 2004b). However, there are also researchers who dispute the scientific credibility of the concept of EI and conclude it as an "elusive construct" (Davies, Stankov and Roberts, 1998; Matthews, Roberts, and Zeidner, 2004).

After about fifteen years of research, it is a good time to review what has been done in the field and whether EI deserves future attention. As an emerging topic, there are very few comprehensive reviews of the construct, which offer a big picture of the current state and future directions of EI research. This is what we want to achieve with this chapter. Specifically, we start with a review of the development of the EI concept and the main works in the field. Following this, we discuss the debates on three major aspects of EI: the nature and domain of the EI construct, its construct validity, and its measurement problems. We then suggest what we see as the most important directions for future development of the field. In particular, we call for research that focuses on the construct validity and measurement of EI, and efforts on the outcomes and antecedents of EI

[*] [1] Telephone: (852)2609-7794,FAX: (852) 2603-6840,Email: cswong@baf.msmail.cuhk.edu.hk

toward developing an EI theory that could guide the field to move forward. This review is concluded with our overall evaluations of the field and suggestions for future development.

I. INTRODUCTION

Emotional intelligence (EI) has been one of the most controversial topics in both practitioner and academic communities in the last one and a half decades. This could be credited to several important articles and books in both the scientific and popular literature (e.g., Salovey and Mayer, 1990; Bar-On, 1997). There are two reasons that those works became so popular. First, the concept of EI is intuitively understandable to a wide audience because it is consistent with our daily experience - We all have such experiences that work, and lives were affected when our emotions were not under good control, and "we can readily call to mind people who are high on cognitive intelligence but quite unremarkable in their social adroitness" (Zeidner, Roberts, and Matthews, 2004: 239). Second, EI involves two important research areas, namely emotion and intelligence, both of which have been broadly studied for a long time. Indeed, it could be rather surprising to some scholars that such an important construct has not been studied till recently.

Irrespective of the enthusiasm that EI has raised, we need rigorous academic research to investigate its validity and utility before we accept it as a valid construct in the academia. Fortunately, since its first introduction into the academic world by Salovey, Mayer and their colleagues in 1990 (Salovey and Mayer, 1990; Mayer, Dipaolo, and Salovey, 1990), there has been a large body of research on EI in various disciplines, such as psychology, education and organizational behavior. Research efforts at validating the EI construct resulted in a number of encouraging results and at the same time, new questions are raised as well. For example, proponents of EI have argued for the utility of EI in predicting important individual outcomes such as academic and career success, life satisfaction and feelings of powerlessness, and organizational outcomes such as employee job satisfaction, job performance, and leadership effectiveness. (e.g., Wong and Law, 2002; Law, Wong, and Song, 2004). A variety of instruments to measure EI have been developed in the literature, including the self-reported scale such as Emotional Quotient Inventory (EQ-i, Bar-On, 1997), Wong and Law Emotional Intelligence Scale (WLEIS, Wong and Law, 2002), and EI tests such as Multifactor Emotional Intelligence Scale (MEIS, Mayer, Salovey, and Caruso, 1999), and its amended version Mayer-Salovey-Caruso Emotional Intelligence Test (MSCEIT, Mayer, Salovey and Caruso, 2002). On the other hand, researchers have also debated heatedly on questions such as what should be the domain of EI, whether EI meets the standard as an "intelligence", whether it has discriminant validity with established constructs such as personality traits and other intelligence dimensions (e.g., Mayer, Caruso, and Salovey, 2000a; Matthews, Roberts, and Zeidner, 2004).

After about fifteen years of research, it is a good time to review what has been done in the field and whether EI deserves future attention. As an emerging topic, there are very few comprehensive reviews of the construct, which offer a big picture of the current state and future directions of EI research. This is what we want to achieve with this chapter. In the following sections, we first review the development of the EI concept and the main works in this area. Then we discuss the debates and our views on three important issues: the nature and domain of the EI concept, its construct validity, and the measurement problem. Finally, we suggest what we see as the most important directions for the future development of the field. In particular, we call for studies that focus on the validity, measurement, antecedents and outcomes of EI.

II. DEVELOPMENT OF THE EI CONCEPT

Despite this recent ferment of interest, the concept of EI has historical roots that are well embedded in psychological thought for the past century. The roots begin with Edward Thorndike (1920), who introduced the concept of "*social intelligence*" and defined it as "the ability to understand and manage men and women, boys and girls—to act wisely in human relations." Following this, Gardner included "personal intelligence" in his seminal work on the theory of multiple intelligence (MI). In his model, personal intelligence is comprised of *intrapersonal intelligence*, which refers to the "knowledge of the internal aspects of a person: access to one's own feeling life, one's range of emotions, the capacity to effect discriminations among these emotions and eventually to label them and to draw upon them as a means of understanding and guiding one's own behavior", and *interpersonal intelligence*, which "builds on a core capacity to notice the distinctions among others; in particular, contrast in their moods, temperaments, motivations and intentions" (Gardner, 1993: 23). Sternberg who worked on human abilities, suggested that we may wish to pay less attention to conventional notions of intelligence and more to what he terms *successful intelligence*, or the ability to adapt to, shape, and select environments to accomplish one's goals and those of one's society and culture. It involves three broad abilities: analytical, creative, and practical abilities (Sternberg, 1996, 1998). Although related, EI is distinct from these earlier concepts in that they have different domains and EI is more focused on "emotion". We will return to this point later in the chapter.

In this section, we summarize into three lines the major works that have contributed to the development of the EI concept and review each of them. The first line is in the popular literature, including work by Daniel Goleman, who popularized the concept greatly by bringing it to the masses, and Reuven Bar-On, who made the first commercially available measure Emotional Quotient Inventory (EQ-i) designed to assess emotionally and socially intelligent behavior. The second line is the research done by Salovey, Mayer and their colleagues, who first introduced the EI concept into academic research and have been continuously active in this area. We would also discuss some recently emerged works by a group of scholars who have debates on Mayer et al.'s works closely. Besides these two lines of work, researchers have also validated and applied the EI concept in many contexts such as educational and organizational settings. Therefore, the third line of research that we review covers some prominent works done by scholars in areas such as organizational behavior.

The Popular Literature

One of the most important reasons for the fast popularization of the concept of EI is the works by Daniel Goleman. His book "Emotional Intelligence: Why It Can Matter More Than IQ" has topped best seller lists around the world for several years after its publication one decade ago (1995). With that book, Goleman first brought the term EI to a wide audience. He argues that the way we have conventionally viewed intelligence (through IQ tests) has been far too narrow and that EI contributes much more to our lives than has been acknowledged. An important part of the book has also been devoted to the discussion on how EI can be developed, especially for young people. After three years, a sequel to this book came out, titled "Working with Emotional Intelligence" (1998a), in which Goleman focused on why EI matters in the workplace. Using examples and anecdotes from various organizations, Goleman explained why EI counts more than IQ to business leaders and outstanding performers. Following this, Goleman further popularized the EI concept in the business world in a series of *Harvard Business* Review articles (e.g., Goleman, 1998b, 2004).

Although popular among the general public, Goleman's work has been subject to numerous criticisms from academic communities. The most serious criticism is on the broad domain of his conception of EI. For example, in his 1995 book, EI is defined in terms of self-awareness, altruism, personal motivation, empathy, and the ability to love and be loved by friends, partners, and family members. His 1998 framework of EI includes subscales such as emotional awareness, accurate self-assessment, self-confidence, self-control, trustworthiness, conscientiousness, adaptability, innovation, achievement drive, commitment, initiative, optimism, understanding others, and so on. This definition of EI has been criticized for being too broad in scope and convoluted with personality traits, human abilities, motivations, and emotional characteristics (Matthews, Zeidner, and Roberts, 2002). In other words, his conception of EI seems "close to a conception of almost anything that matters beyond conventional concept of IQ" (Sternberg, 1999). Moreover, although Goleman's work might have been successful in conveying his conception of EI to a general audience using non-academic languages, many scholars criticize his work as lacking rigorous theoretical basis, his 10-item EI measure as having no validation evidence, and his claims as lacking support by scientific facts (Matthews, et al., 2002).

Compared with the term EI, a more popular term is "EQ" (Emotional Quotient), which has been claimed to be coined by Bar-On, whose works on emotional-social intelligence also popularized the EI concept greatly. According to his model (Bar-On, 2000), *emotional-social intelligence* is a cross-section of interrelated emotional and social competencies, skills and facilitators that determine how effectively we understand and express ourselves, understand others and relate with them, and cope with daily demands. Based on this model, Bar-On developed a self-report measure, the Emotional Quotient Inventory (EQ-i; Bar-On, 1997). It has five composite scales that comprise 15 subscale scores: Intrapersonal (comprising Self-Regard, Emotional Self-Awareness, Assertiveness, Independence, and Self-Actualization); Interpersonal (comprising Empathy, Social Responsibility, and Interpersonal Relationship); Stress Management (comprising Stress Tolerance and Impulse Control); Adaptability (comprising Reality-Testing, Flexibility, and Problem-Solving); and General Mood (comprising Optimism and Happiness). Although EQ-i has received much attention from both popular and academic press, it is not a valid test of EI (Matthews, Zeidner, and Roberts, 2002; Wong and Law, 2002; Mayer Salovey, and Caruso, 2004) for several reasons. First, Bar-On's emotional-social intelligence model is different from the ability-based definition of EI that is currently widely received in the field. Instead, it includes a number of dimensions that are not related to EI directly (e.g., problem solving, social responsibility, etc.). In this sense, it is factually a "mixed model" that fails to map onto the term EI (Mayer, Caruso, and Salovey, 2000b; Mayer et al., 2004). Moreover, empirical evidence for the reliability and validity of this measure from rigorous studies is also sparse in the literature.

III. MAYER, SALOVEY AND THEIR COLLEAGUES' WORK

As noted previously, the introduction of EI is typically credited to Salovey and Mayer who first brought the notion into academic research (Salovey and Mayer, 1990; Mayer et al., 1990). The first definition of EI given by these authors are "the subset of social intelligence that involves the ability to monitor one's own and others' feelings and emotions, to discriminate among them and to use this information to guide one's thinking and actions" (Salovey and Mayer, 1990: 189). Based on this, a more recent and widely adopted definition is "the ability to perceive accurately, appraise, and express emotion; the ability to access and/or generate feelings when they facilitate thought; the ability to understand emotion and emotional knowledge; and the ability to regulate emotions to promote emotional and intellectual growth" (Mayer and Salovey, 1997). This definition represents a four-branch *ability based model* of EI, namely the ability to (a) perceive emotions, (b) understand emotions, (c) manage emotions and (d) use emotions to facilitate thought. The four branches form a hierarchy, with the first branch (emotional perception) at the bottom and management of emotions at the top, and having a distinction between the branch of using emotions to facilitate thought, which uniquely involves using emotions to enhance reasoning and the other three that involve reasoning about emotions (Mayer, Salovey, Caruso, and Sitarenios, 2001).

Based on the above ability based model, a series of instruments have been developed to measure an individual's EI, among which the Multifactor Emotional Intelligence Scale (MEIS, Mayer et al., 1999), and its amended version Mayer-Salovey-Caruso Emotional Intelligence Test (MSCEIT, Mayer et al., 2002) are the most prominent ones. There are four subscales in the MSCEIT, each representing a branch of EI and having two tasks to measure. (1) The branch of *Perceiving Emotion* contains subsets that ask participants to identify how much certain kinds of emotions are expressed in human faces and picture of landscapes and abstract designs. (2) *Emotional Facilitation* is measured by "sensations", for which participants compare emotions to other tactile and sensory stimuli, and "facilitation", for which participants identify the emotions that would best facilitate a type of thinking. (3) *Understanding Emotion* examines how participants make emotional judgments through two types of tasks – "changes", which tests a person's ability to know under what circumstances emotional intensity lessens and increases and how one emotional state changes into another, and "blends", which asks participants to identify the emotions that are involved in more complex affective states. (4) *Managing Emotion* is measured through scenarios and asking how participants would maintain or change their feelings, and how to manage others' feelings so that a desired outcome is achieved (Mayer et al., 2004).

In their debates with other scholars, Mayer, Salovey and their colleagues have continually clarified and developed their conception and measurement instrument of EI. Some of the most notable recent debates can be found in several scholarly journal issues: the special forum on EI in the inaugural volume of a new APA journal *Emotion* (2001), a special issue in *Psychological Inquiry* (2004), and the point-counterpoint section in a recent issue of the *Journal of Organizational Behavior (2005)*. The debates were centered around several core issues. First, what is the nature and domain of EI. Second, what is the discriminant validity of EI with other relatively well-established constructs in traditional research areas such as personality, intelligence, and emotion. Third, how should EI be operationalized or measured. Finally, what is the predictive power of EI on important outcomes beyond the traditional predictors. We will address these controversial issues in greater detail in the next section.

One group of scholars who have debates with Mayer et al. most closely is Matthews, Roberts and their collaborators (e.g., Roberts, Zeidner, and Matthews, 2001; Matthews et al., 2002, 2004). Their 2002 book "Emotional Intelligence: Science and Myth" has been one of the most serious criticisms of the field of EI to date. The authors criticized the popular view of EI (such as Goleman's and Bar-On's works) as being largely overlapped with traditional personality trait and lack of scientific supports. For the academic literature, their critiques were mainly centered on Mayer et al.'s studies and focused on the issue of lack of construct validity. In a more recent study, their comments on the EI research were further developed and summarized into seven "myths" about EI (Matthews et al., 2004). According to these authors, seven barriers need to be overcome before the field could move forward. They are myths about: (1) definitions of EI are conceptually coherent; (2) measures of EI meet standard psychometric criteria; (3) self-report EI is distinct from existing personality constructs; (4) ability tests for EI meet criteria for a cognitive intelligence; (5) EI relates to emotion as IQ relates to cognition; (6) EI predicts adaptive coping; (7) EI is critical for real world success. Interestingly, these scholars did not provide substantial evidence for disputing the validity and utility of EI, nor did they seem to have paid enough attention to the existing empirical evidence. For instance, as to the "Myth" three, Wong, Law and their collaborators (Wong and Law, 2002; Law, Wang, and Song., 2004) have shown the discriminant validity of EI with the Big Five personality dimensions using WLEIS. Responses toward Matthews et al.'s comments can be found in the recent literature. For example, in the same issue, Gohm (2004) discussed each of the seven "myths" and suggested that much of their criticism does not seem to be applied to Mayer et al.'s ability model of EI. Besides these criticisms, Matthews et al. also provided thought provoking questions and interesting discussions for the future development of EI research. For example, in their 2002 book, they addressed such issues as the origin and development of EI, educational programs and the EI intervention programs.

IV. OTHER MAJOR WORKS

Although Goleman's popular books have boosted the importance of EI at the workplace, scientific studies have not appeared until the early 2000s in the area of organizational behavior. One of the most noteworthy streams of work was done by Law, Wong, and their colleagues who conducted a series of rigorous studies to validate the EI concept (e.g., Wong and Law, 2002; Wong, Wong and Law, 2005; Law, et al., 2004b). In their first exploratory study, the authors investigated the argument that EI is a core variable that affects the performance of leaders (Wong and Law, 2002). They first pointed out the lack of psychometrically sound and practically short EI measure that can be used in management studies. Using a standard scale development procedure, they developed a new self-report EI measure, the "Wong and Law Emotional Intelligence Scale" (WLEIS), based on the four-branch ability based model. The WLEIS has four dimensions: 1. *Appraisal and expression of emotion in one's self*, which relates to an individual's ability to understand his/her deep emotions and to be able to express emotions naturally; 2. *Appraisal and recognition of emotion in others*, which relates to an individual's ability to perceive and understand the emotions of the people around them; 3. *Regulation of emotion in one's self*, which relates to the ability of a person to regulate his/her emotions, enabling a more rapid recovery from psychological distress; 4. *Use of emotion to facilitate performance*, which relates to the ability of a person to make use of his/her own (or others') emotions by directing them towards constructive activities and personal performance. This scale is based on the definition given by Davies et al. (1998). It is the result of a comprehensive synthesis of the EI literature by Davies et al. and is essentially consistent with Mayer and Salovey's (1997) definition. Wong and Law (2002) validated the 16-item self-report WLEIS measure through several samples using MBA and undergraduate students as well as full-time employees. Results demonstrated that EI of leaders and followers, as measured by WLEIS, have positive effects on job performance and work attitudes (including job satisfaction and organizational commitment). Moreover, emotional labor of the job, which refers to the emotion-related job requirements, was found to moderate the EI–job outcome relationship.

Law, Wong, and Song (2004) further examined the construct and criterion validity of EI by others-rating of EI using the WLEIS. One strength of the study is that the authors cross-validated their findings on an employee sample with peer ratings of EI, and obtained significant predictions of students' academic performance using parents' ratings of the students' EI. This makes a contribution to the literature, in that, using others' ratings of EI overcomes the drawbacks of self-report scales to some extent. Their findings demonstrated that EI, as measured by WLEIS, is related to, yet distinct from personality dimensions and has incremental predictive power on life satisfaction and feelings of powerlessness after controlling for the Big Five personality dimensions. Following this, Law and his colleagues (Law, Wong, Huang, and Li, 2004) have made another important step in their EI research—they studied the incremental validity of EI over and beyond the general mental abilities (GMA) and demonstrated the predictive validity of EI on job performance after controlling for personality traits and GMA.

Besides the studies of this group of researchers, there are other studies of EI done by organizational researchers that applied the concept of EI in various research contexts. For example, Jordan and his coauthors (Jordan, Ashkanasy, and Härtel, 2002) have investigated the role of EI in the relationship between employee's perceptions of job insecurity and reactions. They proposed a model in which EI moderates employees' emotional reactions to job insecurity and their ability to cope with the associated stress. They proposed that low EI employees are more likely than high EI employees to experience negative emotional reactions to job insecurity and to adopt negative coping strategies. Another study by Huy (1999) presented a multilevel theory of emotion and change, which focuses on attributes of EI at the individual level and emotional capability at the organizational level. The author argues that EI facilitates individual adaptation to change, and emotional capability increases the likelihood for organizations to realize radical change. Both studies adopted Mayer and Salovey's (1997) EI definition. While those applications are innovative and informative, neither of these models has been empirically tested, which limits their values in providing empirical evidence for us to judge the validity and utility of EI in organizational research.

V. THE STATE OF THE FIELD

After an introduction of the major works in the EI literature, we now focus on three key issues to discuss the current state of the field. First, we discuss the nature and domain of the EI construct. We then review the discriminant validity of EI with other constructs such as personality variables, and predictive validity of EI on important outcomes such as individual life satisfaction and job performance. Finally, we discuss the measurement problem.

Nature and Domain

As mentioned, EI has been defined and used by researchers in various forms after its introduction (e.g., Mayer and Salovey, 1997; Davies et al, 1998; Montemayor and Spee, 2004). The first problem of EI research that Matthews et al. (2004) challenged is the coherence of the definitions of EI in the literature. However, this concern does not currently seem valid for the following reasons. Firstly, their review included the definitions given in popular literature (e.g., Goleman, 1995), which is not for scientific research. Secondly, minor differences in construct definition at their early stage of development is a typical phenomenon for many established constructs. Many well established constructs, such as organizational citizenship behavior (OCB) and leader-member exchange (LMX) have undergone similar struggles in their early developmental stage (see, e.g., Organ and Ryan, 1995; Schriesheim, Castro, and Cogliser, 1999). Meanwhile, the convergent trend of the EI definition is becoming clear in the literature. As Ciarrochi, Chan, and Caputi (2000) pointed out, the definitions of EI employed by various scholars "tend to be complementary rather than contradictory". Currently, the most widely accepted one is Mayer and Salovey's (1997) definition that EI is a set of human abilities to process emotional information. According to this definition, EI is a multidimensional construct including four facets of abilities—emotion perception, facilitation, understanding, and managing.

The term "emotional intelligence" implies that EI involves both intelligence and emotion ingredients. Controversies on the nature of EI related to both aspects. Related to the "intelligence" aspect, it is one of the most heated debates in the field that EI meet the traditional standard for an "intelligence" (e.g., Mayer et al., 2000a; Roberts et al., 2001). Mayer et al. propose EI as a standard intelligence because it meets three criteria: first, the conceptual criterion, that is, EI could be measured as an ability for which there are correct answers; second, the correlational criteria, that is, the domain of EI was sizeable in that it could be measured with a set of diverse tasks that are moderately interrelated; third, the developmental criterion, that is, EI develops with age and experience (Mayer et al., 2000a, 2001). This has been questioned by Roberts and his coauthors (Roberts et al., 2001), who assessed the validity of EI using MEIS and found inconsistent findings using expert versus consensus scoring protocols. However, the results also showed satisfactory reliability and convergent and divergent validity of EI, and did not completely disprove EI as one form of intelligence.

Researchers have also raised questions on the "emotion" aspects of EI. These include, for example, whether different types of emotions share certain essential biologically-based features, whether emotions may be fundamentally altered by display rules, and whether emotions and cognitions represent different functions of the mind (Averill, 2004; Mayer et al., 2004). Some of these concerns are valid and may be interesting for future exploration, which we will discuss in the next section. One of the promising approaches to answer these questions is neuroscientists' study on human neural systems. Contemporary studies are discovering the biological and physiological details of how human emotions work. There are scholars who believe that specific brain systems have evolved to handle motivationally significant stimuli. Amygdala, a primitive system in the brain was found to act as an emotional sentinel, without which man is unable to gauge the emotional significance of events (Ekman and Davidson, 1994). Such findings by neuroscientists provide us important evidence for the neuropsychological basis for EI.

Currently, although there may not be enough concrete evidence to fully support EI as an intelligence facet, there is no good evidence to disprove it either. In fact, the current situation in the field is that there is more supporting evidence for the validity and utility of EI derived from usual rigorous academic procedure to investigate this construct than evidence for disproving it. As a result, the EI construct deserves empirical investigations. Based on the extant evidence, we suggest that, it will benefit the field if EI researchers base their study on Mayer et al.'s (1997) ability based model of EI, although validations of this model are still required.

Construct Validity

To establish a new construct, it must be shown that the construct is distinguishable from existing constructs. This is the greatest barrier that proponents of the construct EI have met. Critiques of EI as a new construct centers on whether it is distinct from established constructs, for example, the traditional intelligence dimensions, personality traits, and other existing similar constructs such as social intelligence, interpersonal skills, and so on. In the following, we first focus on the discriminant validity of EI with those constructs.

As Mayer et al. (2004) noted in their discussion on the "intelligence" facet of EI, different types of intelligence are often distinguished according to the kind of information on which they operate (Carroll, 1993). For example, the input information that verbal intelligence processes is vocabulary, sentences, and passages. EI, as defined by the ability based model, essentially represents an intelligence system for the processing of emotional information. Accordingly, EI is different from traditional intelligence dimensions such as verbal or mathematical intelligence, in that they focus on different type of information. In the literature, there is some empirical evidence that EI does not correlate highly with cognitive abilities (e.g., Law et al., 2004; Wong and Law, 2002; see also Mayer et al., 2004 for a review). However, this does not mean that emotion and cognition function independently or they operate in different areas of human mind. There is a long debate on the nature of emotion in the history of psychological and philosophic research. Currently, many scholars agree that affect and cognition are interdependent and may be closely intertwined in human function, and that emotion represents a complex of more basic components: cognition, evaluation, motivation, and feeling (Ben Ze'ev, 2000). This view of emotion fits quite well with the EI construct. Under this view, EI may be conceptualized as the interplay between emotions and intellectual thoughts. The abilities to perceive, understand, manage, and use emotions will involve all the basic components of cognition, evaluation, motivation and feeling. In this regard, it is very likely that individual will differ in their intellectual abilities to process the emotion-relevant information.

Another often raised question about the validity of EI construct is whether it is, in fact, a personality trait, especially when it is measured by self-reported questionnaires. Davies, Stankov, and Roberts, (1998) concluded EI as an "illusive" construct because they found that EI had salient loadings on well-established Big Five personality factors. As EI involves individuals' abilities to deal with emotions, high or low-EI people may show some certain attitudinal and behavioral patterns that appear similar to some individual traits. For example, people with high ability to understand emotions may appear to be more agreeable. Therefore it is reasonable that there is moderate correlation between the two. However, EI and personality are essentially of different domains. While EI is one form of human abilities, personalities are stable individual differences that cannot be classified as ability or intelligence. As an ability facet, it is always preferable to have higher EI. However, one cannot say that it is always preferable to have stronger personality of any type. Researchers have demonstrated the discriminant validity between EI and personality through rigorous studies. For example, Wong and Law (2002) developed an EI measure based on the four-dimensional definition of EI, and demonstrated through several samples that it is reasonably distinct from the Big Five personality factors. Those authors also pointed out that the reason that Davies et al. (1998) did not find discriminant validity of EI with personality traits was that they used a group of "EI-related measures" to test their argument, none of which are based on the ability definition of EI (Wong and Law, 2002; Law, Wong, and Song, 2004). Mayer et al. (2004) also found reasonably low correlations between EI (using MEIS and MSCEIT) and the Big Five personality traits, using large samples of respondents. Another evidence for the difference between EI and personality is that EI as a set of abilities can be improved through training for working people (Murray and Jordan, 2004), while personality traits are relatively more stable in adults.

Finally, there are several constructs in the literature that are similar to EI, such as social intelligence and interpersonal skills. "Social intelligence", as first identified by Thorndike in 1920, refers to "the ability to understand and manage men and women, boys and girls – to act wisely in human relations." The first definition of EI that Salovey and Mayer (1990) proposed is a "subset" of social intelligence. In the later definitions given by these scholars (Mayer and Salovey, 1997; Mayer et al., 2000a), it is clearer that EI has a broader domain in that it not only involves one's ability to deal with others, but also perceiving and understanding emotions in oneself and using it to facilitate performance. Moreover, EI is more focused on emotional aspects than social intelligence. Similarly, EI is different from other seemingly close constructs such as interpersonal skills, social skills, or influencing techniques. Those concepts all involves abilities to deal with interpersonal relationships. While we expect that people need EI to build and maintain good relationships with others, EI covers a broader domain in that it includes dimensions that deal with oneself besides others. Its particular focus on emotions should also make it distinguishable from these concepts. Empirical evidence is still needed to show the discriminant validity of EI with these constructs.

We discussed the discriminant validity of EI, in the next, we focus on its predictive validity. To date, researchers have found considerable evidence on the predictive validity of EI. This is one of the most encouraging parts of EI research. While debate continues, various models supporting the relationship between EI and a variety of outcomes across disciplines are rapidly growing in the literature. For instance, researchers have demonstrated a positive relationship between EI and various personal outcomes, such as life satisfaction and feeling of powerlessness. There was also increasing evidence that EI is associated with important organizational outcomes, such as employee attitudes, behaviors, and performances. For example, in a series of studies, Wong, Law and their collaborators found significant impact of EI on life satisfaction (with an average correlation around.40), job satisfaction (average correlation around.40), and job performance (average correlation around.20) (cf. e.g., Law et al., 2004; Wong and Law, 2002; Wong et al., 2004, 2005). Dasborough (2004) found that follower's EI moderates the relationship between follower attributions of manipulative leader intentionality and follower emotional responses. Researchers have also proposed that EI facilitates individual adaptation to organizational change (Huy, 1999), and EI moderates the relationship between job insecurity and employee emotional and behavioral reactions (Jordan et al., 2002). All of the studies reviewed above adopted Mayer and Salovey's (1997) definition of EI, which provide some evidence for the utility of the ability based model of EI.

Up till now, although we have some findings on the predictive validity of EI, there are still not many studies on the outcomes of EI, especially outcomes in work settings. Moreover, all the previous studies focus on simple correlational relationships between EI and other constructs. For further development of the field, researchers can start developing theoretical models of EI, for example, a nomological network of EI. An obvious gap in the literature is that we know little about the antecedents of EI. Researchers in developmental psychology have studied the origin and development of human emotions and intelligence, which may help us in this direction. We will return to this point in the later part.

A final comment that we want to make on the EI construct validation issue is that, it is unconstructive to suggest that exploration of the utility of EI should only be carried out after its construct validity issues are all solved, as some scholars have implied (see, e.g., Matthew et al., 2002). Let us use the debate on whether EI meet the standards for an "intelligence" as an example. We definitely see this as part of the healthy development of a new construct and agree that it is important to further examine the nature of EI. However, we also believe that one may not need a final full consensus on the definition of EI before scientific investigations on EI can be conducted. Scientific research is advancing everyday. Scholars would continue to change or enrich the definition of existing constructs by bringing in new perspectives. For example, the literature of organizational justice started with a simple definition which consisted only of distributive justice. The construct of organizational justice is, however, expanded into a widely accepted multidimensional view of distributive, procedural, interactive and interactional justice. Similarly, scholars studying leader-member-exchange (LMX) started with a heated debate of whether LMX should be a unidimensional construct. After a general consensus that LMX should be unidimensional, Liden and Maslyn (1998) restated the multidimensional view of LMX with valid supports for its possible multidimensional nature. Based on this earlier evidence of evolution of constructs, we suggest that only focusing on the debate of the definition of the construct may not help the advances of the field of EI.

Measurement: EI Tests Versus Self-Report Scales

Debates in EI research have heavily centered on the measurement problems of EI. Compared with the converging sense on the definition of EI, there is little consensus on its measurement methods (Salovey, Woolery, and Mayer, 2001). In fact, debate on EI in the literature is often caused by the lack of an established EI measure. As Mayer et al. (2000b) noted, the development of theoretical models of EI has been paralleled by the development of tests to measure the concept.

There are two types of EI measures: EI tests and self-report scales. EI tests, which are performance-based measures, akin to the traditional intelligence tests, examine the participants' abilities to deal with emotions. Self-report measures ask participants to evaluate themselves on emotion related descriptive statements. So far, the most prominent EI tests are the scales developed by Mayer, Salovey and their colleagues, i.e. MSCEIT and its predecessors such as MEIS (Mayer et al., 2000b). Compared with tests of EI, researchers have developed more self-report scales, for example, Bar-On's (1997) EQ-i, Trait Meta-Mood Scale (TMM; Salovey et al., 1995), and WLEIS (Wong and Law, 2002) (See Salovey, Woolery and Mayer, 2001, for an extensive review on available measures).

Because the ability view of EI is now generally acknowledged, direct and objective test is arguably more suitable than self-evaluation measures. Nevertheless, EI tests also have their limitations. The first challenge is the scoring problem. That is, whether there are "correct" answers to emotional problems and how to define these correct answers. For EI tests to be considered true tests of intelligence, they must have answers that can be evaluated as more or less correct (Mayer, et al., 2004). Mayer and his collaborators (2000b) argued that there are evolutionary and cultural foundations for the existence of right answers. These scholars proposed three alternatives as the scoring criterion: *expert criterion* that uses emotions experts' evaluation as the correct answer, *consensus criterion* that uses the consensus response of a group of unselected test-takers as correct answer, and *target criterion* that uses the target person's (i.e., the real person who is in the scenario or pictures of the test questions) description of his/her "real" emotion as the correct answer to evaluate participants' answers. The first two methods have been employed more often. Mayer et al. found positive correlations among the three criteria and group consensus criterion was found to be the single best criterion (Mayer et al., 2000b). Roberts et al. (2001), however, have challenged their conclusion. Using MEIS, these authors found contrary findings for expert and consensus scoring protocols. In a recent response to this issue of the validity of the scoring criteria, Mayer et al. (Mayer, Salovey, Caruso, and Sitarenios, 2003) further hypothesized that some aggregation of experts will provide reliable identification of answers that more closely converges to the general consensus. Using more (twenty-one) emotions experts (scholars and researchers drawn from volunteer members of the International Society for Research on Emotions) they demonstrated that these experts endorsed many of the same answers, and exhibited superior agreement, particularly when research provides clearer answers to the test questions (e.g., emotional perception in faces). Unfortunately, we have no information about the EI level of these "emotions experts" and do not have strong evidence of the validity of these highly reliable (in an inter-rater reliability sense) answers.

Another problem of EI tests is related to its cross-culture validity. As EI are studied across cultural boundaries, scholars begin to question the cross-cultural validity of existing EI models and tests, and the predictive validity of EI. These are valid and important questions.

Intelligence involves the adaptation of human to certain environment. It cannot be fully or even meaningfully understood outside its cultural context (Sternberg, 2004). As cultural norms influence the meaning of emotion-relevant information, it is necessary to take culture into understanding when it concerns the ability to understand emotion and to use emotion to facilitate performance. Moreover, because most of the existing EI instruments are developed in Western countries, the content of these EI tests is based on the Western culture. As a result, there may be some problems when we generalize existing findings of the validity of these EI tests to other cultural contexts. For example, as Gohm (2004) pointed out, persons in a culture with low norms for expressiveness, for instance, may rate a particular happy face as happier than persons from a very expressive culture. The author suggested that experts native to the culture and consensus scoring involving cultural natives would be needed if the norms in a particular culture differ greatly from Western norms. Law, Wong, & Song (2004) also argued that norm-referenced scoring criteria may suffer problems in cross-cultural settings. They gave an example in which a non-reactive quiet response by a subordinate to his/her boss who made unreasonable demands may be seen as "smart" among Chinese but probably not among westerners. Those authors also compared the self-report EI measure WLEIS with MSCEIT and found that the former has higher criterion validity with their participants.

In addition to the validation problem, these cross-culture issues may also raise interesting research questions that may add to our understanding of the EI construct. For instance, Gohm (2004: 224) has proposed that perhaps, people who are less outward expression, such as in Asian countries, may be more sensitive to tiny emotional expressions, especially when the culture norm is to be sensitive to how others think, and be faster in developing emotion management skills.

Despite the many drawbacks related with self-report EI measures (such as its subjectivity to social desirability, participants' lack of knowledge to make correct self-evaluation etc.), such instruments may have some apparent advantages. First, they suffers less from the problems associated with tests of EI, such as scoring methods, cross-cultural validity, and possible assessment clues (Law, Wong, & Song, 2004). Second, some of the measures are practically shorter which is especially valuable in some conditions such as the survey study in organizational research. Third, one valid measure that might compensate for the possible biases in self-reporting is to use relevant informants' rating of the focal person's EI. For example, Law et al..demonstrated that other's rating (such as parents and close friends) of EI show satisfactory convergent and criterion validity (Law, Wong, & Song, 2004).

VI. FUTURE DEVELOPMENT

After Mayer and Salovey's (1997) introduction of the construct, EI is still at its early stage of development. In view of the problems and issues discussed above, we suggest three major developmental directions for EI research. First, it is important that we come up with a generally accepted definition of the domain coverage of the EI construct. We also need to have a well-validated measure of EI, preferably a culture-free EI test. Moreover, efforts in developing nomological networks of EI and ultimately a theory of EI are needed. We elaborate these issues in this section.

Firstly, we suggest that EI researchers continue to examine the construct validity of EI. It is encouraging that scholars have almost arrived at a common definition of EI. The four-dimensional EI definition by Mayer and Salovey (1997) is well-received by the academic world. In the future, to validate the EI construct, researchers could base their studies on this definition. Within this domain, to better understand the nature of EI, it is important that the neuropsychological basis of EI can be established. We need more concrete evidence that human abilities to perceive, understand, manage and use emotion is a cognitive process and there are individual differences in their cognitive abilities to process emotion-relevant information.

Secondly, for the development of EI measures which is currently crucial for its construct validation, there are two important directions to go. The validity and reliability of MSCEIT need to be further investigated. Researcher need to study the validity of each scoring methods and their convergent validity, and test the generalizability of EI model and its predictive validity in cross-cultural settings. On the other hand, new tests are needed so that possible problems associated with extant tools may be identified and new evidence for the construct validity may be found. Some initial efforts have already appeared in the literature. For instance, Wong, Law and Wong (2004) have developed a force-choice EI measure—the Wong's Emotional Intelligence Scale (WEIS). The scale has two parts, the second of which has twenty questions that ask participants how they would do in the hypothesized emotion-related situations.

We have two more suggestions on dealing with the problems currently associated with EI tests. First, as one way to solve the cross-cultural generalizability problem, researchers could try to get cross-cultural norm data. Next, one possible means to get "correct answer" to EI tests is to use criterion validity. That is, to use the scoring method with which EI tests get the highest predictive validity on a criterion variable. To do this, we need a theory of EI that could guide us to decide a reasonable criterion variable. For example, if life satisfaction is proved to be such a criterion variable, we can use the answers that predict life satisfaction best as the "correct" answers to the EI test.

Thirdly, EI is a topic that transcends disciplines and fields. Scholars in different areas can explore the utility of EI more broadly. Those explorations help to build the nomological networks of EI which in turn can be the theoretical guidance for our further exploration. Based on the ability based model of EI, we can expect that EI might have impact on three groups of outcome variables: attitudinal, behavioral, and performance outcomes. For instance, as has been studied in the literature (e.g., Wong and Law, 2002), EI should have impact on individual's life satisfaction and feeling of powerlessness. This is because a person with high EI is able to understand his/her own and others' emotions, and draw upon these understandings to facilitate his/her behaviors and attitudes to get positive results. Therefore, s/he is generally easier to be happier in his/her life and has less time of depression or feelings of powerlessness on his/her own life. As another example, EI should also have predictive power on leadership effectiveness, because good leadership obviously involves perceiving and understanding subordinates' emotions correctly. Up till now, studies in the educational, social, clinical, and industrial/organizational psychology literature have provided preliminary but encouraging evidence, including attitudinal outcomes such as life satisfaction, feeling of powerlessness, and job satisfaction, behavior and performance outcomes such as social deviant behavior (Trinidad et al., 2004; Brackett, Mayer, and Warner, 2004), stress coping, academic performance (e.g., Lam and Kirby, 2002; Brackett and Mayer, 2003), job performance and leader effectiveness (Wong and Law, 2002, Law et al, 2004). Despite those findings, before we could make any conclusion such as what percent of major life outcomes is determined by EI, or EI predicts more than traditional intelligence, etc. as in popular press, much more empirical studies need to be done and theoretical supports need to be built and refined.

Fourthly, as the popularity of EI grows in the business world, more and more companies are using intervention programs in order to increase employees' EI levels (Cherniss and Adler, 2000; Murray and Jordan, 2004). However, the validity of such investment has yet to be proved. It is the responsibility of researchers to examine such fundamental questions as whether EI is innate, how much it is developed at different life stages and how stable it is (within person variance). If EI can be trained, then what are the effective training methods in organizations? Researchers can be enlightened by theories and findings in several relevant areas, such as developmental psychology, social psychology, and human emotion. This should not be an easy job but the efforts will surely benefit the field not only by providing guidance to practitioners, but also increasing our understanding of the nature and development of EI. Training, in fact, can be one way to prove the existence and value of EI. We can, for instance, conduct experimental studies that randomly assign trainees to an EI training group or to a control group perhaps of equal time training verbal or math intelligence. The participants can then be evaluated with relevant outcome measures. Within subject design can also be employed, with less between-subject random errors but possible influences between the EI training and traditional intelligence training programs. Through this type of experimental methods, we can find effective ways to improve EI on the one hand, and on the other hand, provide evidence for the existence of EI as a set of abilities. To design valid training programs, one can first come up with a set of behavior predictions and then use these behavior changes as the target and criteria in training programs. Once again, the role of theory needs to be emphasized—the intervention programs should be designed around a clear, theoretically sound model of EI, rather than resorting to preexisting commercially available programs that are not based on scientific research.

Finally, there are several other research questions that we see as interesting directions to explore. These questions include, (1) do people have different ability levels on dealing with different types of emotions? In other words, is it possible that people are more emotionally intelligent at, for example sadness and depression then they are at ecstasy and anxiety? There is evidence in psychology that there may be different mechanisms underlying different emotions and various affective states influences people in different ways (e.g., Raghunathan and Pham, 1999). Scholars have already raised some concerns on this question. For instance, Zeidner et al. (2004) raised question about whether any model of EI generalizes across the universe of basic emotions, given evidence differentiating discrete, universal basic emotions. They suggested that "it is too early to dismiss the possibility of the existence of multiple EIs underlying emotions." We suggest that researchers identify and study some core emotions such as sadness, anxiety, and anger that might affect important personal outcomes. It is expected that, if the ability based EI model holds, individual's abilities (perception, facilitation, understanding, and managing) in dealing with those emotions are correlated and there exists an underlying higher-level overall factor that can be called EI. (2) Should EI be studied on its dimension level or at the construct level? Mayer et al. (2004) have proposed that the four-branch ability based model of EI has a hierarchy, and each branch has different ability focuses. Studies using this model have found some evidence that the four dimensions show diverse relationships with the cognitive intelligence, personality, and outcomes. However, as EI is defined as a latent construct under the four dimensions, the risk of doing so is that it may invalidate EI as a whole construct, according to the argument that hypothesis for multidimensional construct should be tested at the construct level (Law, Wong, and Mobley, 1998). At this exploration stage of EI research, studying the dimensions together with the overall construct may benefit the field, which provides more evidence for the nature and dimensionality of the EI construct. (3) As a set of emotional abilities, EI may be an important moderator to some of the established or unestablished relationships in the literature. For example, Jordan et al. (2002) proposed a model in which EI moderates employees' emotional reactions to job insecurity and their ability to cope with associated stress. Researchers in different areas can explore these issues more deeply and extensively.

VII. CONCLUSION

For the years 2000 to 2005, there were 524 journal articles that have *emotional intelligence* in its title in a search of the PsychInfo database, and 324 master and doctoral dissertations in the dissertations and thesis abstract search in the ProQuest database. The rapid development of EI research during the past one and a half decades is indeed an impressive phenomenon in the literature. The encouraging evidence and challenging debates in the field enable and necessitate a critical review of this stream of research. The purpose of this chapter is to provide a comprehensive review of the EI research so that readers can have a broad picture of the field and to suggest future directions for the field to develop.

Based on our review, we conclude that the EI construct as defined by the ability based model has shown great potential validity and utility for academic research, but evidence is still required to establish it as a valid new construct. We are at an early stage of this area. We believe it is important to balance studies that check its validity to survive and studies that fasten its moving forward. For the currently heated debates in the literature, we also believe that unless there is concrete evidence for disproving the validity of the EI construct, researchers should move beyond the repeated debates. For future development of the field, we suggest that researchers continue to examine the construct validity of EI, to improve the measurement tools, to do more deep and extensive examination on the outcomes and antecedents of EI, and to ultimately build a theory of EI that could guide the field to move forward.

REFERENCES

Averill, J. R. (2004). A tale of two snarks: Emotional Intelligence and emotional creativity compared. *Psychological Inquiry, 15*, 228-233.

Bar-On, R. (1997). *Bar-On emotional quotient inventory: A measure of emotional intelligence.* Toronto: Multi-Health Systems Inc.

Bar-On, R. (2000). Emotional and social intelligence: Insights from the Emotional Quotient Inventory (EQ-i). In R. Bar-On and J. D. A. Parker (Eds.), *Handbook of emotional intelligence.* San Francisco: Jossey-Bass.

Ben Ze'ev, A. (2000). *The subtlety of emotions*. Cambridge: MIT Press.

Brackett, M., and Mayer, J. D. (2003). Convergent, discriminant, and incremental validity of competing measures of emotional intelligence. *Personality and Social Psychology Bulletin, 29*, 1147-1158.

Brackett, M., Mayer, J. D., and Warner, R. M. (2003). Emotional intellience and the prediction of behavior. *Personality and individual differences, 36*, 1387-1042.

Carroll, J. B. (1993). *Human cognitive abilities: A survey of factor analytic studies*. New York: Cambridge University Press.

Cherniss, C., and Adler, M. (2000). *Promoting emotional intelligence in organizations: Make training in emotional intelligence effective*. Alexandria, VA: ASTD.

Ciarrochi, J.V., Chan, A.Y.C., Caputi, P. (2000). A critical evaluation of the emotional intelligence construct. *Personality and Individual Differences, 28*, 539-561.

Dasborough, M. T. (2004). *Follower emotional responses to leadership: The moderating role of emotional intelligence*. Paper presented at the annual meeting of the Academy of Management, New Orleans. LA.

Davies, M., Stankov, L., and Roberts, R. D. (1998). Emotional intelligence: In search of an elusive construct. *Journal of Personality and Social Psychology, 75*, 989-1015.

Ekman, P. and Davidson, R. J. (Eds.) (1994). *The Nature of Emotion: Fundamental Questions*. New York : Oxford University Press.

Gardner, H. (1993). *Multiple intelligences: The theory in practice*. New York: Basic Books.

Gohm, C. L. (2004). Moving forward with emotional intelligence. *Psychological Inquiry, 15*, 222-227.

Goleman, D. (1995). *Emotional intelligence*. NY: Bantam Books.

Goleman, D. (1998a). *Working with emotional intelligence*. New York: Bantam Books.

Goleman, D. (1998b). What makes a leader? *Harvard Business Review, 76*, 92-102.

Goleman, D. (2004). What makes a leader? *Harvard Business Review, 82*, 82-90.

Huy, Q. N. (1999). Emotional capability, emotional intelligence, and radical change *The Academy of Management Review, 24*, 325-345.

Jordan, P. J., Ashkanasy, N. M., and Härtel, C. E. (2002). Emotional intelligence as a moderator of emotional and behavioral reactions to job insecurity. *Academy of Management Review, 27*, 361-372.

Jordan, P. J., Ashkanasy, N. M., and Härtel, C. E. (2003). The case of emotional intelligence in organizational research. *Academy of Management Review, 28*, 195-197.

Lam, L. T., and Kirby, S. L. (2002). Is emotional intelligence an advantage? An exploration of the impact of emotional and general intelligence on individual performance. *The Journal of Social Psychology, 142*(1), 133-143.

Law, K.S., Wong, C.S., Huang, G., and Li, X. (2004). *Beyond general mental abilities: The incremental validity of emotional intelligence on job performance*. Paper presented at the annual meeting of the Academy of Management, New Orleans. LA.

Law, K.S., Wong, C.S., and Mobley, W. H. (1998). Toward a taxonomy of multidimensional constructs. *Academy of Management Review, 23*, 741-755.

Law, K.S., Wong, C.S., and Song, L. (2004). The construct and criterion validity of emotional intelligence and its potential utility for management studies. *Journal of Applied Psychology. 89*(3), 483-496.

Liden, R. C., and Maslyn, J. M. 1998. Multi-dimensionality of leader-member exchange: An empirical assessment through scale development. *Journal of Management*, 24: 43-72.

Matthews, G., Roberts, R. D., and Zeidner, M. (2004). Seven myths about emotional intelligence. *Psychological Inquiry, 15*, 179-196.

Matthews, G., Zeidner, M., and Roberts, R. D. (2002). *Emotional intelligence : science and myth.* Cambridge, Mass.: MIT Press.

Mayer, J. D., Caruso, D. R., and Salovey, P. (2000a). Emotional intelligence meets traditional standards for an intelligence. *Intelligence, 27*(4), 267-298.

Mayer, J. D., Caruso, D. R., and Salovey, P. (2000b). Selecting a measure of emotional intelligence: The case for ability testing. In R. Bar-On and J. D. A. Parker (Eds.). *Handbook of emotional intelligence,* (pp. 320-342). New York: Jossey-Bass.

Mayer, J. D., Dipaolo, M. T., and Salovey, P. (1990). Perceiving affective content in ambiguous visual stimuli: A component of emotional intelligence. *Journal of Personality Assessment, 54,* 772-781.

Mayer, J. D., and Salovey, P. (1997). What is emotional intelligence? In P. Salovey and D. J. Sluyter (Eds.). *Emotional development and emotional intelligence: Educational implications,* 3-31.

Mayer, J. D., Salovey, P., and Caruso, D. R. (1999). Models of emotional intelligence. In R. J. Sternberg (Ed.), *Handbook of Intelligence,* (pp. 396-420). Cambridge, England: Cambridge University Press.

Mayer, J. D., Salovey, P., and Caruso, D. R. (2002). *Mayer-Salovey-Caruso Emotional Intelligence Test (MSCEIT) User's Manual.* Toronto, Canada: MHS Publishers.

Mayer, J. D., Salovey, P., and Caruso, D. R. (2004). Emotional intelligence: Theory, findings, and implications. *Psychological Inquiry, 15*, 197-215.

Mayer, J. D., Salovey, P., Caruso, D. R., and Sitarenios, G. (2001). Emotional intelligence as a standard intelligence. *Emotion, 1*, 232-242.

Mayer, J. D., Salovey, P., Caruso, D. R., and Sitarenios, G. (2003). Measuring emotional intelligence with the MSCEIT V2.0. *Emotion, 3*, 97-105.

Montemayor, E. F., and Spee, J. (2004). The dimensions of emotional intelligence construct validation using manger and self-ratings. *Best conference paper at the Academy of Management, New Orleans, LA.*

Murray, J., and Jordan, P. J. (2004). Emotional intelligence, work skill and training. *Paper presented at the annual meeting of Academy of Management, New Orleans, LA.*

Organ, D. W., and Ryan, K. (1995). A meta-review of attitudinal and dispositional predictors of organizational citizenship behavior. *Personnel Psychology. 48,* 775-782.

Raghunathan, R., and Pham, M. T. (1999). All negative moods are not equal: Motivational influences of anxiety and sadness on decision making. *Organizational Behavior and Human Decision Process, 79,* 56-77.

Roberts, R. D., Zeidner, M., and Matthews, G. (2001). Does emotional intelligence meet traditional standards for an intelligence? Some new data and conclusions. *Emotion, 1,* 196-231.

Salovey, P., and Mayer, J. D. (1990). Emotional intelligence. *Imagination, Cognition and Personality, 9*(3), 185-211.

Salovey, P., Mayer, J. D., Goldman, S. L., Turvey, C., and Palfai, T. 1995. Emotional attention, clarity and repair: exploring emotional intelligence using the Trait Meta-Mood Scale. In J. W. Pennebacker (Eds.). *Emotion, disclosure, and health.* Washington, D. C.: American Psychological Association.

Salovey, P., Woolery, A., and Mayer, J. D. (2001). Emotional intelligence: Conceptualization and measurement. In G. J. O. Fletcher and M. S. Clark (Eds.). *Blackwell handbook of social psychology: Interpersonal processes.* Malden, MA: Blackwell Publishers.

Schriesheim, C. A., Castro, S. L., and Cogliser, C. C. (1999). Leader-member exchange (LMX) research: A comprehensive review of theory, measurement, and data-analytic practices. *Leadership Quarterly, 10,* 63-113.

Sternberg, R. J. (1996). *Successful Intelligence.* New York: Simon Schuster.

Sternberg, R. J. (1998). Human abilities. *Annual Review of Psychology, 49,* 479-502.

Sternberg, R. J. (1999). Working with Emotional Intelligence. Book review. *Personnel Psychology, 52,* 780-783.

Sternberg, R. J. (2004). Culture and intelligence. *American Psychologist, 59,* 325-338.

Thorndike, E.L. (1920). Intelligence and its uses. *Harper's Magazine, 140,* 227-235.

Trinidad, D. R., Unger, J. B., Chou, C.-P., and Johnson, C. A. (2004). The protective association between emotional intelligence with psychosocial smoking risk factors for adolescents. *Personality and individual differences, 36,* 945-954.

Wong, C.S., and Law, K.S. (2002). The effects of leader and follower emotional intelligence on performance and attitude: An exploratory study. *The Leadership Quarterly, 13,* 243-274.

Wong, C.S., Law, K.S., and Wong, P.M. (2004). Development and validation of a forced choice emotional intelligence for Chinese respondents in Hong Kong. *Asia Pacific Journal of Management, 21*(4), 535-559.

Wong, C.S., Wong, P.M., and Law, K.S. (2005). The interaction effect of emotional intelligence and emotional labor on job satisfaction: A test of Holland's classification of occupations (pp. 235-250). In Härtel, C. E. J., Zerbe, W. J. and Ashkanasy, N. M. (Eds.). *Emotions in Organizational Behavior.* Mahwah, NJ: Lawrence Erlbaum Associates, Inc.

Zeidner, M., Roberts, R. D., and Matthews, G. (2004). The emotional intelligence bandwagon: Too fast to live, too young to die? *Psychological Inquiry, 15,* 239-248.

In: Intelligence : New Research
Editor: Lin V. Wesley, pp. 115-132

ISBN 1-59454-637-1
© 2006 Nova Science Publishers, Inc.

Chapter 6

THE APPEARANCE OF INTELLIGENCE IN MUSIC: CONNECTIONS AND DISTINCTIONS BETWEEN THE CONCEPTS OF MUSICAL AND GENERAL INTELLIGENCE-A REVIEW

Wilfried Gruhn
University of Music Freiburg, Germany

ABSTRACT

This article reviews the basic neuro-anatomic foundations and psychological concepts of intelligence, aptitude, talent and giftedness and their relevance to music. There are several academic traditions with different approaches which are based upon various scientific paradigms. Starting with a brief survey of the historical contribution of differential psychology and the European tradition of investigating musicality, different concepts of intelligence from the g-factor paradigm (Charles Spearman) up to the theory of multiple intelligences (Howard Gardner) are reviewed. The neural correlates of intelligence introduce into the discussion to what extent (if ever) music abilities and general cognitive competences interact. For this, the debate on the Mozart effect is critically viewed. From a meta-analysis it can be stated that although a moderate positive correlation between studying the music and academic achievement is observed, there is no empirical evidence to suggest a causal relation between music and verbal or math advancement. In the last section a hierarchical structure of the different aspects of intelligence and how they relate to and possibly interfere with music is outlined. An integrated model of general intelligence and music achievement is finally elaborated.

INTRODUCTION

It is not just in recent times that musicality or music aptitude has attracted psychologists and music educators. It is one of the prominent human faculties which is surrounded by mysticism because of the belief in ingenious traits attributed to it. Nowadays, new technologies of brain research have opened new possibilities to investigate the neuronal conditions for creative behavior and musical information processing. But even since the beginning of differential psychological research, music aptitude has been investigated as a special manifestation of human potential which was partly seen as a talent or some kind of intelligence, and partly as a mysterious gift for very few exceptional individuals. From there, the debate on the impact of nature (genetic inheritance) or nurture (environmental support) has arisen.

Our question is whether musicality in its broadest sense and common use of the term can be seen as a particular domain of intelligence or whether it represents a very special and unique personal characteristic which is separated from and probably opposite to intelligence because musical abilities are related to the body, soul, and emotions whereas intelligence is mainly associated with a cognitive attitude. If musicality is one of many thinkable and reasonable manifestations of intelligence it should be defined and analyzed by means of intelligence research; however, if it is seen as an artistic and aesthetic behavior, then musicality or music aptitude is evaluated as an attitude equivalent to, but different from general intelligence and not as a part of intelligence. In this case, the understanding of musical behavior seems to be opposed to rationality. But the antinomy of rational and irrational ways of thinking present only a pretended contradiction and cause more confusion about the essence of musicality than brings a clearance into the discussion.

For music educators, the understanding of musicality (musical talent, aptitude, giftedness) and its foundations and conditions is vital. Educators should develop and support the given potential, but for this they need to know about the characteristics of individual traits, and how to detect, enhance, measure, and evaluate them. In this chapter, the commonalities, differences, and overlapping ideas of the concepts of musical talent, aptitude, giftedness, intelligence, and musicality will be elaborated in a historical context and will be systematically explicated.

HISTORY OF APTITUDE RESEARCH

In Europe, the first academic reflection on musicality was undertaken by the physician Theodor Billroth (1829 – 1894) who became a Professor of Surgery and Pathological Anatomy in Zurich, an enthusiastic amateur musician and composer, and a life long personal friend of Johannes Brahms. Toward the end of his life he devoted much of his time apart from his academic obligations to put down some "aphorisms on the anatomy and psycho-physiology of musicality". This was the first time that the phenomenon of musicality was addressed by a scientist. Of course, Billroth did not empirically investigate this human potential, rather he speculated more philosophically and psychologically on this issue; therefore he called his sketches "aphorisms". He died before he could finish it; his close friend, the Viennese critic Eduard Hanslick first published the sketches in 1895 adopting the title of the last unfinished chapter "Who is musical?" (Billroth, 1896).

Billroth is a representative of the late 19th century. He refers musicality only to western art music which belongs to the culture of the traditionally educated society. He systematically describes typical attitudes and behaviors of musical amateurs and experts in much detail. But he also differentiates abilities that are innate (*veranlagt*) from those that are developed by education (*gebildet*). This can already be seen as a preparation for the future distinction between aptitude (given potential) and achievement (developed by environmental interaction). In emphasizing both aspects he looks rather modern in terms of developmental psychology. Furthermore, he connects the ability of differentiated sensorial perception with the sensitivity for aesthetic qualities which have to be learned. Finally, he is the first who relates all musical cognitions and affections to cortical and subcortical functions of the brain. In analogy to language, he states that the content of a verbal concept can be referred to the cortex whereas the sound qualities of the verbal pronounciation express emotions which are processed by subcortical functions. He believed that the more intellectual notions appear, the more mechanisms for the processing of sensations are inhibited. However, both the linguistic and the musical perception are based on memory by which the transitory elements of music and language can be connected in the mind and create reasonable expectations.

Thirty years after Billroth, another German physician Johannes von Kries (1853 – 1928), Professor of Physiology at the University of Freiburg, published another essay with the same title as Billroth "Who is musical?" (Kries, 1926). His interest was concerned with the phenomenology of musical individuals by describing the many facets of musicality. Regarding different types of musicality he distinguishes between a productive and a receptive musicality as one dimension, and separates intellectual from aesthetic-emotional musicality on the other dimension. Factors that determine the quality of musical behaviors and activities are referred to the sense of rhythm, to the sensorial differentiation of the ear, to memory, emotional sensitivity, and productivity (creativity).

Interestingly, it is obvious that at the beginning of phenomenological investigations and psychological reflections on musicality we find neither educators nor musicologists nor psychologists, but physicians who were the first authors with particular interest in developing a general concept of musicality. But since then, a series of experiments designed by psychologists and educators has been performed to collect empirical psychometric data for different types of music aptitude or talent and to measure distinct and independent musical skills involved in musical practice.

Géza Révész (1878 – 1955) developed a non-standardized, individual test which measured the sense of rhythm, the absolute and relative pitch identification, the analysis of intervals and chords, the vocal reproduction of tunes, and the play by ear (Révész, 1920). In continuation of Révész's attempt to check musicality, Maria van Briessen was interested in identifying criteria for the existence or absence of musicality in humans. For this, she designed a test battery with the sections of melodic perception and memory, rhythmic and harmonic perception, interval memory, and the sense for consonance and dissonance (Briessen, 1929). Finally, Martha Vidor performed an empirical experiment in her laboratory and developed the chronograph (see Figure. 1) to objectively measure the accuracy of rhythmic performance (Vidor, 1931).

Although all of these psychologists did not develop a clear concept of musicality, they agreed upon the differentiation between cognitive and sensorial abilities. But they had never thought of musicality or explicitly described this phenomenon in terms of intelligence. They coincided in the atomistic view of musicality as a compound ability that comprises several distinct and probably independent skills. Furthermore, there was no clear distinction between the terms of "musikalische Begabung" (music aptitude) and "Musikalität" (musicality) which were mostly used synonymously.

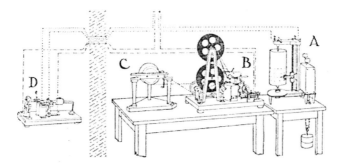

Figure 1. Martha Vidor's experimental apparatus (chronograph) to measure rhythmic accuracy (from: Vidor 1931, p. 5)

Different from the perceptive approach to musicality was another attempt by the psychologist Albert Wellek (1904 – 1972) whose research was originally focused on perfect pitch (*absolutes Gehör*) (Wellek, 1927). From the observation of characteristic mistakes during interval identification he found that musicians tend to orientate their aural imagery on the two components of pitch: a linear progression of height (tone frequency) and a cyclic progression of tone quality that marks a c^1 and c^2 and c^3 with a quality (*Tonigkeit*) which stays the same throughout all octaves. Therefore, he distinguished between a *linear* type of perception which recognizes half steps as most similar, and a *cyclic* or *polar* type of perception which finds half steps extremely different because the cyclic dimension of fifths and octaves is realized as most similar (Wellek, 1938). This typology was first investigated for perception, but was then applied to the entire creative process (*Schaffensprozess*) (Wellek, 1939). Wellek who collected his data from a large field study, exemplified a typology on European composers and demonstrated that Wagner and Bruckner represent the polar type of composer whose thinking is more holistic and integrated, whereas composers like Sweelinck or J. S. Bach represent the linear type of composing which is analytic and disintegrated. By this, Wellek framed a general concept of psychic functions and its appearance in humans' lives. In this concept, music aptitude was seen as a co-variable of basic psychic functions (*psychische Grundfunktionen*). Although he defined the musical potential as an independent gift which always appears in musical activities, his concept of music aptitude was definitely embedded into more general psychic functions. By this, he put music abilities far apart from cognitive functions.

At the same time, we find Carl Seashore (1868 – 1949) in the United States at the University of Iowa, who worked as a pioneer in experimental psychology and developed several tests to measure independent skills in aural and visual perception. His *Measures of Musical Talent* (Seashore, 1919) included six subtests of pitch, loudness, rhythm, time (duration), timbre, and tonal memory. As many others, he understood musical talent (aptitude, musicality) as a bunch of special skills that could be observed and measured independently. In his theory of specifics, Seashore assumed physiological and cognitive limits within the development and the maturation of musical skills. He took the physiological threshold as an innate limitation whereas the cognitive development was seen as a result of environmental factors. By this, he was not far from an understanding of musical talent similar to a general concept of intelligence based on the same two factors.

Seashores' concept was further developed in the US and the UK by many psychologists who continued to create empirical instruments to measure human behavior (Bentley, 1966; Drake, 1954; Gordon, 1965; Kwalwasser and Dykema, 1930; Wing, 1939). Here, the main differences refer to an understanding of the tests as aptitude or achievement tests. Most of them claimed to measure aptitude (or talent which is used synonymously), but only Herbert Wing thought of music aptitude as a form of musical intelligence (Wing, 1939). Evidence from factor analytical studies had taught him that general intelligence functions buildwas an essential component of music aptitude. Therefore, he believed in music aptitude as a complex and general attribute that cannot be divided into separable parts. This was called "omnibus theory" to contrast Seashore's "atomistic theory". Here, we find a direct relation between both concepts: music aptitude and intelligence.

CONCEPTS OF INTELLIGENCE

If one thinks and talks of intelligence one normally refers to higher functions of cognitive processing. A person shows some evidence of intelligence if she or he has a profound and broad knowledge, evaluates situations based on rational reasoning, creates practical solutions for new problems, develops innovative ideas in special domains, and recognizes causal links between facts and ideas very quickly and precisely. If this observation from everyday life is correct, then intelligence could be defined in terms of cognitive brain functions, creative strategies, and processing speed. New connectionist models and chronometric approaches have uncovered remarkable mental differences in time and effort spent on decision making (Fiske, 2004). All of these functions are not domain specific, but refer to a general potential which is founded in genetically determined neurophysiological brain structures and is developmental by environmental stimuli as a consequence of the neuroplasticity of humans' brains.

Obviously, there are remarkable differences in humans' intelligent behavior which can be traced back to mental ability differences. Scientific research was always concerned with the determination of the degree of heritability and environmental influences. Advanced methods in brain research and molecular genetic studies were successful in uncovering specific genes that contribute to individual differences in cognitive functions. However, the effects of genetically and environmentally influenced portions of intelligence are not due to a static gift, rather they develop in a dynamic process. Namely developmental behavioral studies have demonstrated that "as children mature from infancy through adolescence the magnitude of h^2 [heritability] increases and c^2 [environmental influences] decreases" (Thompson and Plomin, 2000).

In the history of psychology, the first who studied the variations of human mental abilities was the British psychologist Francis Galton (1822 – 1911) who strongly believed in the heredity of mental faculties and focused his interest in the individual measurements. For this he developed the first statistical tools and can be seen as one of the founders of differential psychology. In his view, intelligence could be described by the individual differences of intellectual abilities. He assumed that the degree of the intellectual capacity would be reflected by greater sensory acuity. Therefore, he developed the first mental testing center where people could take a battery of tests and receive a report on the results. Since then, differential psychology has developed many psychometric instruments to measure individual human mental ability differences. The underlying concept of intelligence refers to a multilevel hierarchy, "with a general factor at the pinnacle, many specific abilities at the bottom, and separable but correlated group factors of ability in between at one or more levels" (Deary, 2000).

Influenced by Galton and based on statistical results, the English psychologist Charles Spearman (1863 – 1945) regarded intelligence as grounded in a general mental capacity. He presented empirical data from factor analysis to support his concept of a general factor for intelligence and christened it "g-factor" by which he established a two-factor-theory of intelligence with "g" as a general factor and "s" as a specific factor. The empirical result of psychometric data demonstrated that "the first unrotated principal component accounts for a large proportion of the variance in mental test batteries" (Deary, 2000, 8). Therefore, he saw the statistical value of "g" not as an arbitrary mathematical abstraction, but as something real, although he was fully aware that "g" could only *name*, but not *explain* the nature of what this factor represents.

> "But notice must be taken that this general factor g, like all measurements anywhere, is primarily not any concrete thing but only a value or magnitude. Further, that which this magnitude measures has not been defined by declaring what it is like, but only by pointing out where it can be found" (Spearman, 1927).

Spearman himself proposed several explanations of g and referred to the power of attention and the implemented mental energy. Nowadays, the neuronal conditions of mental speed and synaptic dense and transmission speed might serve as the neuronal correlates that determine the general conditions of intelligence (Brand, 1979). But although it has been argued that Spearman's view presents primarily a model than a valid theory which is actually based on only one single factor g, and despite the critique on the uni-dimensionality of g, the idea of a general factor, that influences cognitive achievement in many domains, is still under debate.

At that time, intelligence was mainly regarded as a monolithic global trait with largely innate and immutable limitations. The psychologist who did not believe in this and who developed a new structural concept of intelligence was Paul Joy Guilford (1897 – 1987). In search of a system for classifying the many different mental abilities he came up with his famous "Structure of Intellect" which was first presented to the public in Paris 1955 (Guilford, 1956). This structural model of intelligence resembled six kinds of operations (cognition, memory recording, memory retention, convergent production, divergent production, evaluation), five kinds of contents (visual, auditory, symbolic, semantic, behavioral), and six kinds of products (units, classes, relations, systems, transformations, implications) which were occupying cells in a three-dimensional system (see Figure 2). Contrary to Spearman, he was convinced that the divergent human abilities could not be related to only one general factor. In his view intelligence was a function of a highly differentiated and complex system with many levels of mental abilities that could and should be developed by education. "Intelligence education is intelligent education" became his famous motto. Therefore, he emphasized the intersection of products, operations and contents and the resulting multi-facet combinations. This evolved into a development in psychology to pay greater attention to a multiple intelligence theory.

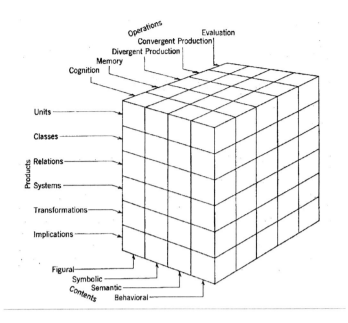

Figure 2. Paul J. Guilford: Model for the complete "Structure of Intellect" (Basic problems in teaching for creativity, in: Taylor & Williams (Eds) (1966). *Instructional media and creativity*. New York, p. 83)

The conception of different intelligences was first developed by Howard Gardner (Gardner, 1983) who was studying human cognitive capacities at Harvard Project Zero. The crucial question was whether intelligence is grounded in one general cognitive ability or whether it combines relatively independent intellectual faculties. Contrary to established theories of intelligence Gardner is convinced that intelligence consists of various intellectual competences. This conception employs the idea of an empirically grounded set of multiple faculties which all meet biological and psychological specifications and could be used to describe intelligences more adequately as a variety of human intellectual competences. This was the starting point for his Theory of Multiple Intelligences (Gardner, 1983) which equals "intelligence" with "intellectual competence". This theory holds for two general claims: first the *account of human cognition in its fullness*, and second the *unique blend of multiple intelligences* (Gardner, 1999). People develop their individual intelligence profile where the different competences interact and can be enhanced by educational or environmental interventions.

According to Gardner, an intellectual competence should fit with the following criteria to be recognized as an intelligence:

- the localization in particular brain areas; potential isolation by brain damage;
- the existence if idiot savants and/or prodigies;
- identifiable core operations;
- a distinctive developmental history;
- an evolutionary history and plausibility;
- support from experimental psychology;
- support from psychometric findings;
- susceptibility to encoding in a symbol system.

According to these criteria he established a linguistic, musical, logical-mathematical, spatial, bodily-kinesthetic, and two personal intelligences, which are recently complemented by a naturalist and eventually a spiritual or existential intelligence (Gardner, 1999). For all of these faculties he claims that

> "intelligences should be thought of as entities at a certain level of generality, broader than highly specific computational mechanisms [...] while narrower than the most general capacities [...]. Yet it is in the very nature of intelligences that each operates according to its own procedures and has its own biological bases" (Gardner, 1983).

Others distinguished between different areas such as academic (cognitive), practical, social, creative, and operative intelligences (Brocke and Beauducel, 2001) which are systematically differentiable, but do not have any empirical evidence of potential interactions between them.

Gardner still uses the venerable terms of human *faculties* and intellectual *competences* instead of skills, abilities, orf talents in his explication of intelligences which he defines as "a biophysical potential to process information that can be activated on a cultural setting to solve problems or create products that are of value in a culture" (Gardner, 1999). In so doing, he remarkably extends the concept of intelligence and opens it toward problem solving and creating culturally valuable products. But this does not necessarily clarify the complex phenomenon of intelligence, it rather waters down the core conceptualization of mental capacities. On the other hand, the wider understanding of intelligence enables him to include creative and aesthetic faculties like musical abilities into his concept of multiple intelligences. This is the first time, that musical competence is explicitly named as an intelligence: musical intelligence instead of mere musical skills or talents. However, it remains open to what degree music aptitude contributes to musical intelligence and if there is a substantial difference between music aptitude and musical intelligence.

Although Gardner claims that the intelligences originate from scientifically proved observations, his conception is nevertheless mainly speculative because the criteria for intelligence as an intellectual competence are not always objectively and empirically evident. But we have to acknowledge that Gardner has opened a new perspective and introduced a broader understanding of what we could or should regard as an intelligence. However, a clear differentiation between related psychological terms such as competence, potential, faculty, ability, and aptitude still remains a desideratum.

As demonstrated there is common agreement on intelligence in a very general sense which refers to *human mental ability differences*. However, a question still under debate is whether intelligence is one singular trait or a combination of many abilities. By an analysis of a collection of intelligence tests it was found "that mental tests tend to collect together in pools that have especially close associations" (Deary, 2001). These pools build sub-groups that relate more highly to each other than to other tests. This calls for the existence of group-factors such as *working memory*, *processing speed*, *verbal comprehension*, and *perceptual organization* (Deary, 2001).

NEURAL CORRELATES OF INTELLIGENCE

Although intelligence is regarded as the total of all mental competences there is no intelligence center in the brain (as there is also not only one music center in the brain). Therefore, it seems reasonable to look for the neural correlates that reflect processes of individuals with higher capacity (or IQ) than others. In the literature three structural correlates of higher intelligence are discussed: brain size, mental speed, and processing efficiency (Eliot, 1999; Neubauer, 2001).

(1) Especially in early childhood, an enormous growth takes place in the brain. This is not due to the growth of new neurons, rather the increase of the volume of the gray matter is a consequence of an exuberant growth of synapses with axons and dendrites. In later years the process of myelination enhances the growth of brain volume. A layer of myelin around the axons functions as an isolation for signal transmission and increases the conduction speed. The higher the synaptic dense, the better and faster the communication between neurons can be performed. Therefore, it sounds plausible, that more gray matter is associated with higher intellectual capacity in discrete areas including frontal, temporal, parietal, and occipital lobes (Haier, Jung, Yeo, Head, and Alkire, 2004). The correlation between brain volume and IQ for adults is reported as r = .35 (Eliot, 1999).

(2) Mental speed generally refers to faster decision making processes and shorter reaction times. One of the factors for mental speed is based on the neural transmission speed which directly relates to myelination as a structural condition for efficient learning. The transmission speed can be recorded from event related potentials (ERP). The highest correlation is exhibited during the first 200 milliseconds (P200) immediately after the stimulus. But this early reaction is mainly an indicator of the sensorial reaction time whereas the P300 wave (which is missing in young children) accounts for higher cortical activities. If we compare the ERPs of children with high and low IQ we find differences not only in the speed, but in the shape of the curve (see Figure 3).

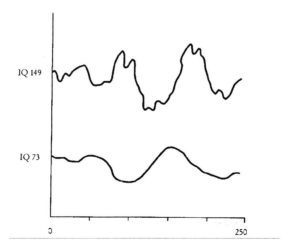

Figure 3. Wave curve of event related potentials of children with high and low IQ (from Eliot 1999, 566).

(3) As brain imaging technologies have shown spend persons with a higher IQ less energy as reflected by the glucose metabolism (Eliot, 1999). It has also been demonstrated that that more effective processing needs less activation power and smaller activated areas (Altenmueller, Gruhn, Parlitz, and Liebert, 2000). With respect to these findings one can state that higher intelligence activates the brain more efficiently and economically.

All three indicators – brain size, processing speed, activation efficiency – are concerned with the entire brain and confirm that intelligence cannot be located in one single area or part of the brain. But there are also indices in the cortex where higher cognitive functions are processed. Here the pre-frontal cortex, where sensory input is processed and information from the limbic system (emotions) and from sub-cortical regions (arousals) are collected and processed, plays a crucial role, namely for the inhibition of distracting activities. In signal transmission of firing neurons we differentiate between excitatory (i.e., stimulating a cell to carry a signal) and inhibitory (i.e., preventing a cell from firing) processes. It can be said that the function of synaptic inhibition is more important for effective processing than facilitating signal transmission by firing neurons. Finally, cortical asymmetry calls for an efficient exploitation of the particular potential of both hemispheres. Therefore, the strength of inter-hemispheric collaboration is another indicator for intelligence.

This neuro-anatomic situation clearly demonstrates that intelligent behavior which is based on the intellectual capacity is a general brain function and not only domain specific. However, there are mental predispositions that are necessary, but not sufficient for the development of special abilities such as musical abilities.

INTERACTION BETWEEN MUSIC AND INTELLIGENCE

From our knowledge of today, the structure of human mental competences forms a hierarchy of abilities (Figure 4) that collect to group-factors which in turn perform close associations to a general factor. If this presents an appropriate model of the structure of intelligence, then musical abilities might relate to processing speed and perceptual organization. Music aptitude, then, determines a given (innate) potential that is developmental within certain limits. Consequently, one might hypothesize that music aptitude, i.e., a given potential, can be recognized as music intelligence if it interferes with mental group factors from that hierarchy. Intelligence presents the cognitive structure for the development of individual abilities like musicality. Therefore, it has to be proven how the cognitive structure (intelligence) and the individual ability (musicality) interact.

It is quite natural and understandable that musicians and especially music educators believe in the benefits of musical practice. If a cognitive effect of music on humans' intellectual growth could be documented the justification of general music in schools and the endowment of the arts in society would no longer be questioned. This is probably one reason that the first report about a measurable effect of listening to Mozart on spatial-temporal reasoning abilities in Nature 1993 (Rauscher, Shaw, and Ky, 1993) evoked an exploding media interest with more newspaper mentions than any other Nature report around that time (Bangerter and Heath, 2004). The astonishing popularity of this only moderate (but significant) and temporary increase of test scores for items that are related to spatial-temporal reasoning from *Stanford-Binet's Intelligence Scale*, which immediately was extended to a general Mozart effect, has obviously many reasons. It seems obvious that cognitive transfer-effects serve as striking arguments for musical and arts education. Wherever one complains about the weakness of the educational system the arts are apt to fulfill a wonderful substitute. Bangerter and Heath found that in states with problematic school system newspapers gave most coverage to the Mozart effect (Bangerter and Heath, 2004). Furthermore, wherever educators are urged to defend the benefits of musical education, they look for empirical evidence that the power of the arts might promote and enhance the learning even in non-arts domains.

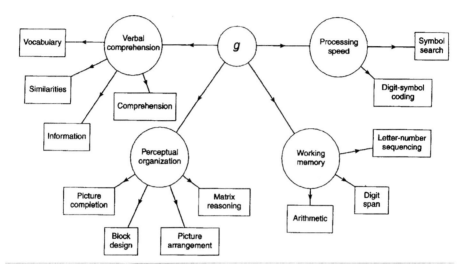

Figure 4. Hierarchy of mental abilities according to the *Wechsler Adult Intelligence Scale* III (from Deary 2001, S.3)

The desire to relate the good to the beauty is deeply rooted in humans' conception and can be traced back to ancient Greek philosophy. Antique thinking was characterized by the concept of "kalokagathía" (*kalós kai agathós* = beautiful and good), i.e., the idealistic identification of sensual (or aesthetic) qualities with ethic values. This has nurtured the idea of the value of the arts, that an aesthetic behavior (as performed in music) could affect an ethic or educational goal (such as cognitive achievement). This sub-conscious occidental roots of thinking are adopted when we apply the arts to educational purposes.

Since 1993 countless experiments on the Mozart effect were performed with the intention to replicate andor confirm the original findings of Rauscher and Shaw (Rauscher, Shaw, and Ky, 1995). In 2000 an extensive meta-analysis was performed based on 1135 studies published in 41 English spoken journals (Winner and Hetland, 2000a). The authors used a quantitative measure by calculating an effect size which was correlated with the results in spatial abilities, mathematics and reading skills. This meta-analysis demonstrated a positive relationship between studying the arts and academic achievement, but did not support any causal link.

"The existing research does not allow us to determine the mechanisms underlying these relationships, however. Further and extensive research would be required to determine whether transfer, when it occurs, is due to transfer of cognitive skills, transfer of working habits, transfer of motivation and attitude, or some other type of mechanisms" (Winner and Hetland, 2000b).

There are many personal and situation dependent factors involved to produce the observed effects. More importantly, if a correlation or interaction between music performance and the improvement of cognitive skills (like spatial-temporal reasoning) can be observed, it does not allow any implications for causality. Rather preference and arousal hypotheses have been applied to explain the effect (Rauscher, Bowers, Dettlaff, and Scott, 2002; Rickard, 2004; Thompson, Schellenberg, and Husain, 2001).

From neuroscience there is no reasonable indication for a "near" transfer (Barnett and Ceci, 2002) because near transfer can only occur between closely connected domains. Therefore, it is appropriate to acknowledge that transfer can only function internally within areas of same or similar functions. All activities and environmental as well as social stimuli cause structural and functional changes in the brain which is defined as neuroplasticity. Consequently, true transfer effects would mean that activities in one domain cause changes in another related domain. But there is no empirical evidence for this. Plastic effects were always observed within the same domain (e.g. the enlargement of the finger representation of the left hand in string players). As from statistical correlations, so from neurosciences there is no support for a transfer from musical activities to an increase of cognitive competence.

However, there are several educational studies that claim for positive results of music on learning in schools and pre-schools (Bastian, 2000; Costa-Giomi, 2004; Rauscher and Zupan, 2000; Spychiger, 1995). These studies do not yield clear and consistent results on extra-musical effects on the quality of learning. Based on her experience with a Swiss longitudinal study, Maria Spychiger states that in general the demonstration of transfer effects decreases with methodological validity (Spychiger, 1995). In her study of the effects of piano instruction on children's academic achievement Eugenia Costa-Giomi found that simple effects did not reveal significant differences in language and math scores between experimental and control groups; the only significant difference was found in self-esteem scores (Costa-Giomi, 2004).

It is evident that "far" transfer from music lessons to intellectual competence are fairly rarely documented. However, extra-curricular experiences in music (instrumental lessons, choir participation, band activities etc.) and other areas play a prominent role in the development of social, personal, and behavioral skills. But a close link between musical and cognitive abilities on a lower level of the pyramid of intelligence is problematic to construe. If there is a connection so that the term of musical intelligence is more than a metaphorical description the missing link must be searched on a higher level of the pyramid.

This link might be found in mental speed. This group factor refers to the time span used in neural processing which is widely independent from formal instruction and intensive training. Saccades (rapid eye movements) can serve as an independent and objective measure for mental speed. In several studies it has been demonstrated that some parameters of saccadic eye movements such as fixation duration and reaction time positively correlate with IQ measurements (Galley, 1998, 1999). Therefore, saccadic eye movements offer an appropriate measure to evaluate the cognitive potential humans.

In an experiment where subjects with different or no musical background were asked to perform an eye movement task measured by an Electro-Oculogram (EOG), a significant interaction between musical activities and mental speed could be observed (Gruhn, Galley, and Kluth, 2003). Young children who participated in different kinds of musical activities exceeded their peers without music in all parameters of mental speed. This reflects a clear and strong interaction, but does not indicate any causal relation. From these results we cannot conclude that it is musical practice that enhances mental speed. On the contrary, mental speed could be regarded as a candidate for fostering musical abilities. However, the role of music aptitude and its function for a concept of intelligence is still unclear.

COMMONALITIES AND DIFFERENCES
TOWARD AN INTEGRATED MODEL OF MUSIC ACHIEVEMENT

To come to a conclusion how musicality and intelligence interact we must clearly differentiate between the assumption, that music possibly has an effect on intelligence as an intellectual competence, and the use of overlapping concepts such as competence, capacity, and ability. As already demonstrated there is no clear evidence that neither music practice nor music instruction demonstrates a causal relation in a sense that it is music that increases intellectual competence. Therefore, we will focus here only on the differences and commonalities in the terminology.

According to the little amount of studies in sciences that focus on musical *intelligence* there is no substantial interest in this connection – except for the Mozart effect. However, this situation changes if we look for musical *talent* or *giftedness*. It has been stated that giftedness is ascribed to individuals who are advanced in scholastic abilities whereas talent refers to exceptional abilities in arts and music (Winner and Martino, 2000). But this cannot be generalized. Very often the terms are used in both domains; one speaks of high talent in sports as well as of a gifted musician or artist. It is more likely that talent is often associated with technical conditions and giftedness with a sublime genius. Furthermore, there are several similarities that are shared in different types of gifted individuals: 1. they have started earlier than peers and learned more rapidly; 2. they are intensely motivated and show obsessive interest in their domain; 3. they learn virtually on their own with a minimum of adult scaffolding (Winner and Martino, 2000).

If we think of everyday colloquial custom we will realize that terms such as cognitive or intellectual *ability*, *competence*, *capacity*, and *potential* are used more or less synonymously. These terms appear on a scale where simple *skills* mark one pole which is more technically determined and relies on training and practice, and talent or gift marks the opposite pole which is more often associated with a genetic predisposition. Conversely, *intelligence* as a cognitive function is often contrasted to musicality as a non-cognitive *aptitude*. However, in general the term of aptitude is related to or interacts with intelligence. Here, the question is whether and when aptitude equals intelligence. If we observe the decisive behavior of highly intelligent people we find the same personal characteristics as in highly musically gifted persons: they are obsessively interested in their domain and extremely intrinsically motivated, they achieve a superb and broad knowledge that exceeds their own domain, and they have access to a remarkable memory. Therefore, there is no structural difference.

However, for musicality it has to be proven whether or not music *aptitude* represents a form of intelligence so that it is suitable to talk about *musical* intelligence. Our proposition is that the group-factors, namely mental speed and perceptual organization, link music aptitude to intelligence. If intelligence is defined as human mental abilities it refers to a structure of mind within which a particular aptitude can develop or can be developed. A survey of the terminology and possible links between levels is shown in Figure 5. However, this hierarchical structure of meanings and references is not always reflected by everyday use, we rather mix those words and often talk about different objects with diverging connotations by using the same terminology.

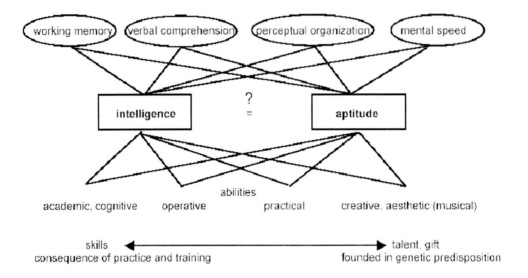

Figure 5. Hierarchical structure of the terminology. Intelligence represents a theoretical construct which becomes concrete in specific domains and can or cannot be equaled with aptitude

Here, we support an understanding of intelligence as the general brain structure for developing aptitudes. The development of the functional architecture of the human brain depends to a great deal on the perceived signals from the different sensorial channels and is, therefore, influenced by all kinds of practical experiences. These activations stimulate the synaptogenesis (growth of synapses) and strengthen the neural connections within the neural network. "Neurons wire together if they fire together" (Singer, 2002). The highly differentiated and specialized brain structure is in debt of evolutionary processes of selection and adaptation. In course of this process the structural conditions for mental activities develop according to the individual social and cultural conditions. These conditions, then, lay the ground for intelligence.

This in mind, we should reflect on some crucial aspects of the interdependence of musical and other abilities or intelligences. If we consider intelligence as a theoretical construct with "g" as a statistical factor, then all different abilities in cognitive, social, artistic, kinesthetic, and similar domains represent concrete manifestations of special aptitudes. Domain specific tests can only measure the magnitude of the a particular aptitude, but it won't be possible to predict the magnitude of a particular aptitude from IQ; even it will be difficult to trace back that magnitude to IQ. Therefore, the crucial questions for further research are

(1) Is a causal link between the theoretical construct intelligence and its many manifestations empirically evident?

(2) Is there a mutual interaction between general intelligence and concrete manifestations and is that connection reversible?

(3) Is it possible to predict from the achievement on a lower level to the quality and magnitude of intelligence on a higher level?

As a possible solution based on recent research findings (Gruhn et al., 2003) we would like to propose an integrated model of music achievement which combines the structural conditions of general intelligence with the particular ability of music aptitude (see Figure 6). Several group-factors of general intelligence in combination with a special aptitude (talent or gift) form the prerequisite that intensive deliberated practice succeeds in an emerging musical achievement.

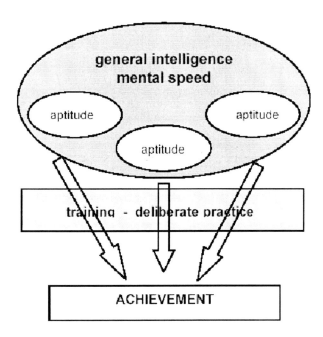

Figure 6. Integrated model of intelligence and aptitude toward achievement.

This model might reconcile the demands of expertise research which emphasizes the importance of accumulated training and deliberate practice but neglects the fact that many individuals drop out and do not succeed by their practice time. On the other hand, the model keeps the question of the priority of general intelligence or aptitude open, rather it emphasizes an interaction of both. There is some evidence to assume that only if a high degree of mental speed interacts with a high music aptitude, adequate practice, parental support and an appropriate formal instruction, this may cause a musical effect which is manifested by a high artistic achievement. Here, we plead for a careful distinction between general intelligence, music aptitude, and music achievement which interact, but are not mutually exchangeable.

REFERENCES

Altenmueller, E., Gruhn, W., Parlitz, D., and Liebert, G. (2000). The impact of music education on brain networks: evidence from EEG-studies. *International Journal for Music Education, 35*, 47 - 53.

Bangerter, A., and Heath, C. (2004). The Mozart effect: tracking the evolution of a scientific legend. *British Journal of Social Psychology, 43*(4), 605 - 623.

Barnett, S. M., and Ceci, S. J. (2002). When and where do we apply what we learn? A taxonomy for transfer. *Psychological Bulletin, 128*, 612 - 637.

Bastian, H. G. (2000). *Musik(erziehung) und ihre Wirkung.* Mainz: Schott.

Bentley, A. (1966). *Measures of Musical Abilities.* London: George Harrap and Co.Ltd.

Billroth, T. (1896). *Wer ist musikalisch? [Who is musical?]. 2nd edition.* Berlin: Paetel.

Brand, C. R. (1979). General intelligence and mental speed: their relationship and development. In J. P. Das and N. O'Connor (Eds.), *Intelligence and learning* (pp. 589 - 593). New York: Plenum.

Briessen, M. v. (1929). *Die Entwicklung der Musikalität in den Reifejahren.* Langensalza: Friedrich Mann.

Brocke, B., and Beauducel, A. (2001). Intelligenz als Konstrukt. In E. Stern and J. Guthke (Eds.), *Perspektiven der Intelligenzforschung* (pp. 13 - 42). Lengerich: Pabst Science Publ.

Costa-Giomi, E. (2004). Effects of three years of piano instruction on children's academic achievement, school performance and self-esteem. *Psychology Of Music, 32*(2), 139 - 152.

Deary, I. J. (2000). *Looking down on human intelligence. From psychometrics to the brain* (Vol. 34). Oxford: Oxford University Press.

Deary, I. J. (2001). *Intelligence. A very short introduction.* Oxford: Oxford University Press.

Drake, R. M. (1954). *Drake Musical Aptitude Test.* Chicago: Science Research Ass. Inc.

Eliot, L. (1999). *What's going on in there? How the brain and mind develop in the first five years of life.* New York: Bantam Books.

Fiske, H. E. (2004). *Connectionist models of musical thinking* (Vol. 112). Lewiston N.Y.: Edwin Mellen.

Galley, N. (1998). An enquiry into the relationship between activation and performance using saccadic eye movement parameters. *Ergonomics, 40*, 698 - 712.

Galley, N. (1999). Fixation durations and saccadic latencies as indicators of mental speed. In I. Mervielde and I. J. Deary and F. F. de Fruyt and F. Ostendorf (Eds.), *Personality Psychology in Europe* (Vol. 7, pp.: 221 - 234). Tillburg: University Press.

Gardner, H. (1983). *Frames of mind. The theory of multiple intelligences.* New York: Basic Books.

Gardner, H. (1999). *Intelligence reframed. Multiple intelligences for the 21st century.* New York: Basic Books.

Gordon, E. E. (1965). *Music Aptitude Profile.* Boston: Houghton Mifflin Comp.

Gruhn, W., Galley, N., and Kluth, C. (2003). Do mental speed and musical abilities interact? In G. F. Avanzini, C.; Minciacchi, D., Lopez, L.; Majno, M. (Ed.), *The neurosciences and music* (Vol. 999, pp. 485 - 496). New York: Annals of the New York Academy of Sciences.

Guilford, J. P. (1956). The structure of intellect. *Psychological Bulletin, 54*, 267 - 293.

Haier, R. J., Jung, R. E., Yeo, R. A., Head, K., and Alkire, M. T. (2004). Structural brain variation and general intelligence. *Neuroimage, 23*(1), 425 - 433.

Kries, J. v. (1926). *Wer ist musikalisch? [Who is musical?] Gedanken zur Psychologie der Tonkunst.* Berlin: Springer.

Kwalwasser, J., and Dykema, P. W. (1930). *Kwalwasser-Dykema Music Test.* New York: Carl Fisher.

Neubauer, A. C. (2001). Elementar-kognitive und physiologische Korrelate der Intelligenz. In E. Stern and J. Guthke (Eds.), *Perspektiven der Intelligenzforschung* (pp. 43 - 67). Lengerich: Pabst Science.

Rauscher, F. H., Bowers, M. K., Dettlaff, D. M., and Scott, S. E. (2002). *Effects of environmental, social, and auditory enrichment on maze learning in rats: Implications for arousal.* Paper presented at the Cognitive Neuroscience Society, San Francisco.

Rauscher, F. H., Shaw, G. L., and Ky, K. N. (1993). Music and spatial task performance. *Nature, 365*, 611.

Rauscher, F. H., Shaw, G. L., and Ky, K. N. (1995). Listening to Mozart enhances spatial-temporal reasoning: towards a neurophysiological basis. *Neuroscience Letters, 185*, 44-47.

Rauscher, F. H., and Zupan, M. (2000). Classroom keyboard instruction improves kindergarten children's spatial-temporal performance: A field experiment. *Early Childhood Research Quarterly, 15*, 215 - 228.

Révész, G. (1920). Prüfung der Musikalität. *Zeitschrift für Psychologie, 85*, 163 - 209.

Rickard, N. S. (2004). Intense emotional responses to music: a test of the physiological arousal hypothesis. *Psychology Of Music, 32*(4), 371 - 388.

Seashore, C. E. (1919). *Seashore Measures of Musical Talent.* New York: Psychological Corp.

Singer, W. (2002). *Der Beobachter im Gehirn.* Frankfurt: Suhrkamp.

Spearman, C. (1927). *The abilities of man.* London: McMillan.

Spychiger, M. B. (1995). *Mehr Musikunterricht an den öffentlichen Schulen?* Hamburg: Kovac.

Thompson, L. A., and Plomin, R. (2000). Genetic tools for exploring individual differences in intelligence. In K. A. Heller and F. J. Moenks and R. J. Sternberg and R. F. Subotnik (Eds.), *International Handbook of Giftedness and Talent* (2. edition ed., pp. 157 - 164). Amsterdam: Elsevier.

Thompson, W. F., Schellenberg, E. G., and Husain, G. (2001). Arousal, mood, and the Mozart effect. *Psychological Science, 12*, 248 - 251.

Vidor, M. (1931). *Was ist Musikalität? Experimentell-psychologische Versuche.* München: C.H.Beck.

Wellek, A. (1927). Drei Typen des Absoluten Gehörs. *Musikblätter des Anbruch, 9*, 420 - 423.

Wellek, A. (1938). *Das Absolute Gehör und seine Typen.* Leipzig.

Wellek, A. (1939). *Typologie der Musikbegabung im deutschen Volke.* München: Beck.

Wing, H. D. (1939). *Wing Standardised Tests of Musical Intelligence.* Slough, Buckinghamshire: National Foundation for Educational Research (England and Wales).

Winner, E., and Hetland, L. (2000a). The arts and academic achievement: what the evidence shows. *The Journal of Aesthetic Education, 34*(3-4).

Winner, E., and Hetland, L. (2000b). The arts in education: evaluating the evidence for a causal link. *The Journal of Aesthetic Education, 34*(3-4), 3 - 10.

Winner, E., and Martino, G. (2000). Giftedness in non-academic domains: the case of the visual arts and music. In K. A. Heller and F. J. Moenks and R. J. Sternberg and R. F. Subotnik (Eds.), *International Handbook of Giftedness and Talent* (2. edition ed., pp. 95 - 110). Amsterdam: Elsevier.

In: Intelligence : New Research
Editor: Lin V. Wesley, pp. 133-149

ISBN 1-59454-637-1
© 2006 Nova Science Publishers, Inc.

Chapter 7

WISC-III PROFILES IN HIGH-FUNCTIONING PERVASIVE DEVELOPMENTAL DISORDERS AND ATTENTION-DEFICIT/HYPERACTIVITY DISORDER

Tomonori Koyama[1,2] and Hiroshi Kurita[2,3]
[1] Department of Mental Health Administration, National Institute of Mental Health,
National Center for Neurology and Psychiatry, Kodaira, Japan
[2] Department of Mental Health, Graduate School of Medicine,
University of Tokyo, Tokyo, Japan
[3] Zenkoku Ryoiku-Sodan Center, Tokyo, Japan

ABSTRACT

To obtain clinical clues for differential diagnosis of high-functioning (i.e., IQ of 70 or over) pervasive developmental disorders (HPDD) from attention-deficit/hyperactivity disorder (ADHD), we compared 79 HPDD children (15 autistic disorder [HFA] [M = 9.3 years, 13 males]; 45 PDD not otherwise specified [HPDDNOS] [M = 8.1 years, 37 males]; 19 Asperger's disorder [AS] [M = 10.3 years, 17 males]) and 37 ADHD children (M = 8.6 years, 30 males) on the Japanese version of Wechsler Intelligence Scale for Children Third Edition (WISC-III) and the Childhood Autism Rating Scale—Tokyo Version (CARS-TV). Compared with the ADHD children, the HPDDNOS children scored significantly ($p < .05$) lower on Verbal IQ (90.5 vs. 103.5) and Verbal Comprehension (90.3 vs. 103.8). The HFA children scored significantly higher on Freedom from Distractibility than the HPDDNOS children (111.9 vs. 97.4). After controlling for Full Scale IQ, the HPDDNOS children scored significantly lower on Comprehension and significantly higher on Block Design than the ADHD children. The HFA children scored significantly lower on Vocabulary than the ADHD children. Although all of the three HPDD subgroups showed the similar profile of low score of Comprehension and high score of Block Design, the AS children showed relatively high verbal ability and troughs on Coding. The latter profile was also shared by the ADHD

---

[1] Correspondence should be addressed to Tomonori Koyama, Department of Mental Health Administration, National Institute of Mental Health, National Center for Neurology and Psychiatry, 4-1-1 Ogawa-Higashi, Kodaira, Tokyo 187-8553, Japan; e-mail: koyama@ncnp-k.go.jp

children but not by the other two HPDD subgroups. Although both HPDD and ADHD groups partially shared some clinical symptoms, the HPDD subgroups were more abnormal in social interaction but less abnormal in hyperactivity and near receptor responsiveness. These findings might reflect underlying brain dysfunction in the three HPDD subgroups and ADHD and may help professionals to distinguish clinically between them.

Key Words: attention-deficit/hyperactivity disorder (ADHD); high-functioning; pervasive developmental disorders (PDD); Wechsler Intelligence Scale for Children Third Edition (WISC-III).

INTRODUCTION

Pervasive developmental disorders (PDD) are a group of developmental disorders characterized by impairments in three areas of development: qualitative impairments in social interaction, communication, and restricted patterns of behaviors and interests. The Diagnostic and Statistical Manual of Mental Disorders fourth edition (DSM-IV) (American Psychiatric Association [APA], 1994) proposed five subtypes of PDD, namely, autistic disorder, Rett's disorder, childhood disintegrative disorder, Asperger's disorder, and PDD not otherwise specified (PDDNOS). International Classification of Diseases 10th Revision (ICD-10) (World Health Organization [WHO], 1993) adopted basically similar PDD subtypes.

Since the end of the 20th century, several epidemiological studies have reported a high prevalence rate of PDD of about 0.6% in the general child population (Baird et al, 2000; Bertrand, Mars, Boyle, Bove, Yeargin-Allsopp, and Decoufle, 2001; Chakrabarti and Fombonne, 2001), which is much higher than previously thought. Such prevalence rising is possibly brought by broadened recognition and early detection of the PDD without mental retardation (IQ $\geq$ 70), called high-functioning PDD (HPDD). For example, from Chakrabarti and Fombonne's (2001) epidemiological study conducted in Great Britain, we can calculate a prevalence of HPDD as 0.445%, about one half of that for schizophrenia. Today, some promising screening tools for HPDD have been developed, such as Autism-Spectrum Quotient (AQ) (Baron-Cohen, Wheelwright, Skinner, Martin, and Clubley, 2001; Kurita, Koyama, and Osada, in press2005).

Attention-deficit/hyperactivity disorder (ADHD) is a highly disabling condition, even though much milder than PDD, with onset in early childhood. ADHD is defined in DSM-IV as a disorder with persistent pattern of inattention and/or hyperactivity-impulsivity that is more frequent and/or severer than that is typically observed in individuals at a comparable level of development. ADHD is about 10 times as common as PDD, with a prevalence ranging from 3 to 7% in school-age children (APA, 2000). Although the diagnosis of ADHD is preempted by that of PDD in DSM-IV and ICD-10, increased awareness of HPDD and its relatively mild autistic symptoms have stimulated clinical studies on the similarityies and differences between HPDD and ADHD.

Although children with ADHD are not socially withdrawn and do not selectively hyper-focus on activities or topics of interest to them, they could show PDD-like features. Stein, Szumowski, Blondis, and Roizen (1995) found that relative to IQ, Socialization, Communication and Daily Living on the Vineland Adaptive Behavior Scales were significantly more impaired in ADHD children than PDD children. Clark, Feehan, Tinline, and Vostanis (1999) noted that 65 to 80% of parents of ADHD children reported significant difficulties of their children in social interaction and communication. On the other hand, many children with HPDD have hyperkinesis and attention deficiency. Ghaziuddin, Weidmer-Mikhail, and Ghaziuddin (1998) reported that a half of children with Asperger syndrome presented ADHD symptoms. Goldstein and Schwebach (2004) and Yoshida and Uchiyama (2004) reported that 59% and 67.9%, respectively, of children with HPDD also met the DSM-IV symptom criteria for ADHD. Due to the mildness of autistic symptomatology, it is common for high-functioning children with PDDNOS to be initially given a misdiagnosis of ADHD (Jensen, Larrieu, and Mack, 1997; Perry, 1998).

Although several studies compared their symptoms in parent-rating scales (Jensen et al., 1997; Luteijn et al., 2000; Roeyers, Keymeulen, and Buysse, 1998), the difference in cognitive function between HPDD and ADHD remains to be clarified. To our knowledge, there has been no study to compare the cognitive profile between HPDD subgroups and ADHD by using Wechsler Intelligence Scale for Children Third Edition (WISC-III). Although Ehlers et al.'s study (1997) using the Wechsler Intelligence Scale for Children Revised (WISC-R) had a similar perspective, their study was conducted on children with Deficits in Attention, Motor control and Perception (DAMP), a broader concept than ADHD, and did not include children with PDDNOS, which seems to be the majority of PDD (Fombonne, 2003).

The purpose of the present study is to obtain clinical clues for differential diagnosis of HPDD including its subgroups from ADHD through a comparison of cognitive function and autistic symptom profiles between them.

METHODS

Instruments

Japanese Version of WISC-III

The Japanese version of the Wechsler Intelligence Scale for Children Third Edition (WISC-III) (Wechsler, 1991) used in this study to obtain cognitive function of children was standardized for 1,125 Japanese children ages 5-16, with good reliability and validity (Japanese WISC-III Publication Committee, 1998). WISC-III yields Verbal IQ (VIQ) from 5 subtests (Information, Similarities, Arithmetic, Vocabulary, and Comprehension); Performance IQ (PIQ) from 5 subtests (Picture Completion, Coding, Picture Arrangement, Block Design, and Object Assembly); and Full Scale IQ (FIQ). In addition, WISC-III produces statistically based 4 Index scores: Verbal Comprehension (from Information, Similarities, Vocabulary, and Comprehension); Perceptual Organization (from Picture Completion, Picture Arrangement, Block Design, and Object Assembly); Freedom from Distractibility (from Arithmetic and Digit Span); and Processing Speed (from Coding and Symbol Search). "Mazes" is not used for any calculation of IQ or Index and was not included for analysis of this study. In this study, experienced psychologists administered WISC-III to subjects introduced in the subjects' section.

Childhood Autism Rating Scale-Tokyo Version (CARS-TV)

The Childhood Autism Rating Scale-Tokyo Version (CARS-TV) with satisfactory reliability and validity (Kurita, Miyake, and Katsuno, 1989) is the Japanese version of the Childhood Autism Rating Scale (CARS) (Schopler, Reichler, DeVellis, and Daly, 1980), one of the most widely used scales to evaluate the degree and profiles of autism in children. CARS-TV consists of 15 items (Relationships with people, Imitation, Affect, Use of body, Relation to nonhuman objects, Adaptation to environmental change, Visual responsiveness, Auditory responsiveness, Near receptor responsiveness, Anxiety reaction, Verbal communication, Nonverbal communication, Activity level, Intellectual functioning, and General impressions), and each item is scored from 1.0 (normal) to 4.0 (severely abnormal) with the unit of 0.5. The total CARS-TV score is obtained by summing-up each item score and thus ranges from 15.0 to 60.0. Experienced psychologists also administered CARS-TV to the subjects of this study based on behavior observation and parental interview.

Subjects

All subjects were recruited from referrals to three clinics (The Child Guidance Clinic affiliated with the National Welfare Foundation for Disabled Children [Zenkoku Ryoiku-Sodan Center], The Nerima Welfare Center for the Mentally and Physically Handicapped, and The Kawasaki Central District Center for Remedial Therapy for Handicapped Children) in and near Tokyo, well known for their specialty in developmental disorders and related conditions. In each clinic, a clinical team consisting of experienced professionals (i.e., child psychiatrists, clinical psychologists, and pediatric neurologists), led by the same child psychiatrist (H. K.) having clinical experiences with developmental disorders including PDD and ADHD for 30 years, diagnosed children by consensus according to relevant DSM or ICD schemes depending on the year of visit of children.

Based on detailed clinical examination at first visit and follow-up observations as well as questionnaires on development and symptoms of children filled out by parents, the clinical teams diagnosed the subjects according to DSM-IV. As to the diagnosis of PDDNOS, which is defined as a residual category of PDD and has no operational diagnostic criteria in DSM-IV, we used modified DSM-IV criteria for autistic disorder to conform to ICD-10 criteria for atypical autism with atypicality in symptomatology as follows: A patient exhibits (1) qualitative impairment in social interaction, (2) qualitative impairment in communication, and (3) restricted repetitive and stereotyped patterns of behavior, interests and activities of criterion A, but does not fully satisfy criterion A for number of areas of abnormality; meets criterion B (i.e., abnormal or impaired development before age 3); and meets criterion C (i.e., not Rett's disorder or childhood disintegrative disorder). All the PDDNOS children in this study satisfied not only the above-mentioned criteria but also the criteria for PDDNOS proposed by Buitelaar and van der Gaag (1998) (i.e., requiring a total of three or more items from (1), (2), and (3), including at least one item from (1), of criterion A of DSM-IV criteria for autistic disorder).

As summarized in Table I, the subjects of this study were 79 HPDD children (15 autistic disorder [high-functioning autism; HFA], 45 PDDNOS [HPDDNOS], 19 Asperger's disorder

[AS]) and 37 ADHD children, with no significant differences between the four groups in sex ratio and chronological age. All of the 116 subjects had WISC-III FIQ of 70 or over.

Table I. Demographics of Subjects

		HFA	HPDDNOS	AS	ADHD
Sex, n	Male	13	37	17	30
χ^2 (3) = 0.82, p = .85	Female	2	8	2	7
	Total	15	45	19	37
Age, years	Mean	9.3	8.1	10.3	8.6
Welch's F (3, 40.3) = 2.41, p = .08	SD	2.5	2.1	3.9	2.0
	Range	5 – 13	5 – 13	5 – 16	5 – 13
WISC-III Full Scale IQ	Mean	99.8	93.0	99.5	100.3
F (3, 112) = 2.10, p = .10	SD	14.6	14.9	11.7	15.3
	Range	74 – 127	70 – 134	79 – 118	71 – 129

Note: HFA = high-functioning autism; HPDDNOS = high-functioning pervasive developmental disorder not otherwise specified; AS = Asperger's disorder; ADHD = attention-deficit/hyperactivity disorder. SD = standard deviation.

Statistical Analysis

For WISC-III IQ and Index scores, differences of mean scores between the four groups were tested by analysis of variance (ANOVA). For WISC-III subtest scores, differences were tested by analysis of covariance (ANCOVA) with FIQ, which was somewhat lower in the HPDDNOS children, as a covariate. Based on the estimated score, we illustrated subtest profile of each group for verbal and performance subtests.

In clinical settings, to grasp strengths and weaknesses of children is useful, so we conducted the following analyses. We converted FIQs of the subjects into subtest compatible scores by assigning score 1 through score 19 for every FIQ range of 5 from 53-57 (score 1) through 143-147 (score 19) (e.g., 58-62 [2], 63-67 [3], 68-72 [4] . . . . 93-97 [9], 98-102 [10], 103-107 [11] . . . . 128-132 [16], 133-137 [17], and 138-142 [18]). With this converted FIQ score, each child was classified according to his/her performance on each WISC-III subtest score relative to his/her FIQ score into three levels: poor (i.e., a subtest score was lower by 3 point or more than FIQ score), fair (different by 2 point or less), and good (higher by 3 point or more). The proportion of children in the three levels between the four groups was compared by chi square test.

The difference of the mean total CARS-TV score between the four groups was tested by ANOVA. For each CARS-TV item score, the difference was tested by ANCOVA with the total CARS-TV score, expected to be higher in the three HPDD subgroups (HFA, HPDDNOS, AS) than ADHD, as a covariate.

All tests were 2-tailed and a significant level was set at p < .05. In the case of significant difference between the four groups was found, post hoc comparisons were made with Bonferroni correction. All statistical analyses were performed with SPSS 13.0J for Windows.

RESULTS

WISC-III IQ and Index

As shown in Table II, VIQ and Verbal Comprehension (VC) were significantly lower in the HPDDNOS children than the ADHD children. The HFA children scored significantly higher on Freedom from Distractibility (FFD) than the HPDDNOS children.

Table II. WISC-III IQ and Index in Four Groups

WISC-III	HFA (n = 15) Mean (SD)	HPDDNOS (n = 45) Mean (SD)	AS (n = 19) Mean (SD)	ADHD (n = 37) Mean (SD)	F (3, 112)
IQ					
FIQ	99.8 (14.6)	93.0 (14.9)	99.5 (11.7)	100.3 (15.3)	2.10
VIQ	98.5 (16.4)	90.5 (19.5)[a]	100.3 (16.9)	103.5 (15.6)[a]	4.02**
PIQ	101.3 (18.5)	97.4 (13.8)	98.8 (10.9)	96.7 (16.8)	0.38
Index					
VC	95.8 (16.1)	90.3 (19.3)[a]	99.6 (17.1)	103.8 (14.7)[a]	4.33**
PO	101.9 (18.4)	98.2 (14.4)	102.0 (11.1)	98.4 (17.4)	0.44
FFD	111.9 (15.7)[a]	97.4 (18.1)[a]	107.1 (16.9)	102.3 (16.7)	3.25*
PS	98.7 (21.8)	94.6 (15.4)	89.1 (13.3)	93.8 (14.9)	1.07

Note: HFA = high-functioning autism; HPDDNOS = high-functioning pervasive developmental disorder not otherwise specified; AS = Asperger's disorder; ADHD = attention-deficit/hyperactivity disorder. FIQ = Full Scale IQ; VIQ = Verbal IQ; PIQ = Performance IQ; VC = Verbal Comprehension; PO = Perceptual Organization; FFD = Freedom from Distractibility; PS = Processing Speed; SD = standard deviation.

[a] Figures with the same superscripts on the same line differ significantly (p < .05) from each other by post hoc comparisons with Bonferroni correction.

*p < .05, **p < .01.

Verbal Subtests

In Figure I, we illustrated the verbal subtest profile of the four groups based on the estimated scores. The ANCOVA with the FIQ as a covariate revealed a significant difference between the four groups on Vocabulary (F = 4.07, df = 3, 111, p = .009) and Comprehension (F = 3.80, df = 3, 111, p = .012). Post hoc comparisons with Bonferroni correction showed that the HFA children scored significantly lower on Vocabulary and tended to (p < .10) score lower on Comprehension than the ADHD children and that the HPDDNOS children scored significantly lower on Comprehension and tended to score lower on Vocabulary than the ADHD children. Digit Span, which is especially high in the HFA children, tended to be different between the four groups (F = 2.39, df = 3, 111, p = .073). There was no significant difference between the AS children and the ADHD children.

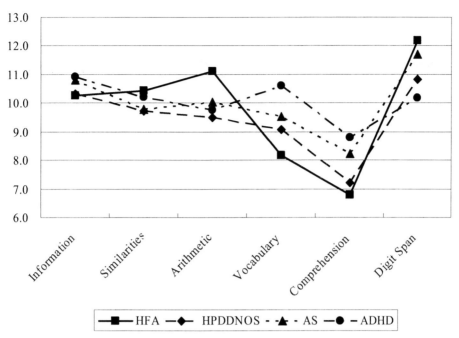

Note: Scores were estimated with mean Full Scale IQ of 97.28. HFA = high-functioning autism;
    HPDDNOS = high-functioning pervasive developmental disorder not otherwise specified; AS =
    Asperger's disorder; ADHD = attention-deficit/hyperactivity disorder.
Vocabulary: HFA < ADHD (p = .013), HPDDNOS < ADHD (p = .057).
Comprehension: HFA < ADHD (p = .052), HPDDNOS < ADHD (p = .033).

Figure I. Estimated Scores of WISC-III Verbal Subtests in Four Groups

Table III showed percentages of children in the three levels of poor, fair, and good in each verbal subtest. Distributions of the four groups were significantly different on Vocabulary and Comprehension. Compared with the ADHD children, more HPDD children (e.g., as high as 60% of the HFA children) were poor at Comprehension.

Performance Subtests

As shown in Figure II, Block Design subtest showed a significant difference between the four groups (F = 3.05, df = 3, 111, p = .032), and post hoc comparisons with Bonferroni correction showed that the HPDDNOS children scored significantly higher than the ADHD children. Coding subtest tended to be different between the four groups (F = 2.63, df = 3, 111, p = .054), and low scores were shared by the AS and ADHD children.

Table IV showed percentages of children in the three levels of poor, fair, and good in each performance subtest. Distributions of the four groups were significantly different on Coding and Block Design and tended to be different on Picture Arrangement. The difference between HPDD and ADHD was remarkable on Block Design; over a half of the HPDDNOS children were good at Block Design. Forty percent of the HFA children were poor at Picture Arrangement.

**Table III. Percentages of Children by Levels of WISC-III Verbal Subtest Scores
Relative to FIQ by Diagnoses**

Subtest	Diagnosis	Level (%)		
		Poor	Fair	Good
Information	HFA	7	67	27
$\chi^2(6) = 2.69$, p = .85	HPDDNOS	13	56	31
	AS	11	47	42
	ADHD	8	65	27
Similarities	HFA	20	47	33
$\chi^2(6) = 6.53$, p = .37	HPDDNOS	16	58	27
	AS	16	74	11
	ADHD	5	73	22
Arithmetic	HFA	7	60	33
$\chi^2(6) = 7.49$, p = .28	HPDDNOS	16	71	13
	AS	16	53	32
	ADHD	8	78	14
Vocabulary	HFA	33	67	0
$\chi^2(6) = 15.51$, p = .02	HPDDNOS	9	78	13
	AS	11	79	11
	ADHD	14	54	32
Comprehension	HFA	60	33	7
$\chi^2(6) = 13.74$, p = .03	HPDDNOS	31	69	0
	AS	21	79	0
	ADHD	19	76	5
Digit Span	HFA	7	47	47
$\chi^2(6) = 4.87$, p = .56	HPDDNOS	4	58	38
	AS	5	63	32
	ADHD	14	62	24

Note: Each child was classified according to his/her performance on each subtest score relative to
his/her FIQ converted by assigning score 1 through 19 for every FIQ range of 5 from 53-57 (score
1) through 143-147 (score 19) into three levels: poor (i.e., a subtest score was lower by 3 point or
more than FIQ score), fair (different by 2 point or less), and good (higher by 3 point or more).
HFA = high-functioning autism; HPDDNOS = high-functioning pervasive developmental disorder
not otherwise specified; AS = Asperger's disorder; ADHD = attention-deficit/hyperactivity
disorder.

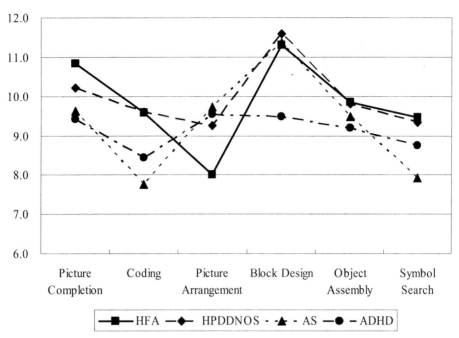

Note: Scores were estimated with mean Full Scale IQ of 97.28. HFA = high-functioning autism; HPDDNOS = high-functioning pervasive developmental disorder not otherwise specified; AS = Asperger's disorder; ADHD = attention-deficit/hyperactivity disorder.
Block Design: HPDDNOS > ADHD (p = .035).

Figure II. Estimated Scores of WISC-III Performance Subtests in Four Groups

Autistic Symptom Profile

As expected, the total CARS-TV score was significantly higher (i.e., more abnormal) in the three HPDD subgroups of children (HFA, M = 22.8; HPDDNOS, 22.0; AS, 22.1) than the ADHD children (M = 18.3), F = 15.73, df = 3, 112, p < .001. However, only 1 (6.7%), 5 (11.1%), and 1 (5.3%) of the HFA, HPDDNOS, AS children, respectively, scored higher than CARS-TV PDD cutoff of 26.0 (Tachimori, Osada, and Kurita, 2003).

Since each CARS-TV item score significantly correlated with the total CARS-TV score, we compared the four groups on the 15 item scores by ANCOVA with the total CARS-TV score as a covariate. As shown in Table V, 7 subtests showed significant difference. Post hoc comparisons with Bonferroni correction showed that the HPDD subgroup (s) of children scored significantly higher than the ADHD children on 4 items: "Relationships with people," "Affect," "Nonverbal communication," and "General impressions." On the other hand, the ADHD children scored significantly higher than the HPDD subgroups of children on 2 items: "Near receptor responsiveness" and "Activity level." On "Verbal communication," not only the ADHD children but also the AS children scored significantly lower (i.e., less abnormal) than the HPDDNOS children.

Table IV. Percentages of Children by Levels of WISC-III Performance Subtest Scores Relative to FIQ by Diagnoses

Subtest	Diagnosis	Level (%)		
		Poor	Fair	Good
Picture Completion	HFA	13	53	33
$\chi^2(6) = 3.47$, p = .75	HPDDNOS	7	64	29
	AS	16	63	21
	ADHD	16	65	19
Coding	HFA	20	60	20
$\chi^2(6) = 13.17$, p = .04	HPDDNOS	18	56	27
	AS	32	68	0
	ADHD	43	46	11
Picture Arrangement	HFA	40	47	13
$\chi^2(6) = 11.09$, p = .09	HPDDNOS	20	56	24
	AS	16	74	11
	ADHD	8	78	14
Block Design	HFA	13	47	40
$\chi^2(6) = 16.37$, p = .01	HPDDNOS	4	44	51
	AS	11	53	37
	ADHD	19	70	11
Object Assembly	HFA	27	47	27
$\chi^2(6) = 7.24$, p = .30	HPDDNOS	13	51	36
	AS	21	63	16
	ADHD	22	65	14
Symbol Search	HFA	33	40	27
$\chi^2(6) = 8.45$, p = .21	HPDDNOS	16	58	27
	AS	37	58	5
	ADHD	24	62	14

Note: Each child was classified according to his/her performance on each subtest score relative to his/her FIQ converted by assigning score 1 through 19 for every FIQ range of 5 from 53-57 (score 1) through 143-147 (score 19) into three levels: poor (i.e., a subtest score was lower by 3 point or more than FIQ score), fair (different by 2 point or less), and good (higher by 3 point or more). HFA = high-functioning autism; HPDDNOS = high-functioning pervasive developmental disorder not otherwise specified; AS = Asperger's disorder; ADHD = attention-deficit/hyperactivity disorder.

**Table V. Childhood Autism Rating Scale-Tokyo Version
(CARS-TV) Items Significantly Different (p < .05) by ANCOVA
(analysis of covariance) with the Total CARS-TV Score as a Covariate**

CARS-TV items	HFA (n = 15) Mean (SE)	HPDDNOS (n = 45) Mean (SE)	AS (n = 19) Mean (SE)	ADHD (n = 37) Mean (SE)	F (3, 111)
Relationships with people	1.32 (0.05)	1.37 (0.03)[a]	1.38 (0.05)[a]	1.19 (0.04)[b]	5.02
Affect	1.50 (0.06)	1.49 (0.03)[a]	1.55 (0.05)[a]	1.34 (0.04)[b]	4.49
Near receptor responsiveness	1.67 (0.14)	1.38 (0.08)[b]	1.50 (0.12)[b]	2.02 (0.10)[a]	8.12
Verbal communication	1.41 (0.06)	1.49 (0.04)[a]	1.27 (0.06)[b]	1.31 (0.04)[b]	5.06
Nonverbal communication	1.45 (0.07)	1.54 (0.04)[a]	1.44 (0.06)	1.30 (0.05)[b]	4.96
Activity level	1.31 (0.07)[b]	1.32 (0.04)[b]	1.24 (0.06)[b]	1.62 (0.05)[a]	8.65
General impressions	1.40 (0.04)[a]	1.34 (0.03)[a]	1.44 (0.04)[a]	1.15 (0.03)[b]	12.75

Note: Scores were estimated with the mean total CARS-TV score of 20.95. HFA = high-functioning autism; HPDDNOS = high-functioning pervasive developmental disorder not otherwise specified; AS = Asperger's disorder; ADHD = attention-deficit/hyperactivity disorder. SE = standard error.
[a, b] Figures with different superscripts on the same line differ significantly (p < .05) from each other by post hoc comparisons with Bonferroni correction.

DISCUSSION

Consistent with previous studies in children with high-functioning autism (HFA) employing the WISC-R (Asarnow, Tanguay, Bott, and Freeman, 1987; Ehlers et al., 1997; Freeman, Lucas, Forness, and Ritvo, 1985; Siegel, Minshew, and Goldstein, 1996) and the WISC-III (Mayes and Calhoun, 2003), the HFA children in this study scored low on Comprehension and Picture Arrangement and scored high on Block Design. This profile seems to indicate the unique intellectual structure in autistic patients, that is, superior in visuospatial ability but inferior in skills related to so-called social intelligence (Beebe, Pfiffner, and McBurnett, 2000). Despite the mildness of their autistic symptomatology, the HPDDNOS children in this study still maintained this cognitive pattern. Although the presence of such an intellectual pattern might be a clue to detect high-functioning individuals with PDD, clinicians should remember relatively high verbal cognitive ability of AS shown in this study.

This study had some discordance with the first WISC-III study of children with HFA (Mayes and Calhoun, 2003), which reported low scores on Freedom from Distractibility (derived from Arithmetic and Digit Span). The HFA children in this study did not show such weakness and were superior to the HPDDNOS children in that ability. Earlier studies of children with HFA using the WISC-R (Asarnow et al., 1987; Ehlers et al., 1997; Freeman et al., 1985; Siegel et al., 1996) did not necessarily report the low score on Arithmetic and according to Siegel et al.'s (1996) summary (Table I, p390-391), Digit Span was one of the best verbal subtest for patients with HFA. Those discordances need further studies for clarification.

According to above Siegel et al.'s summary, the low score of Coding was one of the common characteristics in patients with HFA. In this study, however, the low score of Coding was typically seen in the AS children. Since the concept of AS became popular only after the publication of ICD-10 and DSM-IV in the middle of the 1990's, studies before then did not necessarily differentiate AS from HFA. In other words, the patients with HFA in some previous studies might involve patients with current Asperger's disorder. Future studies using rigorous diagnostic criteria to differentiate between AS and autistic disorder in terms of the presence or absence of delay in language and cognitive development might clarify this issue.

Consistent with previous ADHD studies using the WISC-III (Anastopoulos, Spisto, and Maher, 1994; Mayes, Calhoun, and Crowell, 1998; Mealer, Morgan, and Luscomb, 1996; Nyden, Billstedt, Hjelmquist, and Gillberg, 2001; Prifitera and Dersh, 1993; Saklofske, Schwean, Yackulic, and Quinn, 1994), the ADHD children in this study scored low on Processing Speed (derived from Coding and Symbol Search), which requires visual concentration and carefulness. However, the ADHD children in this study did not show low performance on Freedom from Distractibility (derived from Arithmetic and Digit Span), which requires auditory concentration and carefulness, as has been reported in previous studies. However, as shown in Table VI, all of the three WISC-III studies conducted for sufficient number of Japanese children with ADHD did not show weakness on Freedom from Distractibility. Although this discrepancy remains to be elucidated, it might reflect some differences in educational or cultural backgrounds between Japan and western countries. Future WISC-III studies in Japan and/or East Asian countries where similar linguistic culture and educational system exist might clarify this issue. In Japanese children, visual inattention characterized by low Processing Speed might be a more important clue for identifying ADHD patients than low Freedom from Distractibility.

Table VI. WISC-III Scores of Japanese Children with ADHD

	Arai et al. (2001) (n = 86)	Ito et al. (2002) (n = 64)	Present study (n = 37)
	Mean (SD)	Mean (SD)	Mean (SD)
Age, years	8.5 (2.0)	9.9 (2.8)	8.6 (2.0)
IQ			
Full Scale IQ	95.4 (14.5)	98.6 (14.1)	100.3 (15.3)
Verbal IQ	98.1 (14.8)	101.0 (15.1)	103.5 (15.6)
Performance IQ	93.1 (15.3)	96.0 (15.8)	96.7 (16.8)
Index			
Verbal Comprehension	98.1 (14.8)	100.6 (15.2)	103.8 (14.7)
Perceptual Organization	94.4 (16.2)	97.6 (15.6)	98.4 (17.4)
Freedom from Distractibility	95.2 (14.3)	97.7 (14.2)	102.3 (16.7)
Processing Speed	91.9 (14.8)	93.1 (14.0)	93.8 (14.9)

Note: ADHD = attention-deficit/hyperactivity disorder. SD = standard deviation.

It may be a reason for misdiagnosing ADHD patients as HPDD that ADHD patients could show some PDD-like symptoms as shown in this and previous studies (Clark et al., 1999; Stein et al., 1995). However, the CARS-TV profile was definitely different between the HPDD and ADHD children. In social interaction, such as "Relationships with people" or "Affect," the three groups of HPDD children were more abnormal than the ADHD children.

When clinicians are faced with a difficulty of differentiating between HPDD and ADHD, to pay attention to core autistic symptoms (i.e., disturbances in interpersonal relationships) would help them to differentiate between both conditions.

On the other hand, after controlling for the total CARS-TV score, the ADHD children were more abnormal in two CARS-TV items: "Activity level" and "Near receptor responsiveness." As expected from the diagnostic criteria, the ADHD children were still more active than the HPDD children. Since various abnormalities concerning near receptor (e.g., nail-biting, smelling, pain insensitiveness) were rated, we could not evaluate relative contribution of individual near receptor abnormalities to "Near receptor responsiveness" score in this study, and a study employing a more precise measure is needed to address this issue. Although replication is necessary, the severity of hyperactivity and near receptor abnormality may also aid differential diagnosis between HPDD and ADHD.

Among the three HPDD subgroups, the only significant finding on CARS-TV was that the AS children were less abnormal than the HPDDNOS children on Verbal communication. To our knowledge, two studies compared CARS-TV scores among HPDD subgroups. Kanai, Koyama, Kato, Miyamoto, Osada, and Kurita (2004) compared children with HFA (M = 6.0 years) and high-functioning ICD-10 atypical autism (basically the same as DSM-IV PDDNOS) (M = 8.2 years), found that HFA scored significantly higher on the total and two item scores (i.e., Relationships with people and General impressions) but scored significantly lower on Anxiety reaction. Kurita (1997) compared children with AS (M = 5.7 years) and high-functioning atypical autism (M = 6.1 years), found that AS scored significantly lower on the total and four item scores (i.e., Imitation, Visual responsiveness, Auditory responsiveness and Nonverbal communication). Since the two previous studies assessed much younger children than those of this study, their HPDD children might have displayed autistic symptoms much clearer so that the difference between the subgroups might have been more distinguishable than the HPDD subgroups in this study. If HPDD subgroups of children look more alike as they get older, relevant rating scales to evaluate HPDD symptoms more precisely need to be developed for clinical and research activities to evaluate the difference among them.

The results of this study should be interpreted very carefully, since several fairly large differences were not always significant, possibly due to the relatively small sample size as might often be the case in HPDD studies. Although in a sample size this study was comparable to or even larger than some previous HPDD studies using the Wechsler Intelligence Scale (Asarnow et al., 1987; Freeman et al., 1985; Szatmari, Tuff, Finlayson, and Bartolucci, 1990), a more extensive and detailed study is needed to test the findings in this study. Since this study was clinic-based, the subjects may have involved severer patients than patients in the general population. However, to obtain clinical suggestions, our clinic-based sample seems to be more appropriate than an epidemiological sample. Recently, some studies (Goldstein and Schwebach, 2004; Yoshida and Uchiyama, 2004) raised a major conceptual issue that clinicians should make comorbid diagnoses of HPDD and ADHD for clinical availability. Although the current study did not compare all ADHD defining symptoms except for "Activity level" on CARS-TV, future HPDD studies are expected to do more detailed assessment on inattentiveness, hyperactivity, and impulsivity to evaluate the validity of the current convention of not diagnosing ADHD in PDD patients.

CONCLUSION

This study clarified similarityies and differences in cognitive function and autistic symptom profiles between HPDD subgroups and ADHD children. Although all of the three HPDD subgroups showed the similar profile of low score of Comprehension and high score of Block Design, the AS children showed relatively high verbal ability and troughs on Coding. The latter profile was also shared by the ADHD children but not by the other two HPDD subgroups (autistic disorder and PDDNOS). Although both HPDD and ADHD groups partially shared some clinical symptoms, the HPDD subgroups were more abnormal in social interaction but less abnormal in hyperactivity and near receptor responsiveness. These findings might reflect underlying brain dysfunction in the three HPDD subgroups and ADHD and may help professionals to distinguish clinically between them.

ACKNOWLEDGMENTS

This study was supported in part by the Research Grant for Nervous and Mental Disorders from the Ministry of Health and Welfare, Japan. We would like to thank Ms. Yoko Hayashi, Mr. Hiromi Ishida, and Ms. Mika Tobari for their help in data collection.

REFERENCES

American Psychiatric Association. (1994). *Diagnostic and statistical manual of mental disorders* (4th ed.). Washington, DC: Author.

American Psychiatric Association. (2000). Attention-deficit/hyperactivity disorder. In *Diagnostic and statistical manual of mental disorders* (4th ed.) text revision (pp. 85-93). Washington, DC: Author.

Anastopoulos, A. D., Spisto, M. A., and Maher, M. C. (1994). The WISC-III Freedom from Distractibility factor: Its utility in identifying children with attention deficit hyperactivity disorder. *Psychological Assessment,* 6, 368-371.

Arai, S., Shirokizawa, F., Suzumura, S., Yamada, S., Ichikawa, H., and Sato, T. (2001). Chyuikekkan tadouseishougai no shinrigakutekikensa niyoru kentou: WISC-III wo chyushin-ni [Psychological assessment of attention-deficit/hyperactivity disorder in special reference to WISC-III] [Abstract]. *Archives of Psychiatric Diagnostics and Clinical Evaluation,* 12, 126. (in Japanese)

Asarnow, R. F., Tanguay, P. E., Bott, L., and Freeman, B. J. (1987). Patterns of intellectual functioning in non-retarded autistic and schizophrenic children. *Journal of Child Psychology and Psychiatry,* 28, 273-280.

Baird, G., Charman, T., Baron-Cohen, S., Cox, A., Swettenham, J., Wheelwright, S., and Drew, A. (2000). A screening instrument for autism at 18 months of age: A 6-year follow-up study. *Journal of the American Academy of Child and Adolescent Psychiatry,* 39, 694-702.

Baron-Cohen, S., Wheelwright, S., Skinner, R., Martin, J., and Clubley, E. (2001). The Autism-Spectrum Quotient (AQ): Evidence from Asperger syndrome/high-functioning autism, males and females, scientists and mathematicians. *Journal of Autism and Developmental Disorders,* 31, 5-17.

Beebe, D. W., Pfiffner, L. J., and McBurnett, K. (2000). Evaluation of the validity of the Wechsler Intelligence Scale for Children-Third Edition: Comprehension and picture arrangement subtests as measures of social intelligence. *Psychological Assessment,* 12, 97-101.

Bertrand, J., Mars, A., Boyle, C., Bove, F., Yeargin-Allsopp, M., and Decoufle, P. (2001). Prevalence of autism in a United States population: The Brick Township, New Jersey, investigation. *Pediatrics,* 108, 1155-1161.

Buitelaar, J. K., and van der Gaag, R. J. (1998). Diagnostic rules for children with PDD-NOS and multiple complex developmental disorder. *Journal of Child Psychology and Psychiatry,* 39, 911-919.

Chakrabarti, S., and Fombonne, E. (2001). Pervasive developmental disorders in preschool children. *Journal of American Medical Association,* 285, 3093-3099.

Clark, T., Feehan, C., Tinline, C., and Vostanis, P. (1999). Autistic symptoms in children with attention deficit-hyperactivity disorder. *European Child and Adolescent Psychiatry,* 8, 50-55.

Ehlers, S., Nyden, A., Gillberg, C., Sandberg, A. D., Dahlgren, S. O., Hjelmquist, E., and Oden, A. (1997). Asperger syndrome, autism and attention disorders: A comparative study of the cognitive profiles of 120 children. *Journal of Child Psychology and Psychiatry,* 38, 207-217.

Fombonne, E. (2003). Epidemiological surveys of autism and other pervasive developmental disorders: An update. *Journal of Autism and Developmental Disorders,* 33, 365-382.

Freeman, B. J., Lucas, J. C., Forness, S. R., and Ritvo, E. R. (1985). Cognitive processing of high-functioning autistic children: Comparing the K-ABC and the WISC-R. *Journal of Psychoeducational Assessment,* 4, 357-362.

Ghaziuddin, M., Weidmer-Mikhail, E., and Ghaziuddin, N. (1998). Comorbidity of Asperger syndrome: A preliminary report. *Journal of Intellectual Disability Research,* 42, 279-283.

Goldstein, S., and Schwebach, A. J. (2004). The comorbidity of pervasive developmental disorder and attention deficit hyperactivity disorder: Results of a retrospective chart review. *Journal of Autism and Developmental Disorders,* 34, 329-339.

Ito, K., Shoji, A., Morita, M., Fukuda, T., Kita, M., Fujii, K., Itani, T., Kanbayashi, Y., and Nakata, Y. (2002). ADHD to PDD no WISC-III profile no kentou [Comparison of WISC-III profile between ADHD and PDD] [Abstract]. *Proceedings of the 43rd Convention of the Japanese Society for Child and Adolescent Psychiatry,* 195. (in Japanese)

Japanese WISC-III Publication Committee. (1998). *Nihonban WISC-III chinou kensahou* [Japanese Wechsler Intelligence Scale for Children Third Edition]. Tokyo: Nihon Bunka Kagakusha. (in Japanese)

Jensen, V. K., Larrieu, J. A., and Mack, K. K. (1997). Differential diagnosis between attention-deficit/hyperactivity disorder and pervasive developmental disorder—not otherwise specified. *Clinical Pediatrics,* 36, 555-561.

Kanai, C., Koyama, T., Kato, S., Miyamoto, Y., Osada, H., and Kurita, H. (2004). A comparison of high-functioning atypical autism and childhood autism by Childhood Autism Rating Scale-Tokyo Version. *Psychiatry and Clinical Neurosciences,* 58, 217-221.

Kurita, H. (1997). A comparative study of Asperger syndrome with high-functioning atypical autism. *Psychiatry and Clinical Neurosciences,* 51, 67-70.

Kurita, H., Koyama, T., Osada, H. (in press2005). Autism-spectrum quotient Japanese version and its short forms for screening normally intelligent persons with pervasive developmental disorders. *Psychiatry and Clinical Neurosciences,* 59, 490-496.

Kurita, H., Miyake, Y., and Katsuno, K. (1989). Reliability and validity of the Childhood Autism Rating Scale-Tokyo Version (CARS-TV). *Journal of Autism and Developmental Disorders,* 19, 389-396.

Luteijn, E. F., Serra, M., Jackson, S., Steenhuis, M. P., Althaus, M., Volkmar, F., and Minderaa, R. (2000). How unspecified are disorders of children with a pervasive developmental disorder not otherwise specified?: A study of social problems in children with PDD-NOS and ADHD. *European Cchild and Adolescent Psychiatry,* 9, 168-179.

Mayes, S. D., and Calhoun, S. L. (2003). Analysis of WISC-III, Stanford-Binet:IV, and academic achievement test scores in children with autism. *Journal of Autism and Developmental Disorders,* 33, 329-341.

Mayes, S. D., Calhoun, S. L., and Crowell, E. W. (1998). WISC-III Freedom from Distractibility as a measure of attention in children with and without attention deficit hyperactivity disorder. *Journal of Attention Disorders,* 2, 217-227.

Mealer, C., Morgan, S., and Luscomb, R. (1996). Cognitive functioning of ADHD and non-ADHD boys on the WISC-III and WRAML: An analysis within a memory model. *Journal of Attention Disorders,* 1, 133-145.

Nyden, A., Billstedt, E., Hjelmquist, E., and Gillberg, C. (2001). Neurocognitive stability in Asperger syndrome, ADHD, and reading and writing disorder: A pilot study. *Developmental Medicine and Child Neurology,* 43, 165-171.

Perry, R. (1998). Misdiagnosed ADD/ADHD: Rediagnosed PDD. *Journal of the American Academy of Child and Adolescent Psychiatry,* 37, 113-114.

Prifitera, A., and Dersh, J. (1993). Base rates of WISC-III diagnostic subtest patterns among normal, learning-disabled, and ADHD samples. *Journal of Psychoeducational Assessment,* WISC-III Monograph, 43-55.

Roeyers, H., Keymeulen, H., and Buysse, A. (1998). Differentiating attention-deficit/hyperactivity disorder from pervasive developmental disorder not otherwise specified. *Journal of Learning Disabilities,* 31, 565-571.

Saklofske, D. H., Schwean, V. L., Yackulic, R. A., and Quinn, D. (1994). WISC-III and SB: FE performance of children with attention deficit hyperactivity disorder. *Canadian Journal of School Psychology,* 10, 167-171.

Schopler, E., Reichler, R. J., DeVellis, R. F., and Daly, K. (1980). Toward objective classification of childhood autism: Childhood Autism Rating Scale (CARS). *Journal of Autism and Developmental Disorders,* 10, 91-103.

Siegel, D. J., Minshew, N. J., and Goldstein, G. (1996). Wechsler IQ profiles in diagnosis of high-functioning autism. *Journal of Autism and Developmental Disorders,* 26, 389-406.

Stein, M. A., Szumowski, E., Blondis, T. A., and Roizen, N. J. (1995). Adaptive skills dysfunction in ADD and ADHD children. *Journal of Child Psychology and Psychiatry*, 36, 663-670.

Szatmari, P., Tuff, L., Finlayson, M. A. J., and Bartolucci, G. (1990). Asperger's syndrome and autism: Neurocognitive aspects. *Journal of the American Academy of Child and Adolescent Psychiatry,* 29, 130-136.

Tachimori, H., Osada, H., and Kurita, H. (2003). Childhood autism rating scale-Tokyo version for screening pervasive developmental disorders. *Psychiatry and Clinical Neurosciences,* 57, 113-118.

Wechsler, D. (1991). Wechsler *Intelligence Scale for Children* Third Edition manual. New York: The Psychological Corporation.

World Health Organization. (1993). The ICD-10 classification of mental and behavioural disorders: *Diagnostic criteria for research.* Geneva: Author.

Yoshida, Y., and Uchiyama, T. (2004). The clinical necessity for assessing Attention Deficit/Hyperactivity Disorder (AD/HD) symptoms in children with high-functioning Pervasive Developmental Disorder (PDD). *European Cchild and Adolescent Psychiatry,* 13, 307-314.

INDEX

locus, 13, 25, 26, 35
logical reasoning, 45
long distance, 61, 64, 65, 67, 73
longitudinal study, 126
love, 98
low risk, 33
lower alpha band, 49, 69, 75

M

machinery, 27
magnetic resonance, 14, 61, 74, 80, 81
magnetic resonance imaging, 14, 81
magnetic resonance spectroscopy, 74, 80
malaria, 42
males, viii, x, 28, 33, 39, 42, 47, 48, 52, 53, 55, 63, 65, 68, 69, 73, 74, 75, 133, 147
management, 11, 12, 16, 99, 101, 107, 111
manic, 29, 31, 32, 34
manipulation, 53
mapping, ix, 84
Mars, 134, 147
mass, 24
mathematical achievement, 37
mathematics, 36, 43, 45, 125
matrix, 4, 11, 12
maturation, 76, 118
maze learning, 131
meanings, 93, 128
measurement, ix, 6, 19, 21, 37, 77, 95, 97, 99, 102, 106, 110, 113
measures, viii, ix, 7, 11, 13, 17, 18, 39, 47, 51, 52, 54, 55, 59, 60, 61, 63, 65, 66, 69, 71, 73, 74, 77, 83, 90, 100, 104, 106, 107, 108, 109, 111, 120, 147
media, 39, 87, 121, 124
mediation, 84
medication, 30
memory, 6, 8, 12, 14, 15, 17, 18, 20, 49, 50, 52, 53, 58, 78, 79, 117, 118, 120, 127, 148
memory performance, 79
memory processes, 58, 78
memory retrieval, 53
men, 35, 36, 39, 44, 53, 80, 97, 104
mental ability, 44, 119, 120, 122
mental arithmetic, 80
mental capacity, 120
mental disorder, 33
mental energy, vii, 1, 13, 14, 120
mental health, 93
mental illness, 30, 35, 37
mental image, 14
mental imagery, 14

mental planning, 8
mental processes, 8, 12
mental retardation, 134
metabolism, 13, 20, 77, 124
methodology, 18, 50
military, 42
missions, 90
mode, 41, 44
modeling, 86, 87, 94
models, 8, 9, 20, 51, 81, 85, 86, 93, 102, 105, 106, 130
moderates, 101, 105, 110
moisture, 39
money, 93
monitoring, 9, 11, 22, 89
mood, 29, 78, 131
mood disorder, 78
mothers, 30, 32
motion, 50
motivation, 98, 103, 104, 126
movement, 89
Mozart effect, x, 115, 125, 127, 130, 131
MRI, 14, 81
multidimensional, 17, 102, 105, 110, 111
multiple factors, 24
multiplication, 32
muscle strength, 24
muscles, 39
music, ix, 44, 50, 76, 80, 115, 116, 117, 118, 119, 122, 123, 124, 125, 126, 127, 129, 130, 131, 132
musicians, 51, 118, 124
mutant, viii, 23, 24, 25, 26, 28, 35, 43, 44
mutation, viii, 23
myelin, 53, 123
myopia, viii, 23, 39, 40, 41, 42, 43, 44, 45, 46

N

nanotechnology, 92
natural selection, viii, 23, 27, 28, 42, 45
NCV, 53
nearsightedness, 39, 40, 41, 42, 43, 44
needs, 5, 10, 109, 124
negative affectivity, 54
negative coping, 101
negative emotions, 54
negative mood, 112
neglect, 12, 16
neocortex, 51
nerve, 35, 52, 53, 80
nerve conduction velocity, 53, 80
nervous system, 13, 53
network, 14, 15, 16, 51, 105

R

S